CW00687443

Antony Cummins is the founder of the Historical Ninjutsu Research Team, which has previously published *The Book of Ninja* (Watkins). Antony also works as a consultant and co-presenter of Urban Canyon Films to produce high-end documentaries on Japan that are distributed by National Geographic. He has been recognized by peers as a leading expert in the discovery of military arts of medieval Japan.

Yoshie Minami was born in Tokyo and currently lives in Saitama, Japan. She has a BA degree in Linguistics from the International Christian University. As a translator, she has published *True Path of the Ninja, Secret Traditions of the Shinobi, Iga and Koka Ninja Skills, Samurai War Stories* and has worked with Antony on various projects including the Japanese book *True English.*

THE BOOK OF
SAMURAI

Book I
Fundamental Samurai Teachings

Book II
*Samurai Arms, Armour & the Tactics
of Warfare*

THE BOOK OF
SAMURAI

FUNDAMENTAL SAMURAI TEACHINGS

The Collected Scrolls of
NATORI-RYŪ

ANTONY CUMMINS
& YOSHIE MINAMI

WATKINS
Sharing Wisdom
Since 1893

This edition published in the UK and USA 2015 by
Watkins, an imprint of Watkins Media Limited
Unit 11, Shepperton House, 89-93 Shepperton Road, London N1 3DF

enquiries@watkinspublishing.com

Design and typography copyright © Watkins Media Limited 2015
Text Copyright © Antony Cummins 2015
Illustrations © Antony Cummins 2015

Antony Cummins has asserted his right under the Copyright, Designs
and Patents Act 1988 to be identified as the author of this work.

All rights reserved. No part of this book may be reproduced or utilized in any
form or by any means, electronic or mechanical, without prior permission
in writing from the Publishers.

7 9 10 8

Designer: Clare Thorpe
Calligraphy: Yamamoto Jyuho
Managing Editor: Deborah Hercun
Copy Editor: James Hodgson
Editor: Steve Williamson
Index: Indexing Specialists (UK) Ltd

Printed and bound in Great Britain by TJ Books Limited

A CIP record for this book is available from the British Library

ISBN: 978-1-78028-888-8

www.watkinspublishing.com

CONTENTS

AN INTRODUCTION TO NATORI-RYŪ

Natori-Ryū is a *samurai* school of war founded in the sixteenth century. The school initially focused on its own military tactics, which included the administering of medical aid; adherents were known among their allied clans for producing a salve for sword wounds and tending to the wounded. However, the main focus was military strategy, developed in the service of the famed warlord Takeda Shingen of Kōshū, one of the most feared in Japan. The death of Takeda Shingen heralded the defeat of the Takeda family and in 1582 the well-respected warrior vassals of Kōshū gave their allegiance to the future *shōgun* Tokugawa Ieyasu. At this point the Natori family split into several divisions, one of which settled in the area of Kishū, present-day Wakayama prefecture. Here it served the Kishū arm of the three great Tokugawa houses, branch clans led by three sons of Tokugawa Ieyasu.

In 1654 Natori Masazumi began his service under the Kishū-Tokugawa clan and was to become Natori-Ryū's most influential grandmaster, expanding the school well beyond its existing curriculum. Being born into the generation of children and grandchildren of experienced *samurai* from the age of wars, Natori Masazumi was surrounded by peers of a much older age who had seen the great wars first hand and their sons, a generation who had been taught directly by these war veterans. Faced with a decline in tactical and military prowess and with a lack of wars to refine soldiery, Natori Masazumi set about collecting a vast array of *samurai* arts into an assembly of scrolls, moulding and expanding his family traditions to create one of the most comprehensive warfare schools of his time.

Natori-Ryū grew from its original tactical and medical traditions and was spliced together with the teachings from one branch of Kusunoki-Ryū. Natori Masazumi studied the skills of Kusunoki-Ryū – including the arts of the *shinobi* – through the line of Kusunoki Fuden. He also studied Kōshū-Ryū on the holy Mount Kōya and integrated those teachings into his still-evolving school. Furthermore he undertook the colossal project of compiling a *samurai* encyclopaedia, cataloguing an extensive amount of Japanese equipment, arms and armour, including the weaponry of China and essential aspects and utensils of *samurai* life. All of this was done with the aim of collecting and maintaining the true skills of the warrior class before its members evolved from men of prowess into bureaucrats.

Natori Masazumi became a confidant and close retainer to Lord Yorinobu Tokugawa of the Kishū-Tokugawa clan, who ordered that Natori-Ryū should be renamed Shin-Kusunoki-Ryū – *The New School of Kusunoki*. This alternative name is used in some of the Natori documents. However, official records, castle maps and certification point to a continued use of Natori-Ryū as an umbrella term for all of the above collected skills and traditions. The school was well respected and appointed as the third most important warfare school of the Kishū domain, where it instructed a selection of the *samurai* of the Kishū-Tokugawa clan in military tactics.

Known locally as Issui Sensei,[1] Natori Masazumi retired from active service in 1685 to the village of Ōno at the base of Mount Kōya and died on 5 May 1708. He was interred at Eiunji temple in Wakayama where his gravestone stands to this day. He was given the death name Kyūgenin Tekigan Ryōsui Koji.

The school continued to flourish after him, maintaining his collected teachings with various branches being established away from the central line. The main school finally closed its doors at the end of the *samurai* era. Transcriptions of Natori Masazumi's work found their way into various libraries and collections, each with attached commentaries from later students of the school.

---

1   Also, Tōissui.

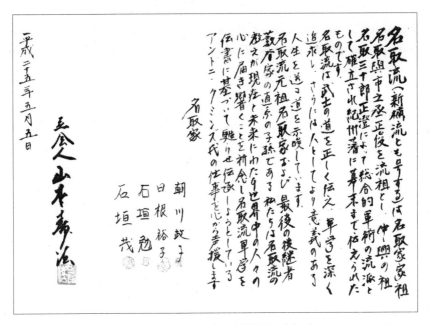

The blessing given to Antony Cummins by members of the Natori family.

Natori-Ryū would have remained among the myriad other dead *samurai* schools if it were not for the fame given to one of its scrolls, the *Shōninki*. This manual is considered as one of the most important works on the arts of the *shinobi*. The fame of the scroll has allowed me to diligently follow the trail of historical documents and to rediscover the story of Natori Masazumi and his school, Natori-Ryū. The first two scrolls have been presented here in this initial volume and the complete school is collected within the whole series. The translation and publication of this series of books, based on the teachings of Natori-Ryū will encompass all of the school's original scrolls and will be accompanied by a reconstruction of the school itself.

On 5 May 2013 at Eiunji temple, a ceremony was held by the monk Yamamoto Jyuhō to reconnect with the spirit of Natori Masazumi. At the end of the ceremony the surviving members of the Natori family gave me their official blessing to re-establish and lead the school into the next generation. Natori-Ryū welcomes any readers to become students of the school, thereby safeguarding the teachings of Natori Masazumi. You can discover more through the website (www.natori.co.uk) and information can be found on major social networking sites.

Antony Cummins

THE SECRETS OF
NATORI-RYŪ

The Collected Teachings of
NATORI SANJŪRO MASAZUMI

當流軍書ノ目録
Tō-Ryū Gunsho no Mokuroku

THE MILITARY WRITINGS OF OUR SCHOOL

The following is a list of the titles of the writings of our school, Kusunoki-Ryū.[1] However, the titles for our secret scrolls have not been recorded.

兵家常談之巻
Heika Jōdan no Maki
DISCUSSIONS ON *SAMURAI* FAMILIES

Containing the military ways and achievements of *samurai* for normal times.

兵具要法
Heigu Yōhō
IMPORTANT WAYS ON MILITARY TOOLS

Containing the use of armour and weapons.

一兵要功
Ippei Yōkō
IMPORTANT POINTS FOR THE INDEPENDENT SOLDIER

Containing military exploits for independent soldiers.

兵役要法
Heieki Yōhō
IMPORTANT WAYS ON MILITARY DUTIES

This scroll consists of two books named *Ken* 乾 and *Kon* 坤, which contain military duties for the commander-in-chief, his retainers, captains, commanders, normal *samurai* and servants.

---

1 Kusunoki-Ryū is used here while Shin-Kusunoki-Ryū is used in other documents such as transcriptions of the *Shōninki*, but the official name used in provincial records is Natori-Ryū.

水戦要法

Suisen Yōhō

IMPORTANT WAYS ON SEA WARFARE

Containing points concerning sea warfare, ship formations and river battles.

君道要法

Kundō Yōhō

IMPORTANT WAYS FOR THE LORD

Containing points on military ways and military orders that a lord-commander should keep in mind.

軍配要法

Gunbai Yōhō

IMPORTANT WAYS ON MILITARY LEADERSHIP AND DIVINATION

Containing military orders, military manoeuvres, the deciding of appropriate dates, times and directions and that which is auspicious and inauspicious. In our school this scroll requires a different oath. This is called *chūken*, the 'middle stage'.

軍気要法

Gunki Yōhō

IMPORTANT WAYS ON MILITARY CHI

Containing points on the sun, moon, stars, wind and rain, smoke, mist and fog, rain and moisture, monsters, the transformation of *chi* and motion and stillness.

軍習要法

Gunshū Yōhō

IMPORTANT WAYS ON MILITARY TEACHINGS

Containing important points on teachings from ancient times.

軍薬要法

Gun'yaku Yōhō

IMPORTANT WAYS ON MILITARY POWDERS

Containing secret recipes for signals, fire weapons, hunger and thirst pills, sword-injury medicines and detoxification medicines.

Apart from the above there are more volumes on the secret traditions in our school. These should be transmitted only after establishing how serious the intended recipient is; therefore, the titles are not recorded here.

Heika Jōdan no Maki

DISCUSSIONS ON
SAMURAI FAMILIES

五始
Goshi[1]

THE FIVE FOUNDATIONS

The *Xingliziyi*[2] states that the life of human beings and objects derives from the *chi* of *in* and the *chi* of *yō* and that originally *in* and *yō* were created from the single *chi* of the universe. *In* and *yō* were generated and became the Five Elements. The duo of *in* and *yō* combined with the Five Elements revolved, flowing while merging and splitting, unevenness occurred and moved away from purity; in some parts it was clear, in others, muddy, thick and also thin. Although human beings and things derive from the same source, human beings have acquired a proper composition of *chi* while things have an unbalanced configuration. Human beings have *chi* flowing through them while things have blockages in their *chi*. Human beings correspond to heaven and earth, for the head is round and is situated aloft, representing heaven, while the feet are at the bottom and represent the earth. Polaris is the centre of heaven and exists in the north, as the *hyakue* point 百会[3] exists at the top of the head, facing the rear while the sun and the moon[4] come and go in the south of the sky, meaning that the eyes of humans are fixed to front. Seas are where all salt water returns and collects in the lower part, [likewise the urine of human beings moves down the front]. All of these are positioned in order to attain a correctness of *chi*. Human beings have a proper composition of *chi*, while things do not; for example, the heads of animals are located at one end and the heads of plants face downwards while branches and leaves move upwards. This is all because the *chi* of things is skewed. For human beings, *chi* flows all throughout and is bright. In things, *chi* is obstructed and stuck. Human beings have acquired what is excellent from the Five Elements; this makes them the highest spirits of creation.[5] For objects,

---

1   The Koga transcription states *genshi* 原始.
2   性理字義 A Chinese text compiled by Chen Chun (1483–1544).
3   Chinese medical point (GV 20).
4   日月 The sun and moon here are known to be the Chinese medical point *jitsugetsu* (GB 24).
5   i.e. the highest level of that which has been created.

chi is stuck and obstructed and without flow, like a depression sinks below a surface; because of this, righteousness passes them by.

The *I Ching* states that the Supreme Ultimate (*taikyoku*) generates two primary forces. The *Zhou yi kouyi* (oral traditions on the *I Ching*) state that the Supreme Ultimate is the origin from which heaven and earth were generated. The Supreme Ultimate is where original *chi* was found in chaos. This can also be known as the Great Origin (*taisho*) and the Great One (*taiitsu*). Laozi says that the Way produced the One, which is the Supreme Ultimate.

To utilize the Supreme Ultimate, know that there are five separate elements and that these concepts mixed together create 'the mind' and that the mind is penetrated by these five. Therefore, the mind is overflowing with the following five.

This means that originally one mind was divided into five. The 'five' means:

1 the Way
2 virtue
3 benevolence
4 righteousness
5 courtesy

If a person understands them thoroughly, then even if they are illiterate then how can they be called ignorant? For this reason I have opened this book with a section on *goshi*.

道

Dō

THE WAY

As a human being, it is never the case that the Way is not present. The righteous Way for a human is:

- *jin* 仁 – benevolence
- *gi* 義 – righteousness
- *rei* 禮 – courtesy
- *chi* 智 – wisdom
- *shin* 信 – fidelity

The Way is so extensive that it covers everything within the world, be it movement, breathing, speech, the written word, in and out, eating and drinking, the beginning and end – this includes all aspects. Wisdom and fidelity exist in everything, from the greater scheme of the world to insignificant aspects of personal situations, such as the four classes: *samurai*, peasants, craftsman and merchants. Make this a realization.

徳
Toku
VIRTUE

If you seek for something in accordance with the Way, it will be obtained without fail. This is the virtue of the Way. To try to catch fish by climbing a tree or to attempt to catch a bird by going through water is found in the ignorance of people. 'Being in ignorance' means to be without correct reason, which will result in no accomplishment. 'No accomplishment' means that a wish to receive a fief will not be fulfilled. In all, heaven will not reward personal desire.

Virtue is that which enables all things to be achieved, be they colossal or trivial. Whether it is lord and retainer, father and son, insects, grasses and trees, from yourself to the collective universe, if a thing has a virtue, anything that is wished for can be fulfilled. If virtue meets the Way it is said to be 'straight'. For virtue to meet the Way you have to be honest within your nature. Do not wish for your own gain, this is heaven's will – so it is spoken.

仁
Jin
BENEVOLENCE

You should develop and master benevolence, starting with the affection and compassion you have for those you associate with. The essence of benevolence is thus:

As with heaven there is nothing it cannot cover, as with the sea there is nothing it cannot envelop, and as with raindrops there is nothing it cannot soak through. Therefore, do not use people without affection or compassion. The world contains benevolence, no single person shall not receive it and nothing will enjoy its existence without it. Benevolence is also the way to fulfil virtue. It is said that, once acquired, the Great Brightness illuminates everywhere, it extends to all without prejudice. Even a despicable man can be a benevolent father. This is *jinshin* – mind of benevolence.

義

Gi

RIGHTEOUSNESS

Righteousness is the way people express goodness. Based on this, know that the good should be praised and the bad punished. With a mindset of righteousness achievement can be attained. Righteousness is where *ri* (reason and truth) exists and every decision should be made from the wellspring of such reason and truth. The good should be praised and the bad should be punished – this is exactly what righteousness is and what reason and truth are constructed of. Attaining achievement is known to be found in conducting righteousness. Righteousness forces people to have a sense of shame and without this mental attitude the ways of benevolence and virtue cannot be followed.

禮

Rei

COURTESY

People should always practise propriety. Work hard from early morning up until late at night and know that courtesy is the foundation of human morality.

From morning to night, never lose sight of yourself but be mindful in everything you do. At all times keep this mindset in terms of your speaking, observation and listening. The goal is not to become angry or fall into dishonesty but practise courtesy spontaneously. With no intention to deceive, you will be accepted into the Way of heaven and can thus demonstrate virtue, benevolence and righteousness.

The above is called *goshi* – the foundation of all things.[6]

---

6   In the Koga transcription the term *genshi* 原始 is written, but we have used *goshi* 五始 for consistency.

十二徳
Jūnitoku

THE TWELVE TOOLS OF VIRTUE

There are twelve tools, each of which has multiple uses. These are considered fundamental for those of warrior families.[7]

鍵縄七徳
Kaginawa shichitoku
THE SEVEN VIRTUES OF THE GRAPPLING HOOK[8]

In our school, the tool known as a *kaginawa* is used:

1 to secure saddles
2 as quick rope[9]
3 to ascend and descend a wall
4 to cook rice in a battle camp[10]
5 to board or alight from a ship
6 to secure luggage
7 for doors, sliding doors and for carrying heads

含帯五徳
Gantai gotoku[11]
THE FIVE VIRTUES OF THE LONG CLOTH

Here this means a *tenugui*.[12] Its uses are:

1 to tie over and hide the head[13]
2 as a spare *obi*-belt
3 to carry rations on the waist

---

7 兵家 – those born to *samurai* families, also a reference to the title of the manuscript.
8 Literally, 'hook and rope'.
9 早縄 *hayanawa* – to quickly bind an enemy with cord or rope.
10 The grappling hook is used to hang a pot over a fire.
11 Possibly read as *Fukumeobi gotoku*.
12 The *tenugui* is a section of cloth normally kept on the person for a variety of uses.
13 忍頬カフリ *shinobi hōkaburi* – to tie the cloth over the top of the head to hide the face.

4 as an identifying mark at night time – use white

5 as a headband

There is a specific place to keep this.[14]

下緒七徳

Sageo shichitoku

THE SEVEN VIRTUES OF THE SWORD CORD

1 to secure a sword in place

2 to bind and capture someone alive

3 when climbing up a wall [using the sword as a step], you can attach the cord to the *obi*-belt [so that the sword can be retrieved]

4 to carry heads

5 for 'three-foot crossing'[15]

6 when staying at an inn, tie the cords of your swords together[16]

7 as an identifying mark between lords and retainers at important times

小柄三徳

Kozuka santoku

THE THREE VIRTUES OF THE SCABBARD-KNIFE[17]

1 to make notes on the back of the tasse[18] – this can also be done on the scabbard of a spear

2 to use as a divided marker

3 to mark a place as evidence that you were there

扇子五徳

Sensu gotoku

THE FIVE VIRTUES OF THE FOLDING FAN

1 to use as a war baton

---

14 In Natori Ryū the *tenugui* is kept around the neck and under the collar.

15 To tie a cord to the man behind so that a team can cross a river or move in the dark.

16 Both swords are tied together when going to sleep, the *samurai* would lie upon them.

17 A small knife blade fitted to the side of a scabbard.

18 A tasse is the upper-thigh protection on medieval armour which is secured in place at the waist of the cuirass. Messages were scratched on the underside if paper was not available.

2 for giving signals

3 to present a head on: ancient tradition states that dappled snow is drawn on fans and is derived from this custom

4 to receive a gift from the lord: during a period of war, heads were placed upon the back face and other items upon the front face of the fan

5 to make notes upon

弓弦五徳

Yumizuru gotoku

THE FIVE VIRTUES OF THE BOWSTRING

1 to use as a rope to hold when crossing a river

2 to make a space in thick vegetation by tying up the grass

3 to form a boundary rope by attaching many together

4 to use as spare horse-reins, to secure a saddle and to secure a horse to grass

5 to be used in any urgent situation as rope

柄頭三徳

Tsukagashira santoku

THE THREE VIRTUES OF THE POMMEL

1 to 'feel' in a dark place

2 as an identifying mark in connection with the *shinobi amigasa* – the hat that hides the face

3 to stab at the eyes through a helmet

They should always be made of metal.

忍指五徳

Shinobizashi gotoku

THE FIVE VIRTUES OF THE HIDDEN DAGGER[19]

1 to use in combat[20]

2 for decapitating heads

3 when in a place where swords are forbidden

---

19 忍指 *shinobizashi* – 'hidden' 忍 and 'to wear' 指; in this context, a 'hidden dagger'.

20 組討 *kumiuchi* – an older term for grappling.

4 for the teaching of *santō issho*[21]

5 it can stay out of sight because it has a smaller hilt[22]

There are various types of the above.

笄指五徳

Kōgaizashi gotoku[23]

THE FIVE VIRTUES OF THE SPIKE

1 for pushing the tongue of a decapitated head back in the mouth

2 to mark a position

3 to put a tag on a decapitated head; use the spike to pierce a hole in the earlobe

4 on a night attack or similar situation; leave it as evidence, marking the fact that you were there

5 to secure a decapitated head to a base to stop it from rolling off

Generally, the reason for making a spike with different features at seven points is so that it can be used as an identification mark.

腕抜三徳

Udenuki santoku

THE THREE VIRTUES OF THE SWORD WRIST-STRAP

1 to stop you from dropping a *katana* long sword

2 with this at your waist, your appearance as a warrior will be most excellent

3 to enable you to hold the strap in your mouth when on horseback

持薬八徳

Mochigusuri hachitoku

THE EIGHT VIRTUES OF CARRYING MEDICINE

1 to treat people's diseases

2 to maintain health

3 to give aid when falling ill while travelling

4 to prevent suffering from poison[24]

21　*Santō issho* is an obscure practice, but it literally means 'stabbing three times at one place'.

22　ハミダシ鐔 *hamidashi-tsuba* – a hilt that is only slightly larger than the scabbard.

23　Possibly read as *Kougaizashi gotoku*.

24　This includes natural poisons such as food poisoning.

5   to avoid illness caused by an epidemic

6   to protect from the cold

7   to prevent heat stroke

8   to treat sword wounds (recipes and treatments are explained in detail in the scroll *Gun'yaku Yōhō*)

南天五徳

Nanten gotoku

THE FIVE VIRTUES OF THE NANDINA PLANT[25]

1   to clean the hands when water is not available

2   to place a decapitated head on

3   to clean the hands after a nightmare[26]

4   after leaving the toilet you may collapse, therefore place a leaf of this plant in your mouth before you enter the outhouse so that all will be fine

5   if you do collapse in the toilet and receive an injury, crumple a leaf from this plant and apply it to the wound; it will heal

Also you can use it as a riding crop when you go to war.[27]

The above are called *jūnitoku* – the twelve tools of virtue.

---

25   *Nandina domestica*, also known as sacred bamboo.

26   Nandina was considered to be a protection from evil.

27   Strip the leaves from a branch and use as a riding crop.

兵家常談目録
Heika Jōdan Mokuroku

SKILL LIST FOR THE SCROLL *HEIKA JŌDAN*

Heika Jōdan is the first stage of our school and hereinafter a list of 290[28] points are written on things that *samurai* should keep in mind at all times. Our master of old used to teach orally – this way is called *zakō*. There was no little concern that the points might be forgotten. Therefore this list was compiled to record a small selection. It does not include every factor, some of which continue to change in various ways. Overall the points mentioned here should be considered as principles and as a basis for other cases. They should be considered to be an aid so that you can be fully flexible according to each circumstance.

At the beginning of the following list the ideogram hei 平 has been written. This is because these points are principles for *samurai* at normal times平世.[29] All these points are things that should be kept in mind so that the principles of the *samurai* may be understood during normal times; they are the teachings concerning preparation.

There are twenty-two points and at the end of this list there are a further eleven points, which are transmitted as secret traditions. Together they add up to thirty-three points and you should be aware of them all, as they are the essence of a *samurai* during normal times.

---

28 The transcriptions state 280, which is an error.

29 The original scroll has the ideogram平 (taken from the term 平世 – 'normal times') just before the list of points starts. This denotes that all the issues should be considered standard points for a *samurai* in times of peace. At the start of each new list the appropriate ideogram was inserted, and the original manual has them written in red ink.

Hei

ARTICLES FOR TIMES OF PEACE

士日用心懸之事

Samurai nichiyō kokorogake no koto

THE FIRST THING THAT A *SAMURAI* SHOULD KEEP IN MIND IN DAILY LIFE

The primary principle that *samurai* should keep in mind during daily life is: 'During a state of order you should consider and prepare for war and in a time of disorder you should think for the best way to bring about peace'. This is called *nichiyō kokorogake*.

兵士差別之事

Heishi sabetsu no koto

DIFFERENTIATING BETWEEN SOLDIER 兵 AND SAMURAI 士

The ideogram *hei* 兵 means 'a soldier with a short reach'. One theory states that the ideogram for *hei* 兵 was created to mean 'those who are strong enough to deal with the weight of twenty *kin*[30] with ease'. Furthermore, it is thought that the ideogram *hei* 兵 was adopted because of its use in the *Seven Chinese Military Classics*, when it was used in the term *gohei* – the five weapons. According to the annotations, these are:

1 halberd 戈 – this has a horizontal head
2 shield 盾 – this is also known as a *kan* 干
3 halberd 戟 – a halberd with a horizontal blade and spearhead
4 pike 夷矛 – this is two *jo* four *shaku* long
5 pike 酋矛 – this is two *jo* long

---

30 斤 – an old unit of weight, 1 *kin* is about 600 grams.

These above are all 'hooked'.

There is another reference saying the five weapons are:

1 bow 弓
2 arrow 矢
3 halberd with horizontal head 戈
4 spear 矛
5 halberd with spiked collar 殳戟

That being said, here and now *hei* 兵 means *samurai*. The *samurai* who rules the country is called *shōgun* or *kubō*, a *samurai* who rules a province or provinces is called a *kokushi*, while the remaining *samurai* are known as *heishi* 平士. Among these *heishi* there are a few subdivisions. However – apart from the two *shinka*, or ministers – each clan has different systems of service and rituals for the positions of *kumigashira* (group captains), *bugyō* (commanders and officials) and other positions. Generally speaking, the term *hei* 兵 is used in the time of war while *samurai* 士 is used at normal times. The word *hei* is often considered as *ikusa kotoba*, the 'language of war'. Details of this are mentioned in the scroll *Ippei Yōkō*.

仕官名目辨之事
Shikan meimoku kore wo wakimaeru koto
UNDERSTANDING THE TYPES OF POSITIONS OF SERVICE

There are different names in each clan for ministers, senior counsellors and various kinds of captains and commanders, etc. Those *samurai* who have served a lord's clan for generations are called *fudai-mono*, 'generational retainers', while those who have newly entered the service of a lord and their family through their skills and abilities in various arts are called *shinzan-mono* – 'newcomers'. Remember, within those above there are *samurai* who have prowess in military matters and they are called *monoshi no ie* (those from a clan of excellence) – or alternatively they are known as *buhen no ie* ('those from a clan of military prowess'); these terms can be applied to both generational retainers and newcomers.

武藝者之品々之事

Bugeisha no shinajina no koto

THE TYPES OF MARTIAL ARTISTS

Bugeisha, or martial artists, are those *samurai* who serve through martial achievements and teach their paths to other *samurai*. The following list displays the kinds of arts in which *samurai* should train themselves:

- *yumi* 弓 – archery
- *uma* 馬 – horsemanship
- *kenjutsu* 劍術 – swordsmanship
- *sōjutsu* 鎗術 – spearsmanship
- *gunjutsu* 軍術 – the skills of war
- *yawara torite* 柔取手 – wrestling and grappling
- *teppō* 鉄炮 – marksmanship
- *suiren* 水練 – aquatic training

There are myriad other styles. However, they are offshoots from the above and branch off into unlimited possibilities. Study each of these arts from someone who is skilled in that way.

主持隠士勇気一等之事

Shūmochi inshi yūki ittō no koto

THOSE WHO SERVE AND THOSE WHO DO NOT SERVE ARE THE SAME IN TERMS OF COURAGE

In addition to those mentioned above, there are other types of *bushi*-warrior, including those who hold grudges against their lords or who cannot adapt themselves to the times and therefore live discreetly in townhouses or in temples and shrines – these people are called *rōnin*. Many of them still follow the path of the *samurai* and are filled with courage. Therefore, whether a person is a *rōnin*[31] or whether a person is a serving *samurai*,[32] valour can be equal to all.

---

31   Here Natori uses the alternative term 隠士 *inshi*, a 'hidden warrior', but in this context he is referring to a *rōnin*, 'one without employment'.
32   主持 – literally, 'one who has a lord'.

軍法軍配軍者差別之事

Gunpō gunbai gunsha sabetsu no koto

DIFFERENTIATING BETWEEN MILITARY PERSONNEL

Gunpōsha

A *gunpōsha* is a person who knows the foundation of morals and who has mastered the *Goji nanakei shidō no hō*[33] in full and who has a godlike understanding of all aspects of victory and defeat in every detail. Furthermore, this person fully understands castles, ground plans, mandates concerning military gear, astrology and astronomy, topography, human affairs and also the arts of *gunbai* [see below]. In the ancient Tang Dynasty the *gunpōsha* had seventy-two people under his command and he knew well the duties of all those below him. If a person does not understand these points wholly and completely, he should not be called a *gunpōsha*.

In the 'King's Wings' chapter of the *Six Secret Teachings* scroll, it says:

> *The general has seventy-two trusted retainers and assistants in order to respond to any events which may happen. This number is according to heaven's way.*

Gunbaisha

A *gunbaisha* is a person who has a full understanding of religious services, manners and customs, and rituals of the army. He is also able to predict the auspicious and inauspicious by considering divination by date, time, direction, lunar mansion, weather and other factors based on the Destruction Cycle and the Creation Cycle.

Gunsha

Gunsha are *samurai* who are engaged in military service.

Gunpōsha, *gunbaisha* and *gunsha*[34] may have similar names, but they are quite different. Some people misunderstand and misuse military titles,

---

33 五事七計四道ノ法. The first part, 五事七計, refers to the five constant factors and seven considerations taken from Sun Tzu's *Art of War*. The latter part, 四道ノ法, consists of the four ways: *jūhō* ('flexible'), *jakuhō* ('weak'), *gōhō* ('rigid'), and *kyōhō* ('strong').

34 All three are based on the ideogram gun 軍 – 'military'.

and not only these three. *Samurai* may misunderstand certain points when discussing other subjects because they are not educated in such ways, but take note: a *samurai* should be educated on *this* subject so that they will not speak ambiguously when discussing military matters; if not, this is considered a misaligned attitude. Do not discuss issues that you do not understand. Once someone talked to their master and used the term *utte iru* – 'to erect war curtains'. The master asked him, 'Do you mean *utte sueru*?' At this the student was embarrassed and blushed with shame saying that he did not know whether to use the verb *utsu* or *haru* for erecting curtains. Although the master did not intend to raise a question on the subject of war curtains, the student was embarrassed due to his lack of knowledge about this matter – be aware of this.

於忠義不畏死心得之事

Chūgi ni oite shi wo osorezaru kokoroe no koto

PREPARING TO BE WITHOUT FEAR OF DEATH IN THE NAME OF LOYALTY[35]

For a *bushi* it is essential to comprehend the following primary principle: as you have been born a *samurai* you must understand the difficulty of devoting and sacrificing yourself for righteousness and loyalty and you must value your name highly. The truth is that *samurai*, just like everyone else, have a fear of death. However, if your understanding deepens it is not so difficult to enter death. It is possible to die from illness, drowning, fire, to be killed in a moment of rage or even through lust. Even humble townsfolk and farmers can die such a death. Of course, for those born into a military family it is natural to die upon the field of battle. Therefore, if you are prepared in full for any destiny, be it glorious or ignominious, and if you are determined upon the above primary principle, then be aware that to die is not such a difficult act.

---

35 The titles from here have *kaeriten*, or speech-order markers alongside them. These show the reader how to decipher the classical Japanese *kanbun* text, by indicating the correct word order.

犬死用捨之事

Inujini yōsha no koto

CONSIDERING A DOG'S DEATH

If someone depends only upon luck then it is as if they are a monk who has failed to reach enlightenment.[36] Such a person will be careless in what he does and will die a dog's death. He is called a *kenkyōnin* – a 'flustered person'. Even in times of peace this is the highest disgrace for a *bushi*. You should avoid a dog's death and take care to die in the correct place. The 'correct place' is in the service of loyalty and justice.

忠義忘身事

Chūgi ni mi wo wasururu koto

SACRIFICING YOURSELF FOR LOYALTY AND JUSTICE

While *chūgi* – loyalty and justice – are aspects that a *samurai* should keep in mind, they are difficult to demonstrate in practice. Loyalty and justice are not reserved just for periods of war but apply to all times. Keep both loyalty and justice in mind and within your conduct throughout your life. On a battlefield this is easy to fulfil. A sense of loyalty and justice means to think nothing of death and to stick to the Way in the service of your lord, but it also means to discipline yourself and follow law and order, and deeply study the philosophies of military conduct. Without conducting these things at all times, loyalty and justice cannot be fulfilled.

士農工商意得差別之事

Shinōkōshō no itoku sabetsu no koto

DIFFERENTIATING BETWEEN THE MINDSETS OF THE FOUR PATHS OF SAMURAI, FARMER, ARTISAN AND MERCHANT

Be aware that the four classes – *samurai*, farmer, artisan and merchant – have very different requirements. Generally it is accepted that farmers, artisans and merchants need less loyalty and justice, while *samurai* should be aware that they are not permitted to lapse in loyalty or justice even for a single moment of their service. They discipline themselves at all times for the sake of *chūgi*.

---

36 悟リ *satori*, a form of enlightenment.

Samurai differ depending on their position but above all things it is essential to cultivate the mental attitude of *budō*, 'the way of the warrior', and to restrain your mind, and avoid amusements, merrymaking, lust and greed.

武藝可學得心之事

Bugei manabubeki tokushin no koto

BE FULLY AWARE OF THE NEED TO LEARN MARTIAL ARTS

Concerning the arts *samurai* should learn, it is recommended that *bushi* should engage in any kind of art and study to the extent where a good knowledge of it is attained. Learn a martial art that you are especially fond of and remain within a single school until its deepest secrets have been discovered – this will also be helpful in the development of other skills. In any one given art, if you do not distinguish yourself or master it, then only empty words will spread out to the world and hollow arguments will be brought forth. In this case you will have not acquired anything for yourself and sometimes ignorance will be permitted to flourish. This is something you should be careful to avoid.

As well as the above, know a little of the tea ceremony, verse linking, *noh* chanting and the reading of Chinese classics, but you do not have to be reputed as good at them – for example, in reading all that is required is to obtain enough knowledge to read the texts with the aid of phonetic markers.[37] If your interest in such subjects increases and you become overinvolved in their meanings, negligence in *budō* will follow.

修身專要之事

Mi wo osamuru wo senyō no koto

THE IMPORTANCE OF INNER DISCIPLINE

Not only *samurai* but also lower people should maintain discipline within. In the chapter of Great Learning in the *Book of Rites* it says, 'Cultivate oneself', therefore *samurai* should hone themselves by first disciplining their minds. Alongside mastery over the mind should be mastery over the body. 'Discipline' means preparation and to be 'prepared in the body' means that a *samurai* must

---

37 *Kana* are small markers that allow the more difficult Chinese ideograms to be spelled out phonetically.

carry certain basic weapons, such as the *katana* long sword and the *wakizashi* short sword and various other kinds of martial tools. The toolsets for peace times and for the battlefield are explained in detail in the scroll *Heigu Yōhō*. Other than the above, there are more things to always be prepared with and these should also be considered among the basics of self-discipline.

遠慮専一之事
Enryo sen'itsu no koto
DISCRETION IS OF THE UTMOST IMPORTANCE

You should keep yourself disciplined and avoid places where trouble may start, particularly in your private affairs. An exception to this rule is when you have been given an order by the lord. Even if you have to venture to such places of trouble and while you may have the ability to quickly settle any issues that may arise, it is best to not be there at all. If you *are* present at such a place then it is better to prevent any issues from escalating.

While the face you are born with cannot be changed, then, as mentioned above, you can still perfect the preparation of your military gear and mindset, but only if you study such matters deeply. First of all you should not forget that you are a *samurai*, this means that you must have loyalty to your lord, filial devotion to your father and your mother and fidelity towards your friends. Even if your *katana*, *wakizashi*, their mountings, scabbard and cord are not resplendent, you should still maintain and sharpen them, carefully inspect the *mekugi* rivet and the *same* shark-skin grip and keep the blade from becoming blunt by polishing and sharpening it. These are the teachings of those who have gone before us and details of this are mentioned later. Correct preparation will encourage discretion – above all, never forget that you are a *bushi*.

家人示置要語之事
Kajin ni shimeshioku yōgo no koto
INFORMATION WHICH YOU SHOULD ALWAYS TELL THE MEMBERS OF YOUR FAMILY

Keep reminding your wife, children and other family members of the position that you hold and that *all* are also indebted to the lord and that if the lord should order so, you must sacrifice your lives to expunge this debt. This is *mononofu no michi* – the way of the warrior. Even lower servants should clearly understand this matter. Everyone, men and women alike, should know the correct procedure in the case of a commotion, fire, earthquake, combat and for when sanctuary seekers arrive. Give specific instructions for each case, so that when you are away at an inn, for example, and others are minding your residence, they will know what to do.

好色用捨之事
Kōshoku yōsha no koto
CONSIDERATION ON LUST

Lust is what *mononofu* military men should especially avoid. In ancient times there were cases where kings and emperors were ruined because of beautiful women. However, if it were not for affairs between men and women the human race would die out – take note that monks are not allowed to participate. Without question, a *samurai* should refrain from overindulgence in love. If you overindulge in lust towards women, you will lose *budō*.

貪欲生基之事
Don'yoku seiki no koto
THE ERUPTION OF GREED

Humans have desire, they desire life and therefore they grasp on to existence. They have desire for sex and therefore they copulate. They have a desire for wealth and therefore they seek gold and silver. Although individual tendencies will depend on the person's nature, they are sometimes triggered by incidents or by friends. Even those who would not normally withdraw from danger may do so if they observe and sympathize with farmers who are in fear of death. If a beautiful woman or man is seen, it encourages people's lustfulness. If people associate with merchants then they may develop a desire for wealth and naturally seek gold. Know that friends reflect upon a person's heart. Those who follow a specific way will talk of the absolute advantages of that way and even evil people or thieves find their own way beneficial. However, it is the same with those on the correct path.[38] Remember that in both Japan and China there have been many cases where people from the lower classes were mentally and physically disciplined and became courageous warriors. Therefore, it is difficult to treat all cases the same. However, the ancient sayings 'If you brush against red you will be stained red' and 'Water will fit into the shape of its vessel' should be remembered.

用心肝要之事
Yōjin kanyō no koto
THE IMPORTANCE OF EXERCISING CAUTION

Samurai should always be cautious. Never leave a *wakizashi* unattended at any point, and in whatever you do keep it at the waist. If you are attacked without a sword to hand, then it will cause you dishonour. It is an indiscretion that a *samurai* should never commit.

Concerning clothes: do not wear garments that have oversized sleeves, or which are too long or are restricted at the legs. Some say that even if the kimono is too long and the sleeves are oversized, the excess length can be tucked into the *obi*-belt or the sleeves can be pulled up, and that only devotion is important for a *bushi*. Taking that into account, if your clothes are too feminine it is considered ill,[39] yet on the other hand, if they are too practical you may resemble a servant, which is also an issue. Warriors should shave the front of their heads and prepare their hair themselves.

It was asked, 'What should you do if an emergency arises while you are shaving your head?' In answer: *bushi* in older times would carry a *sanjaku tenugui*, a three-foot cloth, and if an emergency arose, they would leave straight away even in the middle of shaving.[40] This was the way of a well-prepared *samurai* in older times and they did not forget *budō* at any moment – keep this in mind.

---

38 If a *samurai* engages in correct ways with friends or situations, then a desire for the correct way will emerge. *Samurai* should not place themselves in the way of lust and greed but put themselves in correct situations instead.

39 This implies that to wear clothes that are too fashionable and oversized is detrimental to the *samurai*.

40 If a *samurai* has to leave suddenly he can cover his head with the cloth and hide any unkempt hair.

用心誤而為臆可否之事

Yōjin ayamatte oku to nasu kahi no koto

POINTS ON MISTAKING CONSIDERATION FOR COWARDICE

Some say that being careful is a sign of cowardice as a *samurai*. However, this is completely erroneous. If you do not take care and you lose your life as a result, then this is a dog's death and, as previously discussed, a dishonour for a *samurai*. The correct way for *samurai* is to cherish life and only sacrifice it for loyalty. You must engage in even small matters carefully and sensibly. Consider fire – it starts in minuteness but can escalate into tremendous destruction. Even a small issue can lead to achievement, dishonour or defeat. Remember, 'A journey of a thousand miles begins with a single step.' Be aware that the gods reside in a true and honest heart, therefore take care in your behaviour and do not behave just as you please.

稽古心得之事

Keiko kokoroe no koto

POINTS TO KEEP IN MIND ABOUT TRAINING

There are points you should be aware of when learning various arts. Anyone, including a *samurai*, who is not determined or has not studied any of the arts until he is around twenty-four or twenty-five years of age may be invited by a friend to participate in such arts. However, because of his deficiencies he may be disgraced. This person may suddenly decide upon the study of an art themselves and afterwards have intense devotion, mentally and physically, day and night, for half of a year or even one or two years, but eventually he will become bored and give up. This situation will not produce a skilled person nor one who has mastered that path. It is like when trying to make a fire with Japanese cypress wood – if you suddenly speed up your drilling when you think the fire is about to ignite, the fire will in fact die and you will be exhausted. Instead, steady drilling with a bamboo pipe is required and it is at the point when the wood actually does catch fire that you should start to drill with increased intensity, so that the tinder fully bursts into flames. Likewise, when studying an art, start slowly and carefully and when the 'fire' ignites within, study with intensity. This is the path to excellence. Remember, if you 'drill' in haste then no art can be learned.

家業非ル藝ハ得失之事
Kagyō ni arazaru gei wa tokushitsu no koto
THE ADVANTAGES AND DISADVANTAGES OF ARTS OUTSIDE YOUR FAMILY PROFESSION

Do not spend your time on arts that are of fleeting interest and have no major connection to your own position. In any art, if you venture too far along that path then it will have effects upon you, more than anticipated, and you will neglect your profession. Since olden days it has been said that an excellent swimmer can die in a river or a deer hunter may miss the mountains because they may over-concentrate and forget their own profession. Therefore, a *samurai* should enjoy the warrior arts and keep a loyal death in mind and regard other amusing arts as a pastime only.

日用道具之事
Nichiyō dōgu no koto
TOOLS FOR DAILY USE

- *katana* 刀 – long sword
- *wakizashi* 脇指 – short sword

As mentioned previously, it is desirable that they are well sharpened so they can cut with ease and that they have two rivets.

Items that should be kept on your person:

- a quick rope[41]
- a compass[42]
- a set square
- a stone pencil
- gold and silver
- a mirror

---

41   早縄 *hayanawa* – a thin rope for binding criminals with a hook attached to the end.
42   磁石 *jishaku* – it can also be interpreted as 'magnet'.

- tweezers
- a comb
- a cloth to clean a *katana* blade
- powder to clean a *katana* blade
- a sword-rivet remover
- medicine for sudden illness and breathlessness, be it for a person or a horse
- a fire striker[43]
- a wooden taper[44]
- one or two sheets of paper for the writing of oaths[45]

You should not carry something with writing upon it. However, depending on the situation, you can carry paper with your family name.

The above items should be carried in a *kinchaku* draw-string pouch or a *hanagami-bukuro* small belongings bag. You should also carry a *sanjaku-tenugui* three-foot cloth with you at all times. Be prepared like this when travelling and even during normal times. The above are called *nichiyō dōgu* – tools for daily life.

愛敬専用之事
Aigyō senyō no koto
THE IMPORTANCE OF A FRIENDLY ATTITUDE

Samurai should cherish the concept of *aigyō* – love and respect[46] – and not let their status as *bushi* make them arrogant. Never slander people or talk of a desire for money or complain about the quality of food, be it in word or by behaviour. Consider the following when choosing friends to associate with. While past generations warned against being too selective about people, there is an appropriate way to do this. Keep the concepts of 離 'distant' and 親 'close' in your mind. You may get close to monks and ask them about karma from the path of Buddhism. However, you do not have to become a monk to learn

---

43　火打 *hiuchi* – a striker to create a spark.

44　付木 *tsukegi* – a paper-thin section of wood ignited with the above striker.

45　牛王 *goō* – paper stamped by a temple or shrine and which can be used to write out a written oath if a situation requires it.

46　愛敬 – literally, 'love and respect' – to cherish and to respect others.

Buddhism. It is also beneficial to ask a Zen monk about the meaning of life and of death – you should know about these things at normal times. Understanding the principle of the path to enlightenment may make death less daunting.[47]

Δ Tradition says:

The following eleven points are traditions concerning the previous twenty-two points. You should study them and understand them for what they are. They are called *hiden* – secret traditions – and they should be kept in mind at all times.

忘ルルト不忘ノ三字

Wasururu to wasurezu no sanji

THINGS TO FORGET AND THINGS THAT SHOULD NOT BE FORGOTTEN

Forget the following to aid loyal devotion:

- wives and children
- treasure and properties
- your body and your life

Do not forget the following to aid loyal devotion:

- determination in loyalty
- the name of your family
- parents and ancestors

士者信神ヲ用

Samurai wa shinjin wo mochiiru

SAMURAI SHOULD HAVE A BELIEF IN THE GODS

This is especially true for someone who is a captain of people. If those of a high position do not trust in the gods then lower retainers will become suspicious.

---

47   Literally, 'death will become lighter'.

七三之言語

Shichisan no gengo

SEVEN OUT OF TEN POINTS IN YOUR SPEECH

Nine parts of your mind are for thinking, while one is for speaking. Of this one part, reveal only seven details out of ten and leave three unsaid.

作ル勇之習

Yū wo tsukuru no narai

TEACHINGS ABOUT INSTILLING COURAGE

When discussing war, if someone says he wishes to gain achievements in battle, never tell him that he cannot do so. A proverb says: 'Cattle wish for a ring to be put through their nose.'[48]

一向之劔心

Ikkō no kenshin

TO FACE OFF WITH A SWORD-LIKE HEART

If you avoid soft speech then courage will manifest itself within you. When you 'face off' then have a 'sword-like heart'.[49]

剛臆見分

Gō oku miwake

TO DISTINGUISH BETWEEN THE FORMIDABLE AND THE COWARD

If someone's expression changes[50] at a time of emergency they have no courage, while those who show no surprise are courageous.

武具相應

Bugu soō

HAVING APPROPRIATE MILITARY TOOLS

Make sure you have the correct military tools, as your spirit will rise and fall because of them.

---

48   i.e. people desire hardship.

49   This teaching could apply to any form of confrontation, speech included.

50   There is an underlying message at play with the ideograms. They imply that in such a situation the coward loses colour in his face.

謀計三和一合

Bōkei sanwa ichigō

TACTICS INTEGRATING THREE PLANS INTO ONE

This concept was used while Minamoto no Yoritomo was exiled to Izu and is transmitted in the scroll *Kōketsu*.

刀脇指置様

Katana wakizashi okiyō

POSITIONING YOUR *KATANA* AND *WAKIZASHI*

When going to sleep, place one sword on each side, with them slightly drawn. How to sleep with them when travelling or when under a mosquito net will be explained later.

書證之品付四十八字

Shoshō no shina tsuketari shijūhachi ji

CONCERNING WRITTEN EVIDENCE

Supplementary: the forty-eight-letter *iroha* alphabet

If there is something delicate that cannot be written normally transmit it orally or write in code, remembering that writing can serve as evidence. Here 'forty-eight letters' means the coded communication of the *iroha* alphabet.

位之詞

Kurai no kotoba

WORDS FOR DETERMINING DOMINANCE

Use this way of asserting your dominance when meeting someone for the first time. Avoid strong mannerisms but move your words to strength later on. Also, it is sometimes better to have your servant greet the person or talk to them first and you yourself should say nothing until you have formed a better understanding of the person before you.

The above thirty-three points, including the twenty-two initial points and eleven traditions, are points that *samurai* should use in normal life.

The following seventeen points are on the construction of houses, walls, gates and doors and also paper sliding doors. These seventeen points are secret traditions. At the beginning of the list the ideogram for house 家 has been written. There are also a further seven points, which start at the point marked by the words 'tradition says' – this makes twenty-four points in total.

Ie

ARTICLES ON HOUSES

住宅家屋心得之事

Jūkyo kaoku kokoroe no koto

**POINTS TO KEEP IN MIND ABOUT YOUR HOLDINGS
AND HOMESTEAD**

Although, houses, ground plans, reception halls[51] and entrances[52] can all be constructed according to individual preference, *samurai* do not need to build splendid residences. This is because they may die for loyalty at any moment. It is wrong-minded to spend a lot of gold and silver on your homestead with the intent of securing a future of a hundred years. However, if you have an enemy or someone who has targeted you for vengeance and wishes to murder you, then if your lord has ordered that you should survive and you must cherish your life, a carefully constructed house may be required. Used as a strategy to kill your enemies, constructing an elaborate house will cause them to underestimate you. Apart from cases where a use of tactics is required, most normal *samurai*[53] do not have elaborate houses. That being said, having a well-designed appearance is desirable. Know that merchants and farmers tend to have luxurious houses for the need of family business.

---

51 座敷 *zashiki* – the main room for receiving guests.
52 玄関 *genkan* – an entrance for the taking off of shoes.
53 平士 *heishi* – 'normal *samurai*', the bulk of a lord's force.

門玄関番人心得之事

Mon genkan bannin kokoroe no koto

POINTS TO KEEP IN MIND ABOUT GATEKEEPERS AND ENTRANCE GUARDS

Inform gatekeepers and entrance guards that they should keep watch without being negligent at any time, as they are the first to deal with sanctuary seekers[54] and messengers. If they are dull-witted, their deeds and speech may bring failure and dishonour upon the master. Be aware of this.

同夜分心得之事

Onajiku yabun kokoroe no koto

POINTS THAT GATEKEEPERS AND ENTRANCE GUARDS SHOULD KEEP IN MIND AT NIGHT

Even if someone comes with an urgent message at night, gatekeepers and entrance guards should not open the gate or the door without careful consideration. Tell them to listen to the visitors and study them carefully; making sure to observe what the person's appearance is like in the light. Also, instruct them not to reveal to the visitor without due care and consideration whether you are absent from the premises. During the daytime, it is essential for the entrance guard to observe a messenger's speech, their servants and their facial expressions. However, the process is different if they come from a family that you know very well. Make sure that the entrance guard is aware that someone with an unfamiliar family name is not to be admitted without full attention being given to the situation. Guards should have the same judgement as their master.

門戸撥様之事

Monko hirakiyō no koto

HOW TO OPEN A GATE OR DOOR

In the case of a low-ranking *samurai* who does not have an entrance keeper or when at a villa[55] and so on and there is no one to serve you, you may have

---

54 走込 *hashirikomi* – those who run to find sanctuary after committing an act of vengeance.
55 下屋敷 *shimoyashiki* – a second house or villa. This is advice for *samurai* who are maintaining a lord's villa while they are away.

to open a sliding door or even a paper sliding door yourself. Always open the door with the left hand, then withdraw behind the door and observe the situation. Generally, you do not have enough mobility when opening a sliding door or paper sliding door to the right. When sliding doors are left open, avoid positioning two doors together. This is called *nijūdate* – double-door closing.

忍口習之事

Shinobi-guchi narai no koto

TEACHINGS CONCERNING SECRET ENTRANCES

One or two secret entrances should be incorporated somewhere within the construction or within an outer wall. They should be kept unknown even to servants and other people. Construct them so that they are difficult for others to discover but so that they are easy for you to open. These are called *shinobi-guchi* – hidden exits.

居間得道具置様之事

Ima no edōgu okiyō no koto

KEEPING PRIMARY WEAPONS IN THE LIVING ROOM[56]

In your main room of use, when positioning your *katana*, *wakizashi*, spear, halberd or any other weapon you excel in, long weapons should be placed to the rear and on your right, while your *katana*, *wakizashi* and other things should be placed on the left. Also, position spears and halberds at the main entrance of the living room with the tips of the blades towards the opening. Long weapons and projectiles kept in the main room can be positioned depending on the circumstances of the room itself.

門戸廣狹之事

Monko kōkyō no koto

WIDE AND NARROW GATES AND DOORS

When staying in a house, be it your own or someone else's, for a period of time, make preparations for any sudden incident by investigating the location

---

56 居間 *ima* – the room most frequented by the master of the house.

of doors and the number of *tatami* mats in each of the rooms.[57] Do this so that you are prepared for when you need to move in haste or when you need go in or out of a room. This is also so that you do not hit your body or strike even the tip of your scabbard against anything. If you have not prepared in this way, you may bang your head, foot or tip of your scabbard when you are in a narrow place. Apart from when all is well and depending on the situation, you should consider the layout and size of the rooms. If you have to interact with someone who has come in stealth,[58] do not give out instructions by using names.[59] Things to consider are: marks,[60] prior arrangements, information on gates and doors and the size of rooms. Further details are given in the writing *Shinobi no Maki.*

入忍盗心得之事

Shinobi[61] iru kokoroe no koto

POINTS TO KEEP IN MIND WHEN SNEAK-THIEVES INFILTRATE[62]

If thieves and the like have pierced through into the storehouse or the walls, do not challenge them from inside the house without thinking; instead move to the front area of the house and have someone else call to them from the inside. They will go to the entrance without fail.[63] It is preferable to capture or kill[64] them at this point. If you panic and call out to them from the inside then you may fail to seize them. While the best course of action will vary according to the situation, it is a principle not to force them into a fluster, which is what will happen if you call out to them without preparation.

---

57 i.e. to identify the size of each room.

58 忍来者 *shinobi-kuru mono* – a person who is infiltrating under stealth.

59 Names are to be avoided because infiltrators may use the names of household members to their advantage.

60 目印 *mejirushi* – a mental note or mark to prompt memory.

61 Possibly read as *nintō*.

62 The ideograms 忍盗 are used which imply 'creeping thieves'.

63 The second half of this sentence is only found in the Koga transcription.

64 討 *utsu* – this term has predominantly been translated as 'strike'. However, here the meaning is most likely 'kill'.

有越塀者時之事

Hei wo kosu mono aru toki no koto

POINTS FOR WHEN SOMEONE HAS CROSSED THE OUTER WALL

If someone has crossed over the gate or wall, be it day or night, do not attempt to stab or hook them with a spear or halberd while they are up high; instead, if they are crossing over, wait until they are on the inside and have just landed, *then* strike them. If they are in the process of leaving by climbing over the wall, then, again, attack them when they land. If they are in a higher position, they may take advantage and grab the handle of your spear and fight back. Generally, it is best to attack an enemy when he feels at ease, after he has either entered or departed.

小門出入心得之事

Shōmon deiri kokoroe no koto

POINTS TO BE AWARE OF WHEN MOVING IN OR OUT THROUGH A SMALL GATEWAY

When someone is coming through a small gateway with a door or narrow place, wait until they have exited and *then* strike them. If you strike them at the wrong moment, they may withdraw. If you yourself move in or out through such a place, put your leg out first and do not lead with your head, this is because if you are injured upon the head, with even a slight injury, blood will fill your eyes and mouth and it will prevent you from fighting.

用心塀得要之事

Yōjinbei tokuyō no koto

THE BENEFIT OF WELL-GUARDED OUTER WALLS

These outer walls are *usually* seven *shaku* high and they are called *yōjinbei*; these are the first line of defence. They need not always be seven *shaku* high but should be made so that people cannot jump and grasp the lip; this is why they are called *yōjinbei* – walls of precaution. Walls or thorny shrubs serve as a form of defence even if it is only a minor one. A proverb says, 'Stretching a rope *may* work as a defence.' The same principle applies here.[65]

---

65   i.e. do not overlook any opportunity to create a defence, no matter how simple the idea or construction.

塀裏禦様心得之事

Heiura fusegiyō kokoroe no koto

THINGS TO BE AWARE OF CONCERNING DEFENDING THE INNER SIDE OF AN OUTER WALL

Inform those who are on guard or who are on night-watch duty to patrol the inside of the complex. This is done to prevent the men, including servants, from becoming negligent about internal defence as well as external security. Also, it is a primary security measure to erect defensive spikes[66] on the top of the wall and to scatter caltrops at its base. Know that caltrops are not a measure to be used at normal times but are for when defending places that are deemed unsafe. Details on this are mentioned in the scrolls *Heieki Yōhō* and *Suisen Yōhō*.

忍返心得之事

Shinobi-gaeshi kokoroe no koto

THINGS TO BE AWARE OF CONCERNING DEFENSIVE SPIKES

Infiltrators climbing over walls that have defensive spikes upon them may break the spikes off with a nail remover or, alternatively, place bamboo cylinders over the spikes. Furthermore, there is a tradition called *nunoshiki* – spreading cloth. Further details are in our writing *Shinobi no Maki*. Therefore, it is not safe to rely exclusively on defensive spikes.

屋敷地習之事

Yashikichi narai no koto

TEACHINGS ON GROUND PLANS

If your house is large, give it a layout similar to that of a castle; details are not to be mentioned here. In designing the layout, use the principle of *chigiri no kane*,[67] which will avoid any of the rooms being dark. You should give primary consideration to the well, the toilet and the drainage. To protect against emergencies such as a fire use an underground storehouse. There are other

---

66 忍返 *shinobi-gaeshi* – spiked fence-like defences set on the top of walls to prevent would-be intruders from climbing over.

67 An unknown principle related to light.

points to consider regarding layout design and the master of a house should be aware of all these things.

築山遣水之事

Tsukiyama yarimizu no koto

BUILDING ARTIFICIAL HILLS AND CONSTRUCTING THE FLOW OF STREAMS IN YOUR GARDEN

There are a few things to be aware of when constructing a garden. Do not worry too much about tasteful design or creating handsome views. A master should make sure that the greenery[68] and landscaping have benefits within their layout [in terms of defence]. It is often the case that gardens are unsafe if they have been designed with too much emphasis on creating beautiful views. Furthermore, there are a lot of things to be aware of concerning both the doors and the paper sliding doors of bedrooms, among other things.

境内倒者心得之事

Keidai taoremono kokoroe no koto

THINGS TO BE AWARE OF CONCERNING SOMEONE WHO IS LYING INJURED IN YOUR RESIDENCE

If someone is lying injured in your house, cut and weakened from bloodshed, immediately give notice to the authorities by sending someone out. However, if the injured person is one of your own retainers,[69] all will depend on the situation. If it *is* one of your retainers, you will know how it should be dealt with by the way they usually serve. Overall, it is not desirable to be in haste. Concerning fighting and combat, details will be mentioned later.

門戸鎖様之事

Monko tojiyō no koto

LOCKING GATES AND DOORS

If you detect something suspicious or unsafe, keep the gates and doors open and have lights set up. This is in keeping with the traditional teaching, '*Shinobi*

---

68 Any trees and shrubs.

69 The text does not specify if this is a servant or a low-level *samurai*.

will not infiltrate where lights are lit inside of paper sliding doors.'

Δ Tradition says:

The following seven points are traditions about the above seventeen points. Keep them in mind and understand them as they are said. They are called *hiden* – secret traditions – and are the secret traditions for the above points concerning houses.

小夜枕
Sayomakura
THE NIGHT PILLOW

Place a pillow on the doorsill and then place a folding fan on top of that when you go to sleep. This is done so that when the door moves the fan will fall and wake you up. This is also useful when you have to take a nap.

門戸鎖様
Monko tojiyō
LOCKING GATES AND DOORS

Put holes or nails into the crosspieces of the doors and then pass thin rope through or around them and secure the doors so that they cannot be opened. Know that padlocks and latches are not sufficient.

堀川門
Horikawa mon
THE GATE OF THE IMPERIAL RESIDENCE

In ancient times Minamoto no Yoshitsune opened this gate in anticipation of a night attack.

付火盗賊兼防
Tsukebi tōzoku kanete fusegu
DEFENDING AGAINST ARSON AND THIEVERY

Build with defence and protection in mind so that it stands as a warning to others. There are ways to do this.

鶏眼不睡

Keigan nemurazu

TO BE WITHOUT SLEEP AND TO OPEN YOUR EYES LIKE A BIRD

This means staying up without sleep. On a night when something is critical, there is a teaching which says you should not sleep. This should be done with the feeling of birds, because they wake up immediately alert.

蔀カザシ

Shitomi kazashi

SECURING FROM WITHIN AND WITHOUT

This means securing a house from the inside and from the outside. Securing the outside is called *kazashi*, while securing the inside is called *shitomi*. Many people consider only the outside and care little for protecting the inside. Alternatively, some care only about the inside and neglect the outside. The above is true in most cases.

早晨之心

Sōshin no kokoro

THE ATTITUDE OF RISING AT DAWN

It is a duty for humans to rise early in the morning. Therefore, rise early and search the homestead. An old saying states, 'Make plans for your day when the cockerel crows.' However, if it is a short night it may be difficult to wake at dawn. In such a case wake someone up and inform them of the time that you wish to rise and that they should come to you at this time; this is so that you will not oversleep. This is called *sōshin*.

The above twenty-four points are hints on houses, ground plans and construction. From this point onwards there shall be hints for a master who has guests and for casual conversations. At the top the ideogram for miscellaneous 雑 has been written. There will follow twenty-seven points, with a further nine points on the traditions of this subject. Combined, this comes to thirty-six points in total.

MISCELLANEOUS ARTICLES

虚言可嗜事
Kyogen tashinamu beki koto
REFRAIN FROM TELLING LIES

Samurai should never lie to anyone, even a passing acquaintance. It is essential to show correct manners at all times. When you are invited as a guest in another's house or at a friend's abode then keep this point in mind when you associate with other *samurai*. A single false word from a *samurai* could be disastrous to all present. There have been many cases of this since ancient times.

和睦挨拶之事
Waboku aisatsu no koto
ARRANGING A RECONCILIATION

When entertaining guests as a host, keep the following in mind. If the guests start to fight unexpectedly, make sure to settle the situation so that no one is injured and that grudges do not form. However, when *samurai* argue do not take one side over the other and do not judge which is right and which is wrong. If one side is judged as correct and the other as not correct, then the side judged as incorrect may lose face and if then forced into peace, this may result in them returning to kill their adversary later on. Also, depending on the outcome of the judgement, the side judged as correct may not be forgiving or understanding. Therefore, do not discuss who is correct or incorrect but instead talk to each party with a view to settling the situation. There are various types of incidents that may occur; therefore, good judgement is required.

口論取捌之事

Kōron torisabaki no koto

ARBITRATING IN AN ARGUMENT

If *samurai* argue and you happen to be there, perhaps as a host, and if you have to talk to them to intervene, move between them and sit down – this is a way from old times. The first thing you should do is to calm them down so that they stop arguing. If they say too many things then it will be hard to bring about settlement. Explain to them that they will bring about embarrassment for both the guests and the host – say this as many times as necessary. Moving in between the two is done to prevent them from drawing their *katana* or *wakizashi* swords; once they have drawn a weapon then it will become more difficult to settle the matter. However, even if they have taken a hold of their sheathed swords or even their sword handle, then with arbitration a settlement is still possible. Do not try to convince them in haste or discuss that which is correct and that which is incorrect. Remember the ancient saying, 'Both sides have justice', and therefore as they both have justice, sometimes an arbitrator may decide that he is not needed. Be aware of such a case as this.

詞之虚実用捨之事

Kotoba no Kyojitsu Yōsha no Koto

CONSIDERATION ON INSUBSTANTIAL AND SUBSTANTIAL SPEECH

Samurai should be aware that every single word matters and therefore should try to be reserved at all times. However, in some situations it can be embarrassing if you are *too* reserved. Such an attitude may look like a flatterer pretending to be reserved. It is desirable always to avoid using those words used by women or children, both when you tell a story and when you tell facts. Do not quote fictional stories that are not appropriate to the situation at hand – this will seem improper. That being said and depending on the situation, do not raise an objection if a story is told that is considered slightly incorrect as long as it is told in a spirit of loyalty. The subject of *insubstantial* within *substantial* and *substantial* within *insubstantial* will be explained in detail in the scroll *Ippei Yōkō*.

舊話雑談用捨之事

Kyūwa zatsudan yōsha no koto

CONSIDERATIONS ON CASUAL TALK ABOUT THINGS OF THE PAST

A *samurai*'s words can be counted as more secure than gold or iron. In some stories of military achievements and battles of old, there are episodes involving men of enormous strength. Even though the records talk thus, know that both then and now there are limits to what a human being of normal stature can do. If you tell such stories as if they were literally true, this is embarrassing and people will judge your personality from this. Therefore, there are things you should know about telling stories of rare deeds. For example, if you earnestly praise warriors who did not hesitate to sacrifice their lives, people will think that you must also fight outstandingly. Faced with an emergency, how could any *samurai* be inferior to the brave warriors of yore when fighting at the cost of their lives and for loyalty? Understand that present-day *samurai* happen to be born in times of peace and lead an easy life through a turn of fate. It is desirable to talk with others about various kinds of achievements in warfare.

他人之噂得心之事

Tanin no uwasa tokushin no koto

THINGS TO BE AWARE OF CONCERNING RUMOURS ABOUT OTHERS

If present when rumours or malicious gossip about certain people are being spread, then it is desirable to be very discreet and talk with care. Generally, those who gossip and pass on rumours about others are cowards. If being questioned or asked to confirm what has been said, they will often quote examples of other people's faults and state that 'they did this' or 'they did that'; this is because they lack dignity.[70] Even though *samurai* may sometimes change their words at a later date, in order to present an excuse for a misdeed, they should never pass blame on to others for those actions.

---

70 They will talk about others' faults.

Improve yourself by considering the above points and know that you should never speak of others behind their backs. If you do say anything about someone behind their back then you should repeat those words to their face. Also, know that those who talk to you about people behind their backs will talk about you when you are not with them. If a rumour includes a serious insult in terms of *budō* or something that blights the honour of a *samurai*, then secure evidence of this and a pledge from the person who informed you. The same protocol should be used for words spoken to divide people.

勸盃損益之事

Kanpai son'eki no koto

THE ADVANTAGES AND DISADVANTAGES OF OFFERING ALCOHOL

When entertaining others do not offer too much *sake*. A host should prepare dishes with the utmost of care and not encourage their guests to drink too much wine. All *bushi* have a precious lord to serve and urgent needs and services may arise at any time. Even those who are lord-less but who have acquired and maintain the heart and calling of the *samurai* should drink in moderation. *Sake* slackens the mind and increases the spirit[71] and leads people into confusion; remember the ancient saying, 'Do not fall past the point in which you enter into disarray.'[72] There are myriad cases where people have become intoxicated and have created confusion in important matters. Therefore, this is something that *samurai* should not do. However, there is an old practice that states that you should not totally refuse to drink even a single drop of alcohol, even if alcohol does not agree with you. You should also remember this.

臨席而禮法之事

Seki ni nozonde reihō no koto

POINTS ON MANNERS TO OBSERVE WHEN INVITED AS A GUEST

If you are invited to another's house as a guest and there are various *samurai* present and seated, make sure to bow to those present and to the host. However,

---

71 *Chi*

72 From the *Analects* of Confucius, Book X, Section VIII.

if you are on cordial terms with the people there, be aware that it is slightly against good etiquette to be over-polite to those you are closely associated with at ordinary times. Also it is not appropriate to be polite only at these forms of social gatherings.

There is a correct place for the storage of swords,[73] but remember that if a few *samurai* have already gathered and have left their swords in an alternative place, do not worry about where your *katana* should correctly be positioned but simply leave it with the rest. It is bad manners to put your *katana* in a different place from others', as it implies that such a place is more suitable; however, this may still depend on the situation. When capturing criminals or doing something similar, do not take your *katana* off your waist. However, it is considered a serious breach of manners not to put it aside in other situations.

脇指覚語之事

Wakizashi Kakugo no Koto

THE MINDSET OF THE SHORT SWORD

Do not take your *wakizashi* sword off your waist even when relaxing. This is not only for the sake of personal defence but also as a matter of courtesy to your host and your colleagues. However, this does not apply when in a *sukiya*-style tea house or in a *kakoi* tea-ceremony room or in audience with aristocrats. If a host with good reason asks for side arms[74] to be taken off the waist then they can be taken off. Or if the host asks with respect for swords to be removed, then you should do so. For more on this kind of information, you should ask a practitioner of a school which concentrates on dining and etiquette. Generally keep in mind that a *bushi* should retain his *wakizashi* at all times. If your leg touches another's side arm, then the rule is to hold [his sword] above your head [as you bow]. It is also acceptable [if the owner] lifts up the sword to then just make your bow. It has been recorded here that the *wakizashi* should not be taken off – this is for your benefit.

---

73 This is the act of placing the *katana* in a room or selected position when entering another's house. However, the *wakizashi* should be retained at the waist.

74 腰物 *koshimono* – literally 'things on the waist', which in this context means swords.

座列心得之事

Zaretsu kokoroe no koto

POINTS TO KEEP IN MIND AT GATHERINGS

When attending a dinner, give compliments on the dishes served even if you do not like them. When in the main reception room if the issue of seating position arises and offers of position are given, do not sit in a socially better position than older men who have achieved military success. However, if you are repeatedly and earnestly offered such a position you should not be too reluctant and should accept the offer. Generally, study manners by referring to a specialized source on this subject.

相客心得之事

Aikyaku kokoroe no koto

THINGS TO KEEP IN MIND CONCERNING OTHER GUESTS

When receiving an invitation by messenger or by letter days before the event, ask who else shall be attending and if there are *samurai* invited who hold grudges against each other, turn down the invitation. It is said that to stay away from an event for this reason is actually an act of military cowardice, but do not pay any attention to this. Always keep loyalty in mind – only your lord's orders are of importance, and therefore it is appropriate not to attend such events. If you are unaware of any bad blood then it cannot be helped if a problem does arise. However, it is a wrong mindset to attend if you already know about any such issues.

至愚會釈之事

Shigu eshaku no koto

MEETING AND GREETING IMBECILES

When there are *samurai* among your associates who are ignorant and stupid[75] and talk and behave without thinking, it is essential to keep your distance and know that it is a huge mistake to trick or to make fun of them. As they are

---

75 愚 *oroka* – the implication here is of one who cares little for the correct protocol or decorum and who has stupidity within them. It should be noted that the term has various connotations.

stupid they may suddenly threaten to kill you for the smallest of reasons. There was once a case where an ignorant *samurai* took offence and despite efforts to persuade him that he had taken the situation wrongly, he would not listen and killed the person he thought had insulted him. If you are unaware of a person's stupidity then it cannot be helped, but if you are aware of it and still have dealings with this person, then you are also to be considered stupid.

剛膽言語好嫌之事

Gōoku gengo kōken no koto

PREFERRED TERMS TO BE USED FOR BRAVERY AND COWARDICE

You should take care when talking about episodes of the *samurai*. Do not use words like 'fearful'. When talking about fighting and killing and things of that ilk, do not use 'slack' speech but instead describe fighting as brave and devoted. However, sometimes the situation may demand for care to be taken when you use such words as 'strong', 'horrible' or 'violent'. Also, refrain from talking about amounts of gold and silver, treasure or how expensive things are.

相客争論心得之事

Aikyaku sōron kokoroe no koto

POINTS ON ARGUMENTS BETWEEN OTHER GUESTS

This point concerns arguments between guests. If it is an argument between lower people, your approach will depend on the situation. However, if it is between *samurai*, never call for their parents, brothers or relatives – even if the *samurai* are young – unless the previously mentioned relatives are in attendance. The reason for this is that it will only make for a larger commotion. If things become too difficult for the host to settle himself, he should call for an arbitrator[76] to help him intervene or alternatively he can secretly send for a close friend or older man and make it appear as if he just happened to be passing by and that he was just visiting. Call non-drinkers to deal with non-drinkers and drinkers to deal with drinkers; this is because they know how to talk to each other. In all cases it is desirable to use people who speak with intelligence.

---

76   挨拶人 *aisatsunin* – this implies that someone of good speech should be used to help settle the situation.

士者無口論事

Samurai wa kōron naki koto

SAMURAI SHOULD NOT ARGUE

As a primary rule, keep it in mind that *samurai* should not argue. This is because if an argument continues then it will end up in a killing. If everyone remembers this and maintains self-restraint, arguments should not begin in the first place. If there is an issue that cannot be avoided and something needs to be said, know that if you argue increasingly critically or discuss the right or wrong of a matter, you have to be prepared to make a kill at the end of such a situation. As mentioned earlier there is the tradition of *ikkō no kenshin* – 'facing off' with a sword-like heart – and in this tradition you should speak with determination and directness. This is a way to show your 'inner blade'. If you do not have such determination then it is best to avoid saying words of grave importance.

手帋書状心得之事

Tegami shojō kokoroe no koto

POINTS ON LETTERS AND WRITING

Do not commit important matters fully to paper when writing letters. Generally, when *samurai* compose letters they should not write down specific details. This is because mistakes made orally can be attributed to the carelessness of the messenger, while things written will remain as evidence long after they have been penned and they cannot be erased. When recording someone else's words in a letter you should write in a gentle manner. Writing will sound harsher than speech, so when reading any writings from others keep this point in mind and guess the true inflections behind others' words – if taken wrongly then they will often cause trouble. Details on hidden letters and secret writing are transmitted in our writing *Shinobi no Maki*.

堪忍未發之事

Kannin mihatsu no koto

POINTS ON FORBEARANCE AND REINING IN
PERSONAL OUTBURSTS

Here *kannin* – forbearance – means stopping yourself from speaking out. However, if you restrain yourself at the wrong time, you may appear to be cowardly; therefore, this is a matter of great importance. Restrain yourself by remembering, 'Forbearance as a *samurai* cannot be maintained if you express that which you wish to say.' This is *the* point of this matter. If you bite your tongue when you should speak out, people may think of you as incompetent. On the other hand, if a person is known to be well-versed in *budō*, others may admire his forbearance in keeping going despite being unhappy with a situation. This is the way you should endeavour to be.

他之親族之悪語我時之事

Hoka no shinzoku no aku wo ware ni kataru toki no koto

WHEN HEARING ILL OF SOMEONE'S FAMILY

If someone tells you about ill-mannered behaviour by one of their parents, children or brothers, then know there is a way to respond when listening to such an account. Even if you have already heard or seen such things, you should not confirm or agree on the matter. This is because, above all, it would be discourteous towards the person concerned. Generally, if someone discovers that a member of their family has done wrong then they *could* kill or disown them but they will never admit their relative's faults to someone outside their family. Therefore, if people do discuss such matters with others, they do so in the hope that other people may gain a better understanding. In this case you should give advice such as: 'It may be true, but still they are young and therefore you should advise them on the matter.' Though people may talk to you about their parents, children or brothers, relying on the close relationship they have with you, it is not their aim to receive embarrassing assistance. Sometimes you may have to give them advice that leaves them no option but to make a drastic decision. Perhaps they may decide that their family member cannot be forgiven, and thus they may be forced to take critical action. This should be kept in mind. Every single word matters to a *samurai*. If you fail to adhere to this principle things can easily become ruinous.

万事可知始終事

Banji shijū wo shirubeki koto

KNOWING THAT ALL THINGS HAVE A BEGINNING AND AN END

Be fully aware that things have both a beginning and an end. People normally understand the beginnings of things but do not understand the ends and often advise others to just start or say something without thinking of the ending – this is undesirable. In all things, if you carefully contemplate and pass through thoughtful consideration then you will know how to start and have an idea of how things will end. It is primary to understand this with reference to yourself. According to *The Great Learning of the Book of Rites*: 'All things have roots and branches[77] while affairs have their beginning and an end.' This principle holds true in all matters. If unsure of your own judgements and conclusions then ask those who have prowess in military matters or consult a sage. If a matter cannot be discussed openly with others then there is a technique in our school where you speak to a person who does not know you to discover the information you require. This is called *tamon no tsutae* – the tradition of asking others.

難義不讓他事

Nangi hoka ni yuzurazaru koto

POINTS ON NOT PASSING DIFFICULTIES ON TO OTHERS

Even *samurai* can experience hard times for various reasons. When your body is racked with pain, then so will other people's. Coldness, heat, joy and sorrow are the same to all people and all feel them equally. Therefore, if you are suffering do not pass your suffering on to others, because if it is hard for you to bear then it will be hard for them, too. It is not the way of the *samurai* to be unaware of this issue and to pass on such difficulties. Many farmers and townspeople like to gain prestige through wealth and sometimes create businesses with other people's ideas. This is something *samurai* should not stoop to, no matter how tempting it may be. To have this type of mindset shows a lack of determination and is shameful. Be without blemish where matters of *budō* are concerned;

---

77 本末 *honmatsu* – this can also be seen as 'cause and effect', the 'core and the external', the 'trunk and branches', 'importance and non-importance' and also 'substance and its shadow'.

make sure that you do not suffer disgrace and do not taint yourself to protect others. In ancient times, people sought high honours in battle so as not to be lacking in *budō*. In addition to this, do not discuss or make claim to gold or silver. If you cherish people you will not deprive them of their honour and you will have no enemies in times of peace and if you have no enemies then you shall not enter into arguments or fights throughout your lifetime. Have the determination not to ruin yourself by being short-tempered and do not indulge in momentary and impulsive anger.

下人善悪有主人事

Genin zen'aku shujin ni aru koto

THE RIGHTEOUSNESS OR UNRIGHTEOUSNESS OF LOWER PEOPLE DEPENDS UPON THEIR MASTER

When hiring lower people there exists a major principle, which is to confirm the servant's guarantor and to obtain a certificate to ensure that the person is not a Christian. Obtain the certificate from their family temple[78] – do not neglect this point. Also, find out whether they are righteous or unrighteous and use them according to their character. These issues are discussed in detail in the section *Shō no Hō* – the Way of the General. In addition, observe whether they are cold or hot, joyous or sorrowful. Remember to cherish them and give them compassion when you use them. Basically, lower people do not understand loyalty but if their master is compassionate and addresses them with kindness then they will serve well and only a limited number of them will be ill-behaved. Generally, if servants do not serve correctly then this is because their master has a disloyal attitude – remember that lower people learn from those above. If their master shows loyalty [to his lord] in mind and uses lower people with compassion then they will follow his example. Most immoral acts committed by servants can be traced back to their master.

隠徳専用之事

Intoku senyō no koto

ALWAYS RETAIN HIDDEN VIRTUE

---

78 *Terauke* – a certificate from a family temple.

Farmers, craftsmen and merchants understand only a small amount of this concept, while *samurai* should keep this idea fully in mind. As people have their own interests at heart, they perform good deeds that bring them attention and which allow them to become known to the public, even if it means suffering as a consequence. In contrast, *intoku* – hidden virtue – brings no apparent benefit, so most people consider it useless and do not engage with it; this attitude should be avoided. It should be regarded as absolutely improper to value that which is visible and to disparage that which is hidden. Military tactics should be judged good or bad according to their ability to end disorder. A person without hidden virtue is known as a *hyōri-mono* – a double-sided person. They are despised in the military.

起請文心得之事

Kishōmon kokoroe no koto
POINTS ON WRITTEN OATHS

Since ancient times the written oath has been used as a guarantee when matters appear to be in doubt or to ensure that a vow will not be broken.

Someone asked: 'Consider the following case: a person is in imminent danger of losing his life and he writes a sworn oath to save his life. Although he may incur punishment from the gods [if he later breaks the oath], if he had not written such an oath due to a fear of this divine punishment then he would have lost his life there and then. Therefore, people may write and sign such an oath to escape an immediate danger, but then they may violate this oath by becoming involved in an ill deed. In such a case, the punishment derived from breaking the oath does not arrive immediately; therefore, it seems that the sin of violating the oath does not exist. Am I right or wrong in this?'

The answer: this is similar to what is called *tachishita no chikaibun* – an oath taken under the sword. Originally, the written oath was a way to record a promise or to dispel any doubts that may be held. In another country it is called the *meiyaku* pledge, and the purpose is the same.

Concerning punishment from the gods: unless you are from a family that performs Shintō it is difficult to judge whether divine punishment will be issued and whether this punishment will be light or severe or even whether it will come sooner or later. However, the oath serves as evidence [when needed] and I think that a written oath should be treated in this way. Say you borrow gold or silver from a merchant, then you will need a guarantor or witness. These days there are doubts concerning divine punishment and you may not be able to find an acquaintance who will act as a guarantor for such matters. Instead you will need to make an oath to the gods, thereby making the gods your guarantor. By involving gods as witnesses, you swear not to break your word on such a payment or an agreement made. This is done purely to dispel any doubts. If a person is sinful or dishonest enough to break a promise then why would they use such divine writings? Such written oaths are made on the assumption that there is no intention to break the promise or commit a wrong deed. Basically, those who use a written oath are not serious criminals. Nevertheless, if they ever do break the promise or are guilty of a misdeed after giving the oath then they are the most dishonest and fraudulent of people and do not deserve any respect you may have for them. This is the last thing a *samurai* should ever do. That being said, there is a teaching for breaking a written oath by using *kokoro no kurai* – the stratification of minds. This technique is only for experienced practitioners.

There are various kinds of written oath, including the following:

- *shichimai-gishō* 七枚起請 – the seven-sheet oath[79]
- *kishōmon* 起請文 – the oath written upon papers from a shrine
- *shinmon* 神文 – the oath of divine letters
- *seimon* 誓文 – a written oath

For details of these, ask a Shintō practitioner. In our school the *keppan* blood seal is not used in a pledge as it is kind of *shinmon*. For *samurai* all promises are promises no matter what type they are. The above are the basic issues to keep in mind when considering written oaths.

静行有徳事
Seikō ni toku aru koto
THE VIRTUE OF KEEPING CALM

In all aspects, that which is done in haste should be avoided while that which is done in a serene manner is desirable. There are certain situations that may

---

79   This is a long oath written on seven sheets of *goō* paper which are joined together.

call for quick actions, but in most cases rushing will bring about failure. If you contemplate situations with serenity then rarely will you make mistakes. An old tale says:

> There was once a battle in which a force was marching on in formation while two men went forward in advance to decide the position of camp quarters. When they were at a distance of one or two ri the formation behind them fell into confusion. A dust cloud caused by horses filled the air and all the troops cried out aloud and appeared to be in total disarray. One of the two men said, 'It seems that the hatamoto group[80] has been ambushed and attacked and that a battle has started. This means that we should change the position of the camp quarters, but if we do not know the cause of the commotion then we will not know how to proceed. Therefore, we should return and discover the situation that the hatamoto is in.' The other samurai, who was older and more experienced, took a moment to think and said, 'This is no ambush and if we go back one or two ri then the camp quarters will not be ready in time. Therefore, we should move forward at speed and construct the quarters instead of returning.' The younger samurai remained unsure, but with the reassurance of the experienced man they moved on and built the quarters. Later the whole army arrived at the camp in safety and the younger man asked the experienced one how he had known that there was no ambush, to which he replied, 'I have learned a lot of things about this type of situation from my younger days. In all respects, it is not a positive thing to rush. If you can see confusion or dust clouds then it may appear to be an ambush, but you must listen and notice that there was no sound of musket fire. With this I concluded that it was simply infighting between our troops or that a horse had been freed. I was able to reach this conclusion because I did not rush and I concentrated on listening quietly and, as I had guessed, this disturbance was caused by a horse that had been

---

80 The command group of an army.

released and had moved among the baggage train. Just as in this case, it is best to contemplate everything with a serene heart.'

This episode has been placed here to illustrate points that you should consider.

思案分別差別之事
Shian funbetsu sabetsu no koto
DIFFERENTIATING BETWEEN CONTEMPLATION AND JUDGEMENT[81]

Shian – contemplation – and *funbetsu* – judgement – are similar yet slightly different. Judgement is to weigh up right and wrong, while contemplation is to consider how to follow the righteous path. This holds true not only for *samurai* but for all people. People should contemplate upon their own family business and make judgement on what is righteous. Also, good judgement is required to decide on the way you approach a matter. The foundation of all things is *contemplation*; however, if a situation is deteriorating then use *judgement*.

酒狂不禮取捌之事
Shukyō burei torisabaki no koto
DEALING WITH A VIOLENT DRINKER'S RUDENESS

Violent drinkers may cause unexpected problems. Once at a drinking party with many *samurai* gathered, a man slapped another on the head. Although he was not being serious, the atmosphere suddenly changed and no one spoke a word. The man who had been struck looked to be at the edge of restraint, while the man who had struck him looked bewildered and indifferent and wondered what he should do about such a minor issue. At this point, a sword fight appeared to be inevitable.

The quick-witted host said, 'As we have all partaken of copious amounts of drink, there have been many mistakes. However, as a host I am glad that everyone has enjoyed such a great amount of alcohol. Even if various mistakes have been made due to such a huge amount of drinking, I wish to implore you

---

81 思案 *shian*, which we have interpreted as 'contemplation', literally means 'to look for the righteous way', while分別 *funbetsu*, which we have given as 'judgement', literally means 'to look for a balance between the positive and the negative'.

all not to drag any such mistakes into the future with them. Otherwise, I shall be hesitant to offer another cup of *sake* without worrying. Therefore, though it may seem an unreasonable request, please let me have your written oaths that nothing from this gathering will be spread as rumour later on. After this is done, I will be happy to offer more cups of *sake*.'

Upon hearing this speech, everyone made various responses and all present that night gave an oath which stated that they had drunk excessively, to near unconsciousness, in fact, so that they did not fully remember all the events of the evening and while rude actions may have been performed they did not remember the exact details. This written oath was given by all to the host and in turn the host gave this document to the man who had been struck on the head. Then the host persuaded him to offer his forgiveness and settled the situation successfully. Even when someone tried to talk about it, this drunken episode was not discussed or remembered and in the end no repercussions came from the occurrence. This was all done by the wit of the host. Generally, after such an altercation, the rule is that people should pour drinks for each other.

This has been written here to show the example you should follow in other similar situations.

生得之臆禁好有差事

Seitoku no oku kinkō no sa aru koto

THE DIFFERENCE BETWEEN COWARDS BY NATURE AND THOSE WITH INHERENT AVERSIONS

Samurai are not completely without fear, but there is a difference between a coward by nature and someone who has a particular aversion to something. It may be seen as cowardly to show surprise at natural phenomena, such as thunder, earthquakes and disruption by storms, and to be put into fright by these things may be due to a natural constitution[82] or illness. Apart from the above, there are aversions towards animals and plant life,[83] which can in no way be called cowardice. While a *samurai* may suffer from these aversions, he maintains his composure and therefore it is hard to detect them, whereas

---

82 虚實 *kyojitsu* – 'substantial or insubstantial'.
83 Literally, 'grasses and trees' – in this context it means plant life in general.

they can often be seen in merchants, farmers, women and children. In most cases, those *samurai* who desperately cling to life and are startled at and make a fuss of things and are lacking in martial skills will also shudder upon a field of battle. There is a difference between those who *vibrate with bravery* and those who *shake with a lack of confidence*. Those who have such bravery will cease shaking later on, while those who shake and cringe with fear will turn pale, stammer and become lost in confusion and may even have trouble standing up. Keep in mind the difference between being a coward and having an inherent aversion to something. Finally, be aware that *samurai* should never say that they dislike warfare, even in jest, as this is considered one of the wrong mindsets to have.

Δ Tradition says:

The following nine points are traditions about the above twenty-seven points. Keep them in mind and know them for what they are. They are called *hiden* – secret traditions – and relate to the above military episodes and achievements.

大小暗中不紛亂習

Daishō anchū funran sezu no narai

THE TEACHING OF NOT MIXING UP OR LOSING LONG AND SHORT SWORDS IN THE DARK

In a zashiki room or other such location, it may happen that many swords will be placed together in the dark and therefore become lost from view. Prepare a hidden mark,[84] just like a spear has a *saguri* part.

誤而人之刀指違時

Ayamatte hito no katana sashichigaeshi toki

FOR TIMES WHEN SOMEONE MISTAKES YOUR *KATANA* FOR THEIR OWN

---

84   忍印 *shinobi-jirushi* – in this case, an identifying mark to confirm ownership of the sword.

If you notice someone else has taken your sword by mistake, go to them with their *katana* in hand when giving it back.[85] Take care that you yourself do not make such a mistake. If you do not notice the error until you have parted ways, and the person's house is far away, send a servant to exchange the swords. They should take the sword only as far as the main room or to the front of the entrance.

大小借人心得

Daishō hito ni kasu kokoroe

POINTS TO KEEP IN MIND WHEN LENDING OUT YOUR LONG OR SHORT SWORD[86]

When lending either of your swords, say the following, 'This cuts extremely well, therefore you must use it for a trial cut.' Never just say, 'I will lend this to you', without mentioning trial cuts.

君手討可有時

Kun teuchi arubeki toki

FOR TIMES YOUR LORD WISHES TO KILL IN PUNISHMENT

If your lord is angry and is going to kill someone, you should inform the lord that he should not stain his hands by making the kill himself and you should offer to kill the man instead. At this point take the person away and set him free. Alternatively, you may decide to kill the person immediately given that it is the lord's wish or if they have turned against the lord.[87]

君之刀持時

Kun no katana motsu toki

FOR TIMES WHEN ACTING AS A SWORD-SQUIRE TO THE LORD

---

85 i.e. do not have it in your sash, but have the sword in its scabbard and in hand.

86 This article has an undercurrent of correct etiquette. The lender is giving the borrower permission beforehand to avoid the awkwardness of them having to ask for permission to cut with the sword.

87 The implication here is that it may be a mistake for the lord to have the man killed while under the influence of anger, and therefore the *samurai* should take the man out of sight and give the impression that he is to be killed. However, if the man is in actual violation of the lord or is a real threat and it is not simply a case of misplaced anger, then he must be killed immediately.

When holding the lord's sword, keep it with the hilt pointed towards the lord's right hand. At night hold it to the front. However, follow any orders that he may give you.

朋友頼不頼品

Hōyū tanomu to tanomazaru shina

THE DIFFERENT TYPES OF FAVOUR THAT COLLEAGUES MAY OR MAY NOT ASK

If a *samurai* asks a favour then it is a matter of importance, and if a *samurai* hears that request then it is difficult to decline. Therefore, the following should be said: 'I will accept your request as long as it does not impede the orders of my lord or my father. If it does indeed obstruct those orders then you should not ask it of me.'

善悪場不引

Zen'aku ba wo hikazu

TO NOT WITHDRAW FROM A FIGHT DUE TO WHAT IS RIGHT AND WHAT IS WRONG

When a minor dispute becomes amplified and people will not withdraw, *samurai* do not alter their stance. Therefore, you should make a proper judgement at the outset as to whether an issue is righteous or unrighteous.

鷺烏双論之習

Sagi karasu sōrōn no narai

THE TEACHING OF THE WHITE HERON BEING CALLED THE BLACK CROW

Be aware that in all matters if a discussion moves to the rights and wrongs of an issue then the debate will last forever. It is said that it is never too late to change your mind, but for a *samurai* to do so can be taken as weakness. This point is from an old saying that states that people will insist that a white heron is a black crow.[88]

---

88 The idea is that once a person has taken up a position within an argument, they will generally not move from that position and therefore the longer the debate, the more abstract it may become until it gets to the point where a person will claim white is black.

雑談寸尺之習

Zatsudan sunshaku no narai

TEACHINGS ON CASUAL CONVERSATIONS AND MEASUREMENTS

Sometimes people make exaggerations when they are talking. If something is said to be five *shaku* it may in fact be only two *shaku*, or when something is said to be the amount of one thousand it may actually only be one hundred. *Samurai* should be careful as it can be embarrassing to have their statements corrected.

The above twenty-seven main points are records and points to keep in mind concerning military achievements, conversations, being a guest or being a host. With the secret traditions added, there are thirty-six points in total.

The following are points to keep in mind when travelling, staying in inns, on ships, on horseback or in a palanquin. The ideogram for travel, 旅, has been placed at the top and there are twenty-five points with an additional eleven secret traditions, which adds up to thirty-six points in total.

Tabi

ARTICLES ON TRAVEL

旅行心得之事
Ryokō kokoroe no koto
THINGS TO KEEP IN MIND WHEN TRAVELLING

Remember that not only *samurai* but also lower people travel. In times of peace you may venture thirty, fifty or even one hundred *ri* out of your own area and there are things that should be kept in mind. When travelling, no matter if a person is of noble or of humble origins, there are many things that cannot be done in the way one would prefer them to be done. However, when serving a lord and accompanying them to the city of Edo,[89] there are set customs and schedules for travel which are decided beforehand. This is also a form of travel but is different from the previously mentioned form. The points mentioned hereafter relate to *personal* travel.

旅行金銀可持事
Ryokō kingin motsu beki koto
CARRY ENOUGH GOLD AND SILVER WHEN TRAVELLING

When travelling, teachings say that even if it is only two or three days of travel, make sure to take ample gold and silver. If venturing out on only two or three days of travel then keep as much as ten days' worth of travel

---

89 在府 *zaifu* – this is a period of time in which warlords were required to move their households to Edo, as part of the *sankinkōtai* system (参勤交代), which saw all of the lords of Japan move their affairs to the capital on a bi-annual rotation. This was done to deplete their funds and hinder any form of rebellion.

expenses, as a situation may arise for which you need more gold and silver than expected. Sometimes, greedy scum may rob you of gold and silver and therefore you need to know how to handle your money. Various evil strategies are used to trick travellers – never lower your guard. If those who study at our school become trapped in such schemes then it is classed as a serious blunder. Therefore, it is not proper to forget the advice for travel contained within our writings, such as the *Shinobi no Maki* as well as others – be aware of the issues involved.

旅行大小心得之事

Ryokō daishō kokoroe no koto

THINGS TO KEEP IN MIND ABOUT LONG AND SHORT SWORDS WHILE TRAVELLING

When travelling, make sure that you take with you the *uwa-obi* outer sash and the *shita-obi* loincloth, spare clothes and so on, and use both a scabbard cover and a hilt cover[90] on your *katana* and *wakizashi*. This is not only to protect them from damage but also has other benefits. Concerning the hilt cover, there is a better way to secure it to the hilt which prevents water from running down the opening in rainy weather. If you have killed someone and your *katana* has been bent and you cannot straighten it nor return it to the scabbard, then you cannot withdraw from the situation with a naked blade in hand and it cannot be thrown away. If this is the case, then split the scabbard open and place the scabbard cover over it, so that it will not attract people's attention. Hilt covers do not help you in an emergency but if an emergency arises you can fight with them on and without much difficulty. Soft leather should be used for both scabbard and hilt covers.

他國ノ法令可聞事

Takoku no hōrei kikubeki koto

RESPECTING LAWS IN OTHER PROVINCES

When you are in another province or within lands under ownership, enquire about the laws of that province. Since ancient times it has been said, 'When in

---

90 柄袋 *tsukabukuro* – a cover that fits over the handle of a sword.

another province follow the ways of that province.' When you enter a province, never say that your own district's laws are different or act on the assumption that this province's laws will be the same as yours. The rule that rests over the whole land is that you should not transgress against the laws of other regions.

旅宿可聞置事

Ryoshuku kikiokubeki koto

THINGS TO ASK ABOUT WHEN STAYING AT AN INN

When staying for one or two nights, or especially for an extended period, it is best to ascertain information on the place, the head of the village, local governors, magistrates and district-chiefs. Also make sure to enquire in detail about the clans and houses, famous places and the righteous and unrighteous ways of the locals. In addition to this, find out who are the masters of each house and lodgings, the names of areas in the town, the number of houses and so on. Do this when you arrive because if an emergency arises then the locals will not disclose the information later on. Your success in acquiring this information will depend on how you ask for it, so make an investigation with care and do not raise suspicion. Also, while at an inn do not talk about your home province, and do not talk of yourself carelessly. Do not behave inappropriately or with arrogance, especially when acting as a *kan*-spy or a *shinobi*.

旅可心付品之事

Tabi kokoro tsukurubeki shina no koto

POINTS TO PAY ATTENTION TO WHEN TRAVELLING

When travelling there are many issues that need to be fully considered. First, identify east and west with a compass, as it often happens that you will take the wrong direction in unfamiliar areas. Places that should be checked [in a house you are visiting] are: toilets, wells, the main reception rooms, entrances, the rear entrance and backings, inside and outside of the outer walls, outbuildings, the joints of tatami mats, the backs of hanging screens, the walls, rooms on the ground floor, the inner garden and so on. Make sure that your servants also keep these things in mind.

相宿可心得事

Aiyado kokoroeru beki koto

POINTS TO PAY ATTENTION TO CONCERNING GUESTS IN THE SAME LODGINGS

If there are others staying in the same lodgings, then enquire to the house master about them and find out whether they are merchants, farmers or *samurai*. If they are *samurai*, inform your servants that they should not do anything impolite. However, do not cause your servants to have fear of them by over-stressing this instruction. If the *samurai* wishes to be acquainted with you then all will depend on the situation, but it is generally undesirable to make a move towards introduction as you may be unaware of how people from other provinces think. If they happen to be short-tempered and cause an argument then you cannot leave a fray once you have been introduced.

旅二浴心得之事

Tabi ni yoku kokoroe no koto

POINTS TO KEEP IN MIND WHEN TAKING A BATH DURING TRAVELLING

When in a travelling lodge, you cannot avoid sharing a room with others, or thieves who would steal not only gold and silver but any property. For example, even in the short time it may take to have a cold wash, have your servant keep your clothes and possessions close by and have them hold your *wakizashi* in hand. Also, have them positioned where you can see them. Whether you have hired just one or two rooms or the entire lodgings, always strictly check anyone who enters or leaves. If you are travelling alone beware of the ruse called *sashikomi*, which is where a thief will place a stolen item in your property or clothes with the intention of making it appear that you are a thief instead.

旅行下人申渡事

Ryokō genin ni mōshiwatasu koto

POINTS TO TELL YOUR SERVANTS BEFORE TRAVELLING

Inform your servants to keep watches at night on a rotation of one *toki*[91] or

---

91 A *toki* is one Japanese hour, which is approximately two standard hours.

other set intervals. This should be made clear to them before departure because if they are not informed in full beforehand on matters like how to attend on you or points they need to keep in mind when lodging somewhere unsafe, or even sleeping arrangements, then it is difficult to instruct them once you have set off.

大小置様之事
Daishō okiyō no koto
HOW TO POSITION LONG AND SHORT SWORDS

Your *katana* and *wakizashi* should be placed close to the wall or along the edge of your futon. If you are sleeping in a small area with many people – and this also applies when you are not travelling – sleep with the cords of your *katana* and *wakizashi* passed through each other and then hold the cords or alternatively pass the cords under where you sleep.[92] In addition to this, when you are alone, tie up your travelling bag and other possessions with your grappling hook and rope and put the end of the rope under your body when you sleep.

蚊帳心得之事
Kaya kokoroe no koto
POINTS ABOUT MOSQUITO NETS

If you are sleeping under a hanging mosquito net then place your *katana* and *wakizashi* with the scabbards slightly outside of the net and with the blades drawn two or three *bu*. Do this so that if the scabbards are pulled on, the blades will remain to hand. Also, this way is good if you need to raise the mosquito net for observation.

乗馬荷物心得之事
Jōba nimotsu kokoroe no koto
POINTS ABOUT HORSES AND LUGGAGE

As mentioned above, instruct your servants to closely observe the status of the travelling lodge. In addition, if you are travelling with important items then

---

92 A *samurai* should have one sword on each side of the futon and should cross the sword cords over each other and hold them in hand. Alternatively, pass the sword cords around each other and then under the body.

inform the house master of this and if travelling alone it is advisable to leave the items with the owner of the lodge. If you are travelling on horseback then tell the groom to be careful and, as the master, you yourself should also pay extra attention to your horse and periodically check the horse yourself – this is one of the duties of a *samurai*. Order your servants to pay attention to the stable, feed and allow the horses to interact. Spears should not be left outside of the room you are staying in.

一人旅心得之事

Hitoritabi kokoroe no koto

POINTS TO KEEP IN MIND WHEN TRAVELLING ALONE

As a *samurai* you may have to travel alone from time to time. Therefore, you should always remember these points. On such an occasion, unless you acquire someone as company and make your way together, then you cannot rent a room. However, if you have poor judgement on the company you take up with, you may end up travelling with a thief. If this is the case and if you converse well with them, then you can use our school's *shinobi no aikotoba*[93] and they will help you to cross the area in peace, making them a better travelling companion than a normal person.

獨旅宿心得之事

Hitoritabi yado kokoroe no koto

POINTS ABOUT LODGINGS WHEN TRAVELLING ALONE

If you have not secured any lodging to stay at when travelling alone, then hire a road horseman or palanquin and have them secure lodgings for you. This will make your journey go more smoothly. Even if tiredness has not set in, it is better to travel by horse or palanquin. However, if you cannot use such methods and have trouble finding lodgings, then ask the head of a village[94] to allow you to stay for a single night. If you venture out to a castle town as a *shinobi* you cannot ask anyone for lodgings. In this case visit a merchant's

---

93 忍ノ相詞 – literally, '*shinobi* password'.

94 The implication here is that there are no inns in the village or establishments that take in travellers.

house and buy goods from them, even expensive ones, to gain favour with the house master. If you get close to them, they will offer you lodgings without your having to ask. Alternatively, buy food and *sake* and lavish the house master with it, or think of another way along these lines. If there are no lodgings then use a temple or a shrine.

旅行食物心得之事

Ryokō tabemono kokoroe no koto

POINTS ABOUT FOOD WHEN TRAVELLING

Concerning the arrangements of your meals while travelling

When planning to visit a place where you are not aware of the lodging situation, it is advisable to arrange for lodgings and meals at the earliest possible point.

Concerning rest stops

Take rests in tea houses before you become tired – this is a measure of precaution. However, it is not advisable to rest for too long, as it is good to arrive early at your overnight stop. If you travel too long and arrive at an unknown destination during the night, be aware you will often encounter trouble.

夜盗賊辻切取捌之事

Yoru tōzoku tsujigiri torisabaki no koto

DEALING WITH THIEVES AND ROADSIDE KILLERS AT NIGHT

When travelling long distances there are certain places where you may be attacked at night by roadside killers,[95] highwaymen[96] and the like. When in such a place, move silently and with care and do not become flustered. If someone approaches you to steal gold and silver, kill them immediately and leave it at that. If this occurs in a field then there will be no investigation. If there is more than one robber then simply kill one of them and the rest will flee – remember that the mind of a thief is the mind of a coward. Bravery is not found in those who care nothing about causing difficulty to others for personal gain. If you happen to be in a post-town then go to the head-man[97]

---

95 辻切 *tsujigiri* – literally, 'street killer' or 'street killing'.
96 追ハギ *oihagi* – those who follow pedestrians to rob them.
97 名主 *nanushi* – the leader of a village.

and explain clearly why you killed the man and give them the name of the province and the place where you are from, but do not leave immediately. You only need to do this if people in the town observed the incident. If there is no one who can identify you, then just make the kill and leave, whether it is in a town or a field. If you do have to account to the head-man of the town then obtain proof that you made such a report.

畫盗賊之事

Hiru tōzoku no koto

DAYTIME THIEVES

Be aware that if someone approaches you and offers to tell your fortune, tries to pick your pocket[98] or performs street gambling, then this is a thief. Normally they target only townspeople and if they recognize a *samurai* they leave him well alone. However, the situation may dictate that you have to travel in disguise. If such men follow you, then be patient with them – by giving them a small amount of money, you may then be able to pass. If they approach you in number in a field then just start killing them before they get a chance to initiate a unified attack. When the first one is killed the rest will flee, but make sure to leave as soon as possible.

旅行持薬得用之事

Ryokō mochigusuri tokuyō no koto

THE BENEFITS OF CARRYING MEDICINE WHEN TRAVELLING

You should have a good understanding of medicine and carry it with you. Be aware of the properties of each medicine, depending on whether it is a hot or a cold substance. Essential medicines are those for food poisoning, horse-breathlessness and odour elimination, hunger pills and 'good health' medicine. Be fully aware that there are different ways for each.

舩橋心得之事

Funabashi kokoroe no koto

POINTS TO KEEP IN MIND ABOUT BOAT-BRIDGES

---

98 巾着切 *kinchakugiri* – literally, 'purse cutter'.

When crossing a river by way of a ship or bridge do not complain about the cost of the crossing. It is desirable to pay the fee and cross as soon as possible. Avoid spending time arguing about the toll. Tell your servants to stay close and to keep an eye on your weapons at the point of landing on the other side until all the common people have disembarked and then you yourself should disembark when all the lower people have left. Sometimes you may carry a spear; in this case, when you are disembarking, hold it yourself and when you are on the bank you can pass it back to your spear-carrying servant. The teachings concerning weapon sets are given in detail in the scroll *Ippei Yōkō*.[99]

Boatmen and road-horsemen are often rude, but be patient with them. As with all lower people, you should avoid engaging with them. If you are taking a ferry and a boatman is so rude that it becomes intolerable, then take up the matter with him on the opposite bank once you have landed. If you reprimand him during the crossing then it will take longer than normal.

渡舩心得之事

Watashibune kokoroe no koto

POINTS ABOUT USING A FERRY

It is not recommended that you cross an unfamiliar river on foot, even if it looks shallow. If a ferry is available, then use that instead. If you do begin to cross on foot and find that the water is deep, then unless you are a superb swimmer, use *ikki*[100] – single movement – or make a mental note of the landscape and route before entering the river. The method for crossing a strong-flowing river is 'bounding' on tiptoes. Remember, if there is a ferry you should not walk across and if there are waders[101] then it is desirable to hire them. If there are many people waiting to cross, then stand in line, get on board the litter quickly and disembark quietly. These are ancient ways and you should follow them.

---

99 In fact, information concerning tools and weapons is predominantly found in the scroll *Heigu Yōhō*.

100 一氣 – by context and compared to the skill used later, this is to perform an action with controlled speed.

101 川越 *kawagoshi* – men who carry passengers across rivers upon their backs or on a litter.

渡海心得之事

Tokai kokoroe no koto

POINTS ABOUT TRAVELLING AT SEA

When you are travelling at sea all you can do is depend on the crew and there is nothing to deal with yourself. Rely on the experience of the crew if a storm arises as no one but boatmen have this kind of knowledge. The names of sailing tools and the parts of ships are described in the scroll *Suisen Yōhō*.

里程遠近兼可知事

Ritei enkin kanete shiru beki koto

KNOWING THE DISTANCE TO BE TRAVELLED

In order to increase their fare, palanquin carriers and horse guides tend to exaggerate the distance of travel. Therefore, read other people's reports and travel records and acquire the correct information beforehand or take it from previous journeys. This advice applies to routes you do not take regularly, not those destined for Edo.

雨具心得之事

Amagu kokoroe no koto

POINTS ABOUT WATERPROOF TOOLS

A circular cape is most desirable because of its benefits while fighting. The method of fabrication is given in the scroll *Tōyu no Maki*.

破舩可心得事

Hasen kokoroeru beki koto

POINTS ABOUT SINKING SHIPS

Whether a ferry or a seafaring vessel, ships sometimes capsize. If you panic and think only of escaping then you will often stumble and fall, lose your composure and will inevitably drown when the ship goes down. Therefore, keep calm and hold on to any wooden board or broken part of the ship; cases have shown that this will help you to survive. Be aware that even if the ship does not eventually sink, a flustered and ignorant mind may cause sudden death or seasickness. Also be aware that if a ship is wrecked in a storm and you die as a result, then it is simply your fate and the end of your luck. This information is for when you are in such dangerous situations, and in our school floating aids[102] should be used.

関所心得之事
Sekisho kokoroe no koto
POINTS ABOUT CHECKPOINTS
When encountering a checkpoint remember that this is a requirement of the laws of that province, and so pass through with polite behaviour and good manners. This is not done out of respect for the guards at the checkpoint but for their lord or their governor. The method for passing through new checkpoints established at times of war is mentioned in the scroll *Heieki Yōhō*, and the *shinobi* method of getting through the checkpoint or going over a gate is described in detail in our school's writing *Shinobi no Maki*.

∆ Tradition says:
The following eleven[103] points are traditions for the above twenty-five points. Keep them in mind and know them for what they are. They are known as *hiden* – secret traditions – and relate to travelling, boats, horses and palanquins.

足袋草鞋
Tabi waranji[104]
SOCKS AND STRAW SANDALS
Neither your *tabi* and *waranjigake* foot coverings should have full soles, or they should have some places where the soles are not fully stitched – this is so that you can easily remove gravel from your feet. 'Strong straw sandals'[105] and 'noiseless sandals'[106] are discussed in the scroll *Heigu Yōhō*.

---

102 浮沓 *ukigutsu* – a form of life jacket.
103 There is a transcription error at this point – some versions say twelve.
104 This pronunciation is used in the manual and differs from the modern reading.
105 ツヨワランヂ *tsuyo-waranji*.
106 音無沓 *otonashigutsu*.

食焼様早汁

Shoku yakiyō hayajiru

COOKING MEALS AND INSTANT SOUP

It is desirable to cook with equal amounts of water and rice. If you wish the rice to be harder, use less water; while to make it softer, simply add more. If you put rice into a waist container or normal container while still hot then it will not easily spoil. In order to ensure that the rice is still safe to eat, soak it in hot water[107] – this will also prevent thirst. For instant soup, mix pre-roasted *miso* with hot water.

道迷時

Michi mayou toki

FOR TIMES WHEN YOU ARE LOST

It is advisable to let a horse go ahead of you; Minamoto no Yoshitsune used this method of following an old horse, as horses know their way very well. When walking in the snow and cold, take three seeds of pepper with hot water before you set off in the morning; this can also be done when it is hot. Furthermore, carry roasted soybeans in your kimono to keep you warm. If you become lost, study the grass along a river.

早路不倒足

Hayamichi Taorezaru Ashi

METHODS FOR SUCCESS WHEN TRAVELLING AT SPEED

Pay attention to your feet to avoid damaging them. Also, set up horse relays for quick travel; this will need a correct estimation.

大小鑓印黒白

Daishō yarijirushi kokubyaku

POINTS ON LONG AND SHORT SWORDS AND BLACK AND WHITE MARKINGS FOR SPEARS

Here the term *daishō* is used to refer to carrying your swords in hand when

---

107 i.e. to reheat and eat the rice with boiled water.

you approach a rocky and narrow path.[108] This is done to avoid the ends of the swords becoming stuck. Also, here *kokubyaku* – black and white – means *black* markings for daytime and *white* markings for nighttime. Markings on fire jackets and spears are used to prevent them from becoming lost.[109]

有殺害人而刀改時

Satsugainin arite katana aratameru toki

WHEN YOU HAVE KILLED SOMEONE AND HAVE TO PRESENT YOUR SWORD TO AN INVESTIGATOR

When you are required to draw and display your sword, do not pass it to the man. If asked to pass it over, only draw the sword yourself and show it, while keeping it in hand.

食味噌一日一人之積

Shoku miso ichinichi hitori no tsumori

TO ESTIMATE THE AMOUNT OF RICE AND *MISO* REQUIRED PER PERSON PER DAY

The estimation for one day of rations is five *gō* of rice[110] and thirty *momme* of *miso* – that is fifteen *momme* per meal. Also one *shō* of water is needed.

途中下人咎人云時

Tochū genin toganin to iu toki

FOR THE TIME WHEN TRAVELLING AND YOU ARE INFORMED THAT YOUR SERVANT IS A CRIMINAL

If you are informed that one of your servants has committed a crime, then let it be known you will investigate the matter at a lodging as you are their guarantor. Do not let anyone give explanations along the way. If the complainant carries on making accusations then tell him decisively that he is being extremely rude towards a *samurai*. If someone suggests that he will take the servant under his charge, you should decline and not leave the issue in his hands. Even though

---

108 Take off both the long and short swords from their place at the waist and carry them in hand. They are not drawn from their scabbards.

109 e.g. so a *samurai* can identify his own equipment among others.

110 The scroll *Ippei Yōkō* states six *gō*.

the suspect is in your service, if the crime he has committed was not done on your orders then it is no reflection upon you.

同盗人云来時

Onajiku nusubito to iikitaru toki

FOR THE TIME THAT YOU ARE APPROACHED WITH CLAIMS OF THIEVERY AGAINST YOUR SERVANTS

Unless such a claim comes from the authorities, do not accept it while travelling. If you do so then accusations that the servant of such and such is a thief may follow you. To start with, there is no way that a *samurai* will hand any of his servants over to other people and return without them. Therefore, if someone makes such a claim, tell him that you will address the matter on your return home. Be aware that a *samurai* should not make such an accusation about others.

旅宿不頼状習

Ryoshuku jō wo tanomazaru narai

TEACHINGS ABOUT NOT AGREEING TO REQUESTS TO CARRY LETTERS

If asked to carry a letter, have the person who requests this sign confirmation that he has entrusted the letter to you and to declare that he has not included any money within it. In no other circumstance should you agree to such a request while travelling alone. There are many cases where people falsely claim to have put gold and silver in the correspondence.

無鍋食焼様

Nabe naku shoku yaki yō

COOKING WITHOUT A PAN

After soaking rice in water for a while, wrap it in a straw bundle, then bury it in the ground and make a fire upon the top – this will give you half-cooked rice. Do this when there is no other way. You cannot eat rice unless it has been cooked; therefore, this teaching may be of benefit.

The above twenty-five points were about travelling, lodges, routes, teachings about boat-bridges and palanquins, with the addition of eleven secret traditions. This adds up to thirty-six points in total.

The following points relate to walking at night, as well as the carrying of lanterns and candles. The ideogram for night, 夜, is marked at the top. There are twenty-five points and nine points on traditions, which adds up to a total of thirty-four points.

Yoru

ARTICLES ON NIGHTTIME

夜行心懸之事

Yakō kokorogake no koto

PAYING ATTENTION WHEN WALKING AT NIGHT

Be it far away or close by, you should pay extra attention when you need to walk at night. When you see the outline of a human on the street, prepare yourself. Also, fighting methods are different from those used in the daytime. This is described in the points below.

同道人有之時之事

Dōdōnin kore aru toki no koto

FOR TIMES WHEN YOU HAVE COMPANY WHEN WALKING AT NIGHT

If accompanied by the noble or those who are of age, it is good manners to have them walk ahead of you at night and it is correct to have the lantern-carrying servant come directly after them. However this depends on the situation. That being said, this way is the basic principle for both moonlit and moonless nights.

酔狂溢者心得之事

Suikyō aburemono kokoroe no koto

POINTS TO KEEP IN MIND ABOUT VIOLENT DRUNKS AND RUFFIANS

If violently drunken people or the like are approaching you, make sure to step to the side and get under the eaves of houses. If ruffians try to argue then do not respond thoughtlessly. If there is no way to avoid interacting with them, point a lantern at their faces and have a look at them to form a correct judgement. Most ruffians do not like being seen and will retreat. It is a general rule that *samurai* should have a lantern carried for them at night, even if there is abundant moonlight.

及刃傷燈持心得之事

Ninjō ni oyobi akari mochi kokoroe no koto

POINTS THAT THE LANTERN-CARRYING SERVANT SHOULD KEEP IN MIND WHEN SWORD-FIGHTING BREAKS OUT

If a situation results in sword combat, it is advantageous to have the lantern moved from a rear position to the front, so that your opponent cannot see your body posture. Make sure to inform your servants that when such a situation arises they are not to join the fight. If a torch[111] is carried, it is desirable to have the torch close to and directly pointing at the enemy – this is something that they will detest. At this point they will cut it down, so be sure to move behind them and make the kill.[112]

自身挑燈持事

Jishin chōchin motsu koto

THE METHOD OF CARRYING LANTERNS

When walking alone with a lantern in hand and you unexpectedly become involved in a sword fight in the street, make sure to hold the lantern so that it is pointing at the enemy, do this until they cut it down, then at that moment make your attack. Hold the lantern in the left hand while holding the *katana* in the right. Just stay calm, keep the lantern aimed at the enemy's face and fight in accordance with any developments.

---

111 A torch is a flame upon the top of a shaft, held upright; while a lantern is a flame inside a housing and is held in a lower position.

112 The servant is instructed to push the torch into the face of the enemy while the *samurai* moves to the rear of him. When the enemy makes his cut at the torch the *samurai* makes his kill.

夜中討果行合事

Yachū uchihatashi ni ikiau koto

COMING ACROSS A SWORD FIGHT AT NIGHT

When you come across a sword fight, have your servant hold your lantern up high so that you can observe the whole situation. If you do not know either of the combatants, try to persuade them to stop fighting; if they take no heed of you, there is no need to move in. If you do know one of them, then sometimes you have to give aid. Also, if you happen to see someone striking at the gate of an area of townhouses,[113] then look calm and sit on a stone or such and have your servant hold the lantern. When things settle down, then ask the gatekeeper[114] to open the gate and let you in.

助太刀心得之事

Sukedachi kokoroe no koto

POINTS ABOUT LENDING AID IN A SWORD FIGHT

If you have to help a friend or acquaintance, move to the rear of the enemy and have your servant aim the lantern at the side of his face and allow your friend to strike and make the kill. For example, while moving to the rear say to the combatants, 'Both of you calm down.' This is done to make the enemy lower his guard. Generally speaking, if you talk in a stern manner then the enemy will turn towards you, even if you do not draw your *katana*. This allows your ally to strike him down.

月夜暗夜心得之事

Tsukiyo an'ya kokoroe no koto

POINTS TO KEEP IN MIND FOR MOONLIT AND MOONLESS NIGHTS

When the moon is bright and you do not have a lantern, walk under the eaves of houses. If you move in the shadows then you can easily see those who are in the light and are passing. For combat, be aware of this principle if it is a moonlit night. Furthermore, on a moonless night, the areas underneath eaves and in the shadows of mountains are considerably darker. Keep this in mind for when you do not have a lantern.

---

113 木戸 *kido* – the gate of either a town or a castle.
114 役人 *yakunin* – an officer.

挑燈為持樣之事

Chōchin motaseyō no koto

HOW TO HAVE SOMEONE CARRY A LANTERN

Although a servant with a lantern is normally positioned at the rear, it is recommended that he carry it ahead of you if special caution is required. If someone approaches and wishes to pass on the right then have the servant move the lantern to the right and if the person wishes to pass on the left have the servant swap hands and move the lantern to the left, also make sure to elevate the light towards the opponent's face. This should allow you to observe from the rear with a clear view. Generally, in dangerous situations it is desirable to have someone disciplined, such as one from the *samurai* class, carry the lantern, as it can be disastrous if the lantern bearer becomes cowardly.

夜行杖之事

Yakō tsue no koto

WALKING AT NIGHT WITH A CANE

People of all ages use a cane when walking at night and there are things you should keep in mind about them. If you are attacked with anything bladed or with a staff, then do not fight with the cane. Otherwise you will not have time to draw your own sword later on. Therefore, be aware that canes are only an aid for walking in the street. This is *not* the case with a *shikomizue*, a cane with a hidden element, as it can become a *chigiriki* – a cane with a chain.

夜溢者合時之事

Yoru aburemono ni au toki no koto

FOR TIMES WHEN YOU COME ACROSS RUFFIANS AT NIGHT

When coming across ruffians at night, they may attempt to block the road and stop you from passing. This may happen by day or by night but it will most likely happen at night – this is commonly called *otokodate*[115] and is done to cause trouble to a person's journey. When they come across such situations *samurai* should not rise to the provocation but talk to the ruffians softly and

---

115 男タテ 'To show form' – this is the act of harassing people to display power.

gently so that they may pass through them. If you anticipate that this is about to happen then it is best to take a different route to avoid entering a situation that pushes the limits of your patience.

夜行倒時之事

Yakō taosaruru toki no koto

FOR TIMES WHEN YOU ARE BROUGHT DOWN TO THE GROUND WHEN WALKING AT NIGHT

If the above ruffians try to force conversation upon you or if there is a fair reason to break from forbearance, then it may become a fight to the death. This is not an impossible outcome. In such a case, strike and finish them with speed. It is best to strike when you have drawn them in close. Fighting with them will not be so difficult; this is because they have misaligned minds. However, you may be taken down to the ground at times and if you attempt to stand and fight they may force you back down to the floor. If this is the case, draw your *katana* or *wakizashi* and speak out to them so that they will come in for another strike. At this point, cut horizontally at their legs or the sides of their body while you are in the prone position. It is essential to keep this in mind.

夜行手籠合事

Yakō tegome au koto

GROUP ATTACKS WHEN WALKING AT NIGHT

Sometimes you may be surrounded by a large number of people who simultaneously attack you; there are things to keep in mind to prepare for such a situation. However, if you are attacked all of a sudden there is no way to prepare. In such a case, first apologize and keep your hands down so that your attackers lower their guard, then, when a gap appears, strike out. If their reason for attacking you is to disgrace you, they may seize your swords. Again, say something apologetic and try to retrieve the swords but then be determined to risk your life at once.[116] If they do not return the swords and leave with them, follow them and discover where they are residing, then return to your home. After preparation, carry out a raid when they are not expecting it. Remember,

---

116 i.e. to attack and kill them.

there is no way to do this if you lose sight of them, so do not return without identifying who they are. Beware that if such an event occurs then it is fate and the end of heaven's protection.

夜行燈被借時之事

Yakō akari karirareuru toki no koto

FOR SITUATIONS IN WHICH YOU ARE ASKED TO LEND A LIGHT WHEN WALKING AT NIGHT

If ruffians approach you and ask to borrow your lantern, their aim is to find a pretext for a quarrel if you refuse them. Know that if a *samurai* lends out his light, it may cause problems later. Therefore, in such a situation you should kill the ruffians. If you encounter this situation, tell the ruffians you will gladly lend them your lantern and hand it over to them. Then, as they turn around to leave, strike them down. Alternatively, let them take the lantern away and have someone follow them and inform the local officials that they should investigate the matter. If their lodgings cannot be identified and the situation becomes intolerable, then it goes without saying that you should just kill them and leave. If this happens then be aware that it is not a good idea to have the illumination of the lantern around you.

夜騎馬駕心得之事

Yoru kiba kago kokoroe no koto

POINTS ABOUT HORSE RIDERS AND PALANQUINS AT NIGHT

If there are palanquins or horses approaching at night, warn those who are with you. If you are in a town, step to the side and move under some eaves. If you are in a small alley, move to the side and stay there. If they approach and strike out all of a sudden, it is best that you do not provoke an argument by calling them rude. If they push you to the ground or injure you, then do not just retreat. Instead you should examine the circumstances, strike and leave them – this is dependent on the situation. It is most desirable to have correct judgement in these matters, as to be without such judgement is a failure of *budō*.

夜行乗輿心得之事

Yakō norikoshi kokoroe no koto

POINTS ABOUT USING VEHICLES AT NIGHT

When travelling by palanquin or by horse, it is desirable to have a lantern bearer ahead of you to pay attention to the conditions around and have the servant call out from time to time. If the light goes out it is best to get off the horse or out of the palanquin and walk. If this happens it may still be possible to ride a horse, but never continue to ride in the palanquin as you may receive an injury on a dark path.

座席燈之事

Zaseki akari no koto

CONCERNING LIGHTS WHEN SITTING

There are certain methods for providing illumination at night. Whether you use a candle and stand or a floor lamp, a light should be positioned where a person of importance will sit. If you have a place in mind for such a guest to sit, then make sure to put the light there beforehand. Then, when the guest arrives you can offer him the seat close to the light. A host should make arrangements of this kind beforehand. Also, when expecting a guest, prepare a portable candle so that it can be fetched at any time if required. Note that lamps have oil and therefore cannot be moved in an emergency.

黄昏燈心得之事

Tasogare akari kokoroe no koto

POINTS ABOUT LIGHTS USED AT TWILIGHT

It is a principle that if a guest is leaving as night descends and even if it is not so dark, you should have your servants strike up a light to give to the departing guest. When you are away from home and due to return in the evening, you should have someone strike up a light and carry it on your return journey. If no one has prepared a light then one should be requested. Always make sure you have a light at the ready when it is getting dark.

If a guest takes the wrong sword or loses something, you should take care of the situation for him. Finally, when you put out an oil lamp make sure to put it out with the wick left high, so that it is easy to light the next time it is used.

夜中討者之事
Yachū uchimono no koto
STRIKING AT NIGHT

If you are to strike at people at night, do this by listening for any utterances they make, otherwise you may lose 'sight' of the enemy. If there are many enemies and it is a dark night and there is no light, move to a fence or wall or any place that provides a barrier to one side and use it as a shield to your rear, it is of no benefit if an enemy positions himself behind you. Also, it is effective at night to crouch down and swipe horizontally at a lower target area. There are many other ways to strike effectively at night. Darkness can enable a small number of men to defeat a larger number.

夜中咎他事
Yachū hito wo togamuru no koto
QUESTIONING SOMEONE AT NIGHT

If at night you ask someone to identify himself and he hesitates, call out to him by using your own name. If he confirms that as his own identity, capture him immediately. If you yourself are questioned by someone, then you should not give your own name but give that of a close friend, then in return ask who they are. This is a way to be used in situations where care is needed.

夜退口燈之事
Yoru nokiguchi akari no koto
LIGHTS WHEN WITHDRAWING AT NIGHT

If you are being pursued by many people who have torches and lanterns, it is best to retreat by cutting down the torch bearers. If this is too difficult, just cut down the actual torches or lanterns themselves. If cutting from the right then there will be movement to the left, and if cutting from the left there will be movement to the right. The enemy will defend themselves from the direction they are cut at, therefore be aware that you should move around towards the rear of them and strike from behind.

被追懸心得之事

Oikakerareru kokoroe no koto

POINTS TO KEEP IN MIND WHEN BEING PURSUED

Be it night or daytime, when you strike someone and retreat you may have multiple people pursue you. Townspeople and farmers are most likely to throw stones because they are cowards. If they were capable of following, catching and killing you, then they would not be throwing stones – therefore, know that they actually fear getting close. In such a case, be decisive and return towards them, suddenly catch one or two and injure or kill them – this will make the others stop throwing stones. To do this, defend yourself by holding your sleeve out tight[117] and cover your face when you return to attack. Also, when hiding in a bush, grassy place or forest and being hit by stones that have been thrown, use the same way as above, covering your head and face. You can also use bamboo or wood as a shield. You should not come out of the bush in a panic when they are throwing stones. They are doing this because they are suspicious and are attempting to investigate.[118] There is no need to have fear of the enemy. You should not throw stones yourself; however, if you do decide this is the best course of action, draw the enemy in close while defending yourself from the stones being thrown and pitch fiercely at them, making sure to hit their heads. Know that it will be a battle of one *ken* and five *shaku* distance.

夜中捕者之事

Yachū torimono no koto

CAPTURING PEOPLE AT NIGHT

If the enemies are defending themselves in a thick coppice or within bushes, then it is best to throw torches into the area and not to venture into the darkness without care. Know that as it is darker on the inside, they will be able to see the outside with ease while it is difficult to see them. *Gandō* lanterns[119] are suitable in this situation. It is the same if an enemy is in a townhouse or a

---

117 The *samurai* raises his arm to protect his head and pulls the bottom of his sleeve tight to form a cloth shield in front of his face.

118 i.e. they are trying to flush people out who are in hiding.

119 カントウ挑灯 *gandō chōchin* – a directional light housed in a tube and mounted on a gimbal system.

narrow place. If you have to grapple and pin him to the ground at night, keep talking regularly. This is done because it is difficult to identify who is an ally if there are no lights.

To find a route when there is no illumination, wrap white paper around stones and leave them as children do, as they act as markers for your return. If it is pitch dark then place paper under the straps of your straw sandals so that your feet can be seen no matter how dark it is. As mentioned earlier, at gates it is proper at night to let high-ranking people go through first.

夜中妖怪之事

Yachū yōkai no koto

CONCERNING MONSTERS AT NIGHT[120]

In this world there are many tales of people who have come across mysterious monsters when they have been walking alone at night. However, they are most likely invented. From my childhood I have heard various stories of this kind and have dared to walk in the middle of the night in the places that are rumoured to be frequented by monsters, but I have never encountered anything mysterious. That being said, it is difficult to conclude that they really are fake just because I have not seen one. If the *chi* of creation acts on the Five Elements it is possible that they may move and appear in various shapes, but still most cases are imaginary. Even if you actually experience such things, it is still hard for a *samurai* to talk about supernatural beings with any certainty. The people who claim to have seen a monster usually say that it happened when they were out late at night on their own or with one other person on a deserted street. This would suggest monsters fear large numbers of people; but if monsters truly existed, surely they would show themselves to any number of people? If a *samurai* believes he has seen a monster he should be reserved in this matter and not talk too much of it to others. There are very few cases where trustworthy *samurai* have seen one and most cases are reported by men of loose words. Since ancient times there have been too many unproven reports of this nature and many of these stories have come from women and children.

---

120 妖怪 *yōkai* – monsters and goblins etc., weird and strange creatures common in Japanese folklore.

Foxes and racoons are said to transform themselves and if a person's *chi* is not strong enough then evil spirits will take advantage of this weakness. With this in mind, it seems unlikely that a *samurai* of spirit, bravery and strength would encounter one of these monsters. There are many other cases of mysterious omens and the like. Know that *chi* may arrive in advance as a presentiment. Details of this are mentioned in our school's scroll on *chi* called *Ki no Maki*. One theory holds that only people who are extremely strong-minded or extremely weak-minded will see such monsters; this would suggest that their observation is dependent on the mind.

約路不変事

Yakuro kaezaru koto

TO PROMISE NOT TO CHANGE YOUR ROUTE

Not only at night but whenever a *samurai* leaves his lodgings, he should inform those who stay behind of his route, destination, and estimated time of departure and return. That way, if there is an urgent need or emergency, a servant can find him without fail. However, there should be a distinction between official business and private business.

Details on teachings concerning nighttime are given in the section on night attacks in the scroll *Ippei Yōkō*.

Δ Tradition says:

The following nine points are traditions that should be kept in mind. Understand them for what they are. Therefore, they are known as *hiden* – secret traditions. The following points are secret traditions for walking at night and the carrying of lights.

歩行足下

Hokō ashimoto[121]

FOOTSTEPS

---

121 足下 *ashimoto* – the point where the foot touches the ground, also the walking gait.

Walk quietly and smoothly and pay attention to the way your feet connect to the ground. This is particularly important in dangerous areas. If you are filled with fear and lose heart then it is not good because it will manifest itself in your form. Anything concerning combat should be done with the above in mind.

盲目杖之習

Mōmoku tsue no narai

THE TEACHING OF THE BLIND MAN'S CANE

Blind people cannot see yet they can remember ways, they cross log bridges and visit houses. Be aware that in all cases you should have 'eyes from within the mind'.[122]

路次俄ニ暗時

Roji niwakani kuraki toki

ENTERING DARK AND CONFINED PLACES

When entering a dark place, close your eyes for a short while and open them again. Also, your vision may sometimes all of a sudden turn black when you walk out of a house which is illuminated. Furthermore, this may occur when you have an increase in *chi*.[123] People say that this is something mysterious but it is not: In these cases, simply crouch low and settle down and reflect logically and all will become clear. If you view this as mysterious and become nervous, then things will only grow darker.

暗夜明眼

An'ya meigan

BETTER 'VISION' IN THE DARK OF NIGHT

As mentioned above, in all cases it is best to see with your mind. In addition, wear white *tabi*-socks or attach paper to your feet. To avoid relying too heavily on your eyes, sometimes walk with your eyes closed.

---

122 *Mei no kokoro* – to depend on all the senses of the body and perceive the area not only with the eyes but through a heightened sense of awareness.

123 心気 *shinki* – 'mind-*chi*'.

懷中燭

Kaichū shoku

THE POCKET CANDLE

Mix camphor, *shochu*[124] and glue into a ball and carry it with you always. A ball of about twenty *momme* in weight will give you light for a journey of ten *chō*. It can also be helpful when you are in a difficult place to venture, like a log bridge or in water. It can be held in the palm of the hand or can be thrown into a dark place and it will not spread fire.

難所之大小

Nansho no daishō

SWORDS IN DIFFICULT AREAS

You may have to travel with your swords in hand when in a difficult place. When in dark and difficult places they should sometimes not be worn on the waist. It is best to sling them over your back.[125] Keep this in mind.

暗夜之人相

An'ya no ninsō

IDENTIFYING PEOPLE ON A DARK NIGHT

Stay along the sides of townhouses or under their eaves. Generally, on a dark night your ears are your eyes. Bear in mind that:

- large men walk with a loud step
- small men walk with a lighter step
- suspicious fellows come quietly
- ruffians come in haste
- violently drunk people breathe heavily and their steps are confused

暗夜目印

An'ya mejirushi

MARKINGS ON DARK NIGHTS

---

124 Japanese alcohol.
125 The swords are still in their scabbards.

When visiting someone's house, if it is a townhouse, identify its place in the row and try to remember the entrance, the colour of the walls, what is to the left, the right or to the east or west and have different ways to make a mental note of this identifying information, be it day or night.

足下一二三
Ashimoto ichi ni san
GAUGING DISTANCE

Understand the roads – in both safe and dangerous areas – by knowing the number of steps there are until you get to a hazard such as a moat or a ditch. When you are in an unfamiliar place use the way of walking called the 'probing step'.[126] If you move forward with probing steps and a serene mind, you will not fall. It is better if you can walk with speed and without failure.

The above twenty-five points are teachings on travelling at night and the positioning and carrying of lights. With the nine points on secret traditions, there is a total of thirty-four points.

The following articles are on emergencies and sudden events. There are also points on fires and earthquakes. The ideogram for sudden emergencies, 變, has been put at the top. There are twenty-five points and six secret traditions, which adds up to a total of thirty-one points.

---

126 サグリ足 *saguriashi* – to probe with the feet in the dark to test an unknown area which lies ahead.

Hen

ARTICLES ON EMERGENCIES

不意可心得事

Fui kokoroeru beki koto

POINTS ABOUT UNEXPECTED EVENTS

Fui means anything that happens unexpectedly – for example, fires, earthquakes, rain storms, gales, thunder storms, blizzards, floods, fights, attacks by gangs of thieves, people running at you in madness, people coming to you for sanctuary and people who have collapsed on the street. There are more than can be listed here. However, in any unexpected situation it is most likely that you will become confused. Therefore, the first thing to do is to settle your mind before dealing with the situation at hand. If you are unaware of this, more often than not you will lose the initiative because you will feel rushed. Therefore, always calm your mind and be prepared for this type of situation – this is a key aspect of our school.

有常備事

Tsuneno sonae aru koto

ALWAYS BE PREPARED AT NORMAL TIMES

Both natural phenomena and emergencies in human affairs can be predicted through *kiki* – sensitivity to *chi*. Those who are experienced in military matters show acute discernment in this regard, but this is not a level normal people can reach. Therefore, normal folk should just try to deal with an emergency by being prepared at all times; details on this were mentioned earlier. When actually dealing with an emergency there are some things to keep in mind and these are mentioned in the upcoming points. This includes points on fights, gangs of thieves, sanctuary seekers and fights to the death.

聲音不可驚事
Seion odoroku bekarazaru koto
NOT ACTING SURPRISED WHEN AN ALARM IS RAISED
You may be surprised when someone informs you of an emergency. The level of the emergency can be gauged by the person's speech pattern; some report minor matters as if they were more urgent or talk of an emergency as a minor matter. There are many points to be learned so that you can judge the urgency of a situation.

妻子片付之事
Saishi katazuke no koto
EVACUATING WIVES AND CHILDREN
Whether you are engaged in official duties or at home, if an emergency arises know in advance how you are going to evacuate your wives and children appropriately after reporting to your section captain or the section commander. It is often the case in such a situation that you spend too much time dealing with wives and children. Even if you are away, be prepared and instruct them beforehand, specifically on how they should evacuate in any given situation.

地震火事風雨心得之事
Jishin kaji fūu kokoroe no koto
POINTS ABOUT EARTHQUAKES, FIRES AND STORMS
Large earthquakes are as if a huge boulder has been thrown to the earth and all the ground shakes. Before earthquakes, there is a strong wind called a *jifū*.[127] This will help you to pre-empt larger earthquakes. Also, small fires can grow into infernos depending on the wind. Floods happen after large rains, gales break even bamboo groves and houses, wind tends to accompany rain and fires often happen after earthquakes. The saying, 'Jishin no atama kaze no

---

127 地風 'earth-wind'.

naka' means, 'Earthquakes are strongest at the start while wind is strongest in the middle.'[128]

出火心得之事

Shukka kokoroe no koto

POINTS TO KEEP IN MIND AT THE OUTBREAK OF A FIRE

Most fires happen at night. Instruct everyone in your house, down to the servants, of how to evacuate in this situation. For example, tell them in advance and have them understand that if a commotion or fire occurs and they need to leave the house in haste then they should meet at a specific place so that there will be no confusion. In a fire, if you leave your property and treasure behind and exit without greed then all will be well, no matter how suddenly the fire comes on. If life is lost in a fire it is because people have tried to save their property or their treasures. Important items should be kept in a storage pit to protect them from fire.

群聚騒動心得之事

Gunshū sōdō kokoroe no koto

POINTS TO KEEP IN MIND WHEN CROWDS ENTER INTO CONFUSION

When you are out in public and find yourself in the middle of a commotion, various problems may occur, such as your servants losing their sandals or becoming separated from you. You should prepare your servants to deal with such issues in advance.

In the case of a commotion caused by a fire during the daytime, have something to be used as a marker in front of the gate and at night have a lantern or marker pole, positioned at the front gate that has the family crest on it. Also, position lights at various places around the residence and try to be calm. If you rush, you will always become flustered and lose composure – never allow this to happen. Keep this in mind at all times.

---

128 地震ノ頭風ノ中 – 'Earthquakes from the head, wind from the middle.'

火事羽織之事

Kaji-baori no koto

CONCERNING FIRE JACKETS

Old teachings say that it is preferable for a fire jacket to be made of leather. However, cloth ones work better because if cloth garments are soaked well and then put on they will not catch fire, no matter how intense the blaze. Leather will shrink if it comes too close to the flames, so make fire jackets of cloth instead of leather and have the family crest upon them. It is up to the master to decide on the pattern.

行儀不失心得之事

Gyōgi ushinawazaru kokoroe no koto

POINTS ABOUT MAINTAINING GOOD MANNERS

In emergencies people normally become flustered. *Samurai* should keep themselves from wearing a single-wrap sash, a sash with the knot turned to an improper position, a sash with the knot to the front, long hair that is not tied up and so on, as such lapses of decorum will cause even more agitation. Calm your mind and work on all things serenely. Some people say that if you keep a calm mind then you cannot work at speed, but you can if you follow *hichō no hō* – the way of flying birds.[129] As a *samurai*, remember that in emergencies fear is born from a confusion of the mind. It is important to concentrate your *chi*.

地震可心得事

Jishin kokoroeru beki koto

POINTS ABOUT EARTHQUAKES

During an earthquake immediately open the doors and paper sliding doors and get outside. However, if you panic and are too eager to get outside you may injure yourself. On the other hand, not being fast enough is negligent. Being crushed and killed by a house is a dog's death, so exit quickly. The way to walk in an emergency is called *ashinami*. This involves concentrating on the big toe.

---

129 i.e. the mind should be calm and the body should move with speed.

急火心得之事

Kyūka kokoroe no koto

POINTS ABOUT SUDDEN FIRES

If a fire breaks out close to your residence, have people climb onto your roof to defend against the fire. You yourself should not go up there. Have the servants climb up while you hold the ladder and give orders. If you climbed up and the ladder fell away it would cause a problem. Also, if you were up on the roof it would be difficult to determine what needed to be done regarding any people in confusion or any goings on at ground level.

防火心得之事

Hi wo fusegu kokoroe no koto

POINTS ABOUT PREVENTING FIRES

Fire-fighting tools are called *hikeshi no dōgu* and there are many kinds in existence, so not all of them can be mentioned. The first thing to note is which direction is windward and which is leeward. A large fire will be difficult to extinguish, therefore the surrounding houses should be broken down and removed. However, if it is extremely windy then there is not much point taking away the surrounding houses. Instead, give orders that will prevent people from becoming injured. Confucius says, 'Ask about people and not their horses.'[130]

旅行地震心得之事

Ryokō jishin kokoroe no koto

POINTS ABOUT EARTHQUAKES WHILE TRAVELLING

If you are at the bottom of a mountain during an earthquake, consider that the mountain may collapse. If you are close to the sea, take the correct measures in case of a *tsunami*; furthermore, if you are below the level of a body of water, know that the bank may collapse. Make sure to stay clear of valley entrances. If you are in a house you should have no problem as long as you leave the house immediately.

---

130 Taken from an incident where the house of Confucius burns down and he enquires about humans over horses, even though the horses are considered of higher value. Found in Book X of the *Analects*.

大風心得之事

Ōkaze kokoroe no koto

POINTS ABOUT GALES

In a gale, keep doors shut. In such cases, take to and hide in the mountains. Sometimes houses collapse, but they do not do so in an instant; instead they will make a groaning noise before they actually fall. Also, do not get too close to large trees. People have their own ways to prepare for rain storms and floods; therefore, they are not dealt with here.

火事訪他家事

Kaji take wo tomurau koto

HELPING SOMEONE WHOSE HOUSE IS ON FIRE

If a fire breaks out in a nearby house and you help to put it out, then you should inform the master of the house of this and start work in either the interior or exterior. Wear a fire jacket, and do not start helping until you have announced yourself to the house master, even if you are close friends. Remember, it will be difficult not to lose any tools due to the crowds. Always inform the master of the house, in a loud voice that 'I [insert name] have come to give aid' and do not start to help until the house master accepts your offer. If done like this, the master will remember you; otherwise, they will often not remember any assistance you gave due to the large number of other people fighting the fire. In fires and commotion, it is difficult for normal people to remember others. That being said, there are different points for dealing with relatives.

火事居所之事

Kaji idokoro no koto

WHERE TO POSITION YOURSELF DURING A FIRE

If there are rules in place for where *samurai* should go, then just follow these guidelines. If you are called to an audience with the lord, work in accordance with his orders. It is ungraceful to be moving around by yourself and making a fuss.

隣家出火之事

Rinka shukka no koto

IF A FIRE BREAKS OUT NEXT DOOR

If a fire breaks out next door, whether during the day or the night, first send someone to observe the status of the fire itself. If the source of the fire is under control and if all flames have been extinguished then there is nothing more to worry about. Know that it is difficult for people to abandon property and treasure. Their first thought is normally how to save as many possessions and treasures as possible, which means that they are often too busy to fight the fire itself, and a small fire can get out of control. Therefore, if a fire breaks out in the neighbourhood or among the townhouses, collaborate and get there with speed, identifying how strong or fair the wind is and extinguish the fire by giving orders to your men. There are more things that should be kept in mind.

煙勢凌キ様之事

Ensei shinogiyō no koto

ENDURING SMOKE

If smoke is strong in the leeward direction and it is hard to breathe then it is best to put a piece of Japanese radish in your mouth. Also, medicine for breathing is mentioned in the scroll *Gun'yaku Yōhō*. If you are surrounded by fire, then make your escape by holding onto the mindset of *gunshi no kokoro* – a military death. It is known that smoke does not go lower than one *shaku* from the floor. Therefore, if you crawl with your face downwards you will not choke on the smoke.

盗賊心得之事

Tōzoku kokoroe no koto

POINTS ABOUT THIEVES

Here are things to keep in mind for when thieves infiltrate. Sometimes a number of them may come and break into a virtuous person's house. Thieves steal gold and silver to suppress the hunger of that day and have minds that allow them to indulge in ease at the cost of other people's hardship, so they are not brave warriors in the truest sense. How can a *samurai* who has a sense of loyalty and justice fear them? They always fight in large numbers – this shows that they are weak.

異相心得之事
Isō kokoroe no koto
POINTS ABOUT STRANGE APPEARANCES

Lower-class people tend to be afraid of those whose looks and outfits are out of the ordinary. Many of those who cultivate a fearsome image turn out to be thieves and the like. Even though they look strong, they actually do not have the mindset that a loyal *samurai* has, making it easy to defend yourself against them. If this is understood then it is easy to fight off roadside killers and murder-thieves without endangering your own life.

Concerning defence against intruders:[131] ways to deal with people who have pierced a hole in your storage house or are climbing the outer wall were mentioned previously and will be expanded on later.

亂心者取捌之事
Ranshinmono torisabaki no koto
HOW TO DEAL WITH THE INSANE

If all of a sudden an insane person enters through your gate, send him back to his parents or brothers. If he does not have a home or you do not know who he is, then immediately inform the local authorities. If he is carrying a blade or grasping a drawn *katana*, strike it with a staff so that the blade drops to the floor and send him back home at once. Generally speaking, if you talk gently to those who are insane, giving them an impression of timidity, their insanity will become more intense. This also applies to people who are violently drunk. Insanity develops because of insubstantial *chi*. If they injure someone with a bladed weapon, you should not forgive them; however, this will of course depend on the situation. Sometimes the person may be one who has been possessed by a fox, but know that these people will not fight those skilled in our school. Also, violently drunk people will return to their true self as time passes.

---

131 逃籠 *nigekomori* – people who hide or take refuge in a *samurai*'s property without permission when fleeing from someone.

If you are sitting in the company of a crazy person and he draws his *katana* or *wakizashi*, strike it out of his hand with intent using any weapon – his spirit will deflate. Make sure the person actually is insane, as it is an intolerable slight to strike the weapon of someone who is in full possession of his sanity.

群集下知之事

Gunshū gechi no koto

GIVING ORDERS TO A CROWD

When a large crowd of people is creating a commotion, instruct the heads of neighbourhood units to restore order. If the commotion does not settle, know that the people will not calm down even if you go there yourself and repeatedly tell them to be quiet. In this case, summon five or ten of their leaders and reason with them. Then these key people will return to the crowd and go around telling everyone to settle. While this is happening, you take a position at a higher place and have illumination so that you can see everything and then order the crowd to be quiet from this vantage point. At this they will settle. There are things to learn about how to address a large audience from a higher position.

雑説計知之事

Zōsetsu hakarishiru no koto

KNOWING AND JUDGING CURRENT RUMOURS

Zōsetsu are rumours and people of all ranks need to know where they come from. If you discover that they are in fact orders from district governors or local governors then they should be taken seriously, but for other kinds of circulating news do not become flustered, no matter what people say. During times of war it is possible that some of these rumours will be fabrications, although this is much rarer during times of peace. Also, be suspicious of any report of a thunder storm, a large flood, a large earthquake, the death of a governor or *shōgun* through illness, or any other disaster.

狂気者可遠慮事

Kyōkimono enryo subeki koto

MAINTAIN A DISTANCE FROM THE INSANE

There are ways to identify someone who is acting out of insanity. Be aware of these traits when you are sitting in a room with other people. Know that insane people may be silent and then erupt into speech, or they may talk constantly and then suddenly fall silent – the point is that their pattern of speech is inconsistent. Also, carefully observe the look in their eyes and the tone of their voice. If you believe someone to be insane, take a seat at a distance from them, even if in the same room. There are many points to be kept in mind.

不意急出之事

Fui kyūshutsu no koto

TO DEPART UNEXPECTEDLY

If you have to leave urgently for a certain destination, sometimes you may have to wear long undergarments, a chain-mail headband and a chain-mail shirt; therefore, have them prepared and ready in a set place. However, in some cases you may not have time to get dressed in these items. If so, instruct a servant to bring them after you have gone ahead. When you arrive, if there is no time to don such garments then it cannot be helped, but put them on if there is time. As a general rule, you should be prepared with these things at all times. Concerning the outfit to wear in the case of a fire, when you leave inform your servants to bring it to the destination; this should also be arranged beforehand. These points are also to be kept in mind at normal times. When having to leave urgently, take grilled rice with you. However, if you wait for any servants to prepare such things then you will be late. Therefore, inform those servants of the destination and have them catch up to you. In short, if you simply leave your position quickly, you will arrive sooner, so leaving your lodgings should be done as quickly as possible.

Δ Tradition says:

The following six points are traditions for the above twenty-five points. Keep them in mind and know them for what they are. They are known as *hiden* – secret traditions –and are points for urgent events, fires and earthquakes.

早速ノ門出

Sassoku no kadode

LEAVING URGENTLY

If a situation is truly urgent, just leave immediately and have your servants catch up with you. Also, you cannot spend time preparing a meal, so have grilled rice ready to carry. For an emergency, have straw sandals, long undergarments and a three-foot cloth stored together. For a *samurai* it is preferable to be early – know that having someone wait for you shows a lack of preparation on your part. Keep this in mind and it will become a part of your being.

謀計求別

Bōkei betsuni motomu

CREATING INTENTIONAL MEASURES

When things are hectic or if all of those below you are complacent and unprepared, then intentionally create trouble so that they *will* become prepared. An example is leaving tools for setting fire.[132]

變化不恐

Henka osorezu

DO NOT FEAR CHANGE

If you cannot stop worrying about death, then you will fear everything. It is said that nothing is a greater change than your own death – think on this. This is the same as to stop breathing through a fear of ageing.

水中不燒

Suichū yakazu

TO NOT BURN IN WATER

This is the same as the *suichū ikki* used in water as mentioned earlier. If you are determined when dealing with fire and if you move at speed, then you will not

---

132 火付ノ道具 – tools for arson. The idea is that when the servants discover the arson tools, they will think that someone has tried to break in, which will make them more attentive in future.

be burned. 'Fire cannot burn you and water cannot drown you.' Remember, if you draw your hand across fire pokers with speed you will not burn.[133]

怪夢早醒

Kaimu sōsei

STRANGE DREAMS AND WAKING UP ON TIME

A children's saying states, 'If there is a specific time you wish to wake, then think of that time and bite your thumb three times and you will wake at that hour.' If you have a calm mind then you can wake up at any time that you wish.

A poem states:

いも起て朝寝ハ人のずひきかな

Your wife has risen and you remain in pleasant slumber.

早足不倒

Hayaashi futō

FAST WALKING WITHOUT FALLING

Putting power and thought into the big toe when walking at speed will prevent you from falling and will prevent cramp in your calves. Walk like this in an urgent situation.

The above twenty-five points are about urgent situations, emergencies as well as teachings on fire and earthquakes, with the addition of six secret traditions. This adds up to thirty-one points in total.

The following points are for fights and duels, as well as *seppuku* and killing people. The ideogram for 'strike', 討, has been put at the top. There are twenty-three points and nine points on traditions, which adds up to a total of thirty-two points.

---

133 The reference to *ikki* concerns 'controlled speed' – to do things with a single-minded determination but with control.

Utsu

ARTICLES ON STRIKING

喧嘩討果之事

Kenka uchihatashi no koto

FIGHTS AND DUELS

These occur when *kannin* – patience – runs out, which can sometimes happen to *samurai*. A *kenka* is the kind of fight that may unexpectedly break out at any time, in any place and in any company, when anger can no longer be contained, resulting in the clash of swords. An *uchihatashi* is a form of duel where feuds are settled and a written declaration of intent is given in reference to a dispute. There are a small number of points to be kept in mind concerning bravery, cowardice and victory – these are discussed below.

客人喧嘩心得之事

Kyakujin kenka kokoroe no koto

POINTS ABOUT FIGHTS BETWEEN GUESTS

If one guest kills another in a *kenka* and then tries to leave, the general rule is that he should not be allowed to withdraw. He should not be excused even if the fight was caused by the rudeness of the host or if it was because of a feud between the guests. It is a dishonour for the host that two of his guests were engaged in a fight to the death. Therefore, you should be fully aware of the judgement required in deciding whether to allow the survivor to retreat or not.

討果可心得事 ·

Uchihatashi kokoroeru beki koto

POINTS ABOUT *UCHIHATASHI*

Undertake *uchihatashi* only when you are fully determined beforehand. The combatant who is killed will be the one who lacks determination. Also, there are varying opinions on whether to retreat or to remain after you have succeeded in killing an opponent. Some believe that if a *samurai* retreats after he strikes another *samurai* it is a sign of cowardice, while others consider it advisable to retreat after a successful attack. This all depends on the situation and the opponent, but in our school to retreat afterwards is considered strong and is mentioned in detail in the following points.

喧嘩之場行懸之事

Kenka no ba ikigakari no koto

FOR WHEN YOU HAPPEN TO PASS BY A FIGHT

If you chance upon a *uchihatashi* combat in a field or similar location, then you should inform the local people to intervene by using ladders or with wooden doors or with bamboo that has leaves and branches still attached. Also, talk to each of the duellists about the reason for the issue. If the fight has been provoked by an unexpected accident or such, persuade them to abandon the dispute. However, sometimes the *uchihatashi* was started by one side deliberately and therefore there is no way to stop it. If you pass by a fight in a field where no one else is present, then try to settle the affair. However, if the combatants ignore you and complete the fight, then there is an old way to follow, which goes thus:

First, say the following to the victor when he is about to leave: 'I was talking with you before for a short while, trying to mend this affair, yet I was unsuccessful and you have struck the opponent down and are leaving, but it is not fair that you simply leave after you have struck the man down.'

He will answer as follows: '*Samurai* should support one another. Is it possible that you will drop this matter and that we can just go our separate ways?'

Ancient customs dictate that you should take evidence in this situation, so say the following: 'Having witnessed a fight, a *samurai* cannot simply leave unless he is engaged in official duties that he has to fulfil. Therefore I wish to acquire evidence to avoid any problems that may arise in the future.'

However, this kind of thing rarely happens where *samurai* tread. If you do come across someone who has been attacked and left in a field – or anywhere else, for that matter – inspect the cuts and return. If there are guards present, then you can leave it all to them.

討果詞請樣之事
Uchihatashi kotoba ukeyō no koto
RESPONDING WITH SPEECH DURING COMBAT

If someone is provoking you to fight, do not become impatient. Just say to the person something along the lines of, 'I understand your point but please be aware that you have taken the situation wrongly.' Do not talk with timid words, so be sure *not* to say something like, 'Please be patient and I will apologize.' Furthermore, if you are in a discussion with lower people, never threaten to cut or strike them down because you should never say you will do that unless you mean it. Fighting between *samurai* will depend on the situation, but keep the following in mind:

- Swords may stick in ceilings or in the timber framework of a building.
- If you are in an open field it is best to move to higher ground.
- If you are outnumbered by your opponents seek protection to the rear – this can be a rockface, wall, bamboo groves or woods.

Focus your mind so that you will not retreat even a single *sun*.[134] This is called *doshi no yū* – the courage of a furious *samurai* – and in such situations it is not beneficial to have any hesitation in mind.

於他門逢有鬪諍事
Tamon ni oite tōsō aru ni au koto
OBSERVING A FIGHT OR ARGUMENT IN ANOTHER'S HOUSE

If when patrolling near another's house you come across a retainer making his escape after having struck down a colleague of that family, generally the first

---

134 i.e. 'will not budge an inch.'

thing to do is to attempt to stop him from leaving so that the master of the house will not have difficulty later on. If the master or his retainers are finding it difficult to stop the retainer from escaping, you should kill him and offer the kill to the master as his own feat of arms. Also, if you are a guest at someone's house and sword-fighting breaks out in the back area,[135] then make sure to have a good view of the building entrance or the gate and stay at that point while calmly observing these entrances. If someone tries to leave the complex then stop him. Also, if there is a commotion in the back area of another man's house, do not enter without care. If while you are at another man's house he kills one of his retainers, then enquire about the situation and state that you understand that the victim was an inconsiderate man. See things through until all settles down before you leave. Know that *samurai* should not return to such a place and do not talk much about such an incident. Furthermore, you should not answer anything unless being directly questioned.

Change expands into myriad forms.

助太刀心得之事

Sukedachi kokoroe no koto

POINTS ABOUT ASSISTING IN COMBAT

If you know one of the combatants in an *uchihatashi* feud, then you are obliged to assist him. Firstly say out loud: 'I [insert name] have no part in this dispute, this unexpected fight, but I will give assistance if exhaustion comes upon you.' Next, draw your sword and move to the rear of the opponent. Remember that you will not be asked for help but your ally will make a statement to the effect that your offer is much appreciated. Most cases are like this. If your comrade is defeated, you must fight in his stead; otherwise you should let your ally strike the opponent himself. Even if you do strike in assistance you should let your ally have the finishing blow. For as long as your associate is still capable of fighting, do not intervene – except by talking out loud.

---

135 勝手 *katte* – this area is normally restricted to guests.

留メ三所之事

Todome mitsudokoro no koto

THE THREE COUPS DE GRÂCE:

Since old times there have been three places to which a coup de grâce is administered:

- the first is the windpipe
- the second is the solar plexus or around the heart
- the third is the lower leg[136]

When killing by stabbing with a *yari*-spear, *naginata*-halberd[137] or a *katana*, then it is not necessary to give a coup de grâce. But even if you have inflicted two great wounds upon someone, you should still give him a coup de grâce; this is a principle of *bu*. If no coup de grâce is given it is like a death offered by townsfolk or farmers.

刀抜心得之事

Katana nuku kokoroe no koto

POINTS ABOUT DRAWING A *KATANA*

If a person provokes you beyond endurance and you resolve to kill him, it should not matter if he is of importance or not. You should have patience with people of low status and know that it is even more desirable to be patient with those who are of high status.[138]

Never reprimand your servants or such by hitting them with the back of the blade of a *katana* or *wakizashi*,[139] because if they try to grab the blade it may end up accidentally killing them. If you do need to beat them, do so with a staff. Also, it is wrong to call someone a coward if he announces that one of his servants is to be killed and draws his *katana* or *wakizashi* in readiness, but then does not kill him. Know that not only in the above scenario but in

---

136 足ノ裏 – literally 'leg/foot' and 'beneath', in Japanese this normally means 'sole of the foot'. Here it has been translated as 'lower leg'.

137 This weapon is found listed only in the Koga transcription.

138 The original text uses a distinction between 'heavy' and 'light'. We have taken this to refer to social standing, but it might refer to the level of severity of the person's actions against the *samurai*.

139 The words *katana* and *wakizashi* are found only in the Koga transcription.

all situations, to sheathe a *katana* after acquiring a fuller understanding of a matter is the proper way to correct a mistake. To cut is undesirable, while to not cut is virtuous; never shy away from an act of virtue. However, if two *samurai* have drawn their swords and are about to fight, sometimes they cannot just sheathe them. If a *samurai* draws his *katana*, it means he intends to kill. Do not underestimate this intention or try to adopt makeshift measures such as *meodoshi* – threatening through an aggressive posture.[140] These situations arise through hot-headedness, but if you keep a serene mind and remain settled they can be avoided.

刃ノ血落様之事

Ha no chi otoshiyō no koto

REMOVING BLOOD FROM A BLADE

Place horse droppings inside some paper and wipe it over a blade that has been used to cut someone. This will leave traces of the wiping and the blood will no longer be seen. If there are no horse droppings available to wipe the blade with, use the back of your straw sandals or soil inside paper. Furthermore, there is something called *hayanetaba* quick sharpening, which involves wiping the blade with a moleskin. This will make the blade cut well and is also good for wiping away blood. This way is good because it oils the blade; if you do not use this method, you will notice a deterioration in cutting. Sword handles should have two rivets. A sword with a handle containing only one rivet will cut through a total of three ribs fewer – this is not good enough.[141] It is best to have a sword with a handle containing two rivets with a proper space between them.

人ヲ切ル手之裏之事

Hito wo kiru tenoura no koto

THE WAY OF THE PALM WHEN CUTTING SOMEONE

On the subject of cutting someone: when he moves in to meet you, unless you bring him in close – close enough so that you think you could strike him with

---

140 目ヲドシ – an unknown term, literally 'threatening eye'.

141 Meaning that each rivet in a sword handle will add strength, giving power to the sword cut. A two-rivet handle will enable the sword to cut through three more ribs than a sword with a one-rivet handle.

the hilt – you will not be able to land your blow with the *monouchi*[142] part of the blade, and if it is not done in this manner then you will only hit with the tip.

There are three teachings for striking someone:

- Out of ten parts: three tenths is in the mind; three tenths is in the hand; three tenths is in the sword; and one tenth is in momentum. Remember that even if you have a master-class sword, unless you use mind, hand and momentum you will not make a cut.

- When striking with the sword, keep the inside of the hand relaxed, hold the hilt tightly with the rear fingers, push slightly forward and then cut by pulling. Hold your breath on the strike. To perform this, hold this action as a feeling in your mind.

- When the opponent is moving in towards you, you will make a deeper cut than expected. Conversely, when you are following up on the opponent as he is withdrawing, you will most likely end up striking with only the tip.

For further details you should receive the traditions of a swordsman's school.

Commentator two

Receive traditions from a school of *iai* sword-drawing or *suemono* object-cutting.

突不突事
Tsuku to tsukazaru koto
THRUSTING AND NOT THRUSTING

With weapons shorter than one *shaku* five *sun*, it is best to thrust. If in a narrow space, it is good to thrust even with a *katana*. Make sure the hilt and sharkskin grip are kept in good condition. In principle, you should study under people from the appropriate schools.

士之討果分様之事
Samurai no uchihatashi wakeyō no koto
HOW TO SEPARATE DUELLING SAMURAI

During duels between *samurai*, if townsfolk or farmers approach you to help

---

142 物打 – this is three *sun* down from the tip and is the curved cutting section of the blade.

settle the matter, have those people arm themselves with staffs or such weapons and take them with you. When you arrive say the following:

> *I was just passing by and have observed the goings on here. I am unaware of the grudges harboured between you gentlemen, but please take a moment to calm yourselves as this may cause trouble for the local people of this town. I am saying this as a* samurai. *If you do not heed my words and if you do not hold yourselves back, I will have the townsfolk and farmers strike at you with their staffs until you divide and then neither of you will achieve your aims. Therefore, restrain yourselves for now and leave this area and continue your purpose at any other place that you wish.*

If you take time trying to separate them they will become settled in the end, but if they do not settle divide them by using the staffs and send someone for the local officials and report the situation. Make sure not to leave before the officials arrive. Do not think the above is the only method to use in this matter.

下人討果分様之事
Genin uchihatashi wakeyō no koto
HOW TO DIVIDE LOWER PEOPLE FROM DUELLING

During duels between lower people, if townsfolk or farmers approach you to help settle the matter, as in the above point, inform them that as the duellists are just lower people they should strike at them with staffs and that if they do not calm down after that, then you will come and intervene. The way to talk to those duelling is as follows:

> *Both of you, of lower birth, lack respect for those above you and have created such a fuss as this. If you do not calm yourselves, then I will have these people divide you with staffs.*

They will calm down in most cases, but make sure to also report this matter to the officials. You can simply pass by such a situation without paying attention to it in most cases. However, if you are in a location where the nearest officials are far away, for example, outside a town or in the countryside, and you, as a *samurai*, happen to be seen by the local people and they ask you to intervene, it is difficult to refuse their request. Also, if the lower people are taking their time in starting the duel, it means that they are waiting for someone to intercede. Know that *samurai* never delay their fights in this way.

一人曖遠慮之事

Hitori no atsukai enryo no koto

AVOID DEALING WITH ARBITRATION AS A SINGLE PERSON

A *samurai* should not venture alone if taking a message concerning reconciliation or any other important matter. This is done to avoid missing out a part of the message given or part of the return message. This only concerns personal issues and messages, and is not the case when acting as an official messenger carrying the orders of the lord, or during a military campaign.

介錯心得之事

Kaishaku kokoroe no koto

POINTS TO KEEP IN MIND WHEN ACTING AS A SECOND[143]

Cutting open your guts as a result of fighting or because of your own mistake is just suicide and there is nothing to be learned about this. If it is done by a criminal or at the lord's command, at a temple, empty residence, graveyard or so on, matters will depend on the sentence given by the lord. When attending a performance of *seppuku* and after arriving at the appointed place, you may sometimes be asked by colleagues present to act as a second for the man committing suicide. As a *samurai* you may not refuse this and you should say the following: 'As I am familiar with the person who is about to die then I agree that I should perform this deed. However, what were the details of the lord's order?'

Next talk to the official in charge and say: 'As I am a colleague of the condemned I would like to assist in this matter.'

---

143 介錯 *kaishaku* – the second is a person appointed to decapitate someone who is about to commit *seppuku* (ritual suicide).

In most cases you will not be refused this task. However, during the Sengoku Period sometimes you may have been exempted.

If your offer is accepted, the man committing *hara-kiri* will sit on a fur rug, a futon or a mat and you may ask him if he is satisfied with you as the choice for his second. At this stage the condemned man may then ask you to perform the act of second in a withholding manner.[144] This is because they may wish to cut themselves profusely – you should confirm your acceptance of this. When the *wakizashi* – which will have been wrapped in paper and placed on a pedestal – is brought forward, the person committing suicide will hold it up. After this, they will stab themselves. At this point you should make your cut and do it quickly. When acting as a second it is recommended that you decapitate the man speedily,[145] but if you fail to make the cut it is a dishonour to you. Another reason for cutting quickly is that the condemned man may try to fight back with the *wakizashi*.

切腹古實之事

Seppuku kojitsu no koto

ANCIENT MANNERS ON *SEPPUKU*

In some cases the condemned man's belly should be opened at the temple to which he belongs. According to ancient tradition, a criminal who has committed the most deplorable of crimes is supposed to wear the clothes of a monk, but some say that this should be avoided, because it may be difficult to obtain such garments. Also from ancient times, when *seppuku* was conducted at the condemned man's temple the monks would throw a farewell gathering. These days, officials sometimes may allow the holding of a party in accordance with official orders. In such a case the ones entrusted with the criminal, as well as the messengers and inspectors, would join the gathering. Officials should not take off their swords. After the meal is served hot water is poured, first for the criminal then for everyone else. A while after serving hot water each person

---

144 The original text says 'quietly', which in this context means 'unhurriedly'. The condemned man is asking for the second to give him time to perform the cuts correctly in a show of his dedication to the ritual.

145 Even though the person has asked that time be taken, the instruction is to kill them in a speedy manner which is considered best for all situations.

carries his own tray to the next room, one by one, and stacks it away. If *sake* is being served, the second should pour some for the criminal who will receive it first of all. Then the criminal should drink. Next the criminal pours for the second. This should be repeated four times in total. During the *sake* serving, the men should be positioned on either side of a threshold. When this is finished, cold water is put in a jug and served in a cup, at which point the monk and the criminal drink it. This is called *mizusakazuhi* – the 'cold water cup of eternal separation'. Make sure to put a sprig of the Japanese anise tree in the jug. After this, the monk will conduct the Ceremony of the Fundamental Cause of Suffering and the Lineage of the Buddha over the condemned man. Sometimes the memorial tablet of the one to be killed is presented and incense is offered to it. After all of this, the *seppuku* victim will be executed at the temple.

In keeping with the ancient way described above, the following traditions are still observed to this day:

- Guests take off their swords throughout.
- The condemned man receives hot water before the guests.
- Guests do not stand up with their tray [until it is their turn].
- Cold water is not poured in a cup [that is used for hot water].
- The offering of *sake* four times does not take place across a threshold.

After the second has carried out his duty, another cup of *sake* is prepared for him. To leave before this cup is prepared is deemed as rude to the host and is, therefore, unacceptable.

切腹之品被問時之事

Seppuku no shina towareru toki no koto

BEING ASKED ABOUT HOW TO EXECUTE *SEPPUKU*

If a young person is going to open his belly and asks you how he should spill his guts, do not say that you do not know. Say something like: 'As you are young, it is understandable that you do not know about this matter. All you have to do is imitate the actual cutting.'[146] This will give them strength of mind so that

---

146 Here the victim is young and therefore he does not have to make the cut fully. He can make the gesture of the cut and the second will take off his head.

they can gracefully perform *seppuku*. Young people may ask you about splitting open the guts, because they respect you as a *samurai*. Therefore, if you answer that you do not know you will appear to be a bumpkin.

This is how to teach *seppuku*.

For certain crimes, criminals may be subjected to *uchikubi* (beheading) or *haritsuke* (crucifixion). The latter is sometimes known as *hatamono*.

刑法之事
Keihō no koto
CRIMINAL LAW

Punishments such as *hiaburi* (burning at the stake), *nokogiribiki* (death by sawing) and *haritsuke* (crucifixion) are used as a warning to others. The method of execution depends on the crime committed. The carrying out of a death sentence is official business and not the kind of thing you should casually observe. *Samurai* who wish to observe such a ceremony should accompany an official or make sure they put on their *hakama* before attending the execution site. Generally, issues concerning the condemned are under the control of the provincial governor and the law of the land. Do not just stand there casually watching. However, as a *samurai* you may observe the spectacle if you happen to be passing by.

宰領心得之事
Sairyō kokoroe no koto
POINTS ABOUT SUPERINTENDENTS

Generally, superintendents,[147] be it of criminals and prisoners or any other kind, should follow at the rear. When moving thieves and other criminals from one place to another, the superintendent – who is superior to the other officials – should be at the rear of all.

討者詞掛様之事
Uchimono kotoba kakeyō no koto
POINTS ON WHAT TO SAY WHEN KILLING SOMEONE [AT THE ORDER OF THE LORD]

---

147 宰領 *sairyō* – the person in command of the situation.

Here, *uchimono* means to be sent to someone at the request of the lord to inform the person of his crime and then to kill him. However, as he is a *samurai* he may fight back. Therefore, there are points to keep in mind, so as to not fail to make the kill. With extreme rapidity, inform the person of his crime, then immediately strike and finish him. Only *afterwards* should you say out loud: 'and for this reason the lord has asked me to kill you'.

If you think you have to explain yourself in full beforehand, it may end in the opponent drawing his sword and fighting back. It is a principle that the executioner should not say a word but that the messenger should inform the criminal of these things. However, everything will depend on the crime and the mind of the lord. There are teachings on how to document crimes. As all this may be taking place at the criminal's home, be aware that his servants and retainers may join the fight. Also, whatever the circumstances, do not say the phrase, 'Do you remember that you did commit...' until after you have struck. It is not good to say it beforehand and then fail to kill the target. There may be an investigation at a later point as to whether you did or did not correctly inform the target of your intent[148] – *samurai* should be aware of this.

尸血穢臭之事

Shiketsu oshū no koto

THE OBNOXIOUS ODOUR OF BLOOD AND DEAD BODIES

Generally in sword-fighting, duels or cutting open a stomach, there will be blood. This lifeblood will spread. Even the smallest amount of crimson blood will look like there has been great bloodshed, and if you are not used to this the stench of the blood will knock you sick and turn you pale – something which is inappropriate for a *samurai* because it suggests cowardice. Young *samurai* should accustom themselves to the stench of blood by taking any opportunity to observe executions and punishments,[149] etc. Otherwise they may be reputed as squeamish around blood and therefore unsuited for bloody deeds.

---

148 This is why Natori advises to make the announcement with speed and then strike the target down immediately. After striking, the *samurai* can then slow down and explain in full as the target is dying, in order to satisfy regulations.

149 成敗 *seibai* – punishment, including execution. Young *samurai* must become accustomed to bloodshed by observing the spilling of blood.

闘諍下人發事

Tōsō genin ni hassuru koto

CONFLICTS THAT OCCUR BECAUSE OF LOWER PEOPLE

Samurai do not think much of death when someone provokes them beyond the limit of their patience or when they are acting on loyalty and justice. However, they do not usually kill others or die without good reason. Keeping this principle in mind at all times, *samurai* tend to restrain themselves – so the number of fights they engage in is actually quite small. There are many cases of unscrupulous servants doing things that enrage their master, draining him of patience. To avert problems from this age-old source, a master should always instruct his servants against improper manners or becoming violently drunk. It is traditionally said that disaster and mishap are often caused by lower people.

Δ Tradition says:

The nine points below are the *hiden* – secret traditions – for the above twenty-three points. Keep them in mind and know them for what they are. They are traditions and points for teachings on fighting and duels, as well as *seppuku* and killing at the order of the lord.

大小柄取之品

Daishō tsuka-dori no shina

FOR WHEN THE HANDLES OF YOUR SWORDS ARE GRABBED

If your opponent grabs hold of the handles of your long and short swords to draw them, take hold of the hand-guards with your left hand and strike the opponent between the eyebrows using the your right hand. Strike quick and hard – this will make the opponent let go. If he just has hold of your *katana*, you should draw your *wakizashi* and stab him in the side. To allow this it is recommended that your *wakizashi* should have a *kaeri* – scabbard hook.[150] The *wakizashi* should be short.

---

150 カヘリ – a small hook-like feature on the scabbard which hooks under the lower edge of the *obi*-belt and stops the scabbard sliding upwards when the sword is drawn.

大群之中刀抜様

Taigun no naka katana nukiyō

HOW TO DRAW A *KATANA* IN A CROWD

Place the *katana* between your thighs and draw it with the blade away from your body, making sure to draw it upwards. In such a situation a shorter *katana* will be best.

左之手刀抜様

Hidari no te katana nukiyō

HOW TO DRAW THE *KATANA* WITH THE LEFT HAND

Take and hold a sharp breath to secure the *katana* against your belly.[151] Next, draw the sword (it is best to have the sword slightly pre-drawn). Use this technique when your right hand has been restrained and you cannot draw normally. Again, a shorter *katana* is preferable.

刀曲反時

Katana magari soritaru toki

FOR WHEN YOUR *KATANA* IS WARPED OR BENT BACKWARDS

When cutting someone, a *katana* may bend – although this will not happen with a good *katana*. If you carefully tap the blade with something soft on the convex side of the bend then it will become straight. However if you hit it on the inside of the curve it will snap.[152]

腹ヲ切ヲ指ト云時

Hara wo kiru wo sasu to iu toki

FOR WHEN SOMEONE SAYS HE CANNOT OPEN A BELLY BECAUSE OF INTERFERENCE[153]

---

151 Breathing in sharply pushes the stomach outwards and tightens the *obi*-belt, which helps to hold the scabbard in place so that the sword can be drawn out more easily.

152 If the sword has bent to one side, hammer it gently with the bend protruding upwards and the tip of the blade curving downwards. Do not hammer the blade on the inside with the tip curving upwards.

153 This is a reference to people who are reluctant to attack and kill their enemies because they fear they may have to commit suicide as a punishment.

This is something only a coward will say. A brave man will just kill the opponent he is facing. Do not deal with such cowards, and know that there are plenty of them. Also know that these situations are just a way of shifting personal dishonour onto others.

敵卜見違時

Teki to michigau toki

FOR WHEN YOU ARE MISTAKEN AS THE ENEMY

It is considered a great wrong to be mistaken as someone's enemy and is something that should never be forgiven. However, if the person who has made the mistake is clearing the name of his parents, keep in mind that his filial devotion may have confused matters. In such a case you should forgive him. However, if you have been injured it may be that he cannot be forgiven. Again, this depends on the situation.

刃傷上中下

Ninjō jō chū ge

LEVELS OF SWORD-FIGHTING

Here *ninjo* is the same as *uchihatashi* – feud-fighting. There are three levels:

- *jō* 上 – upper level: to strike the enemy successfully and leave without a scratch
- *chū* 中 – middle level: to strike successfully and to perform *hara-kiri*
- *ge* 下 – lower level: to fail in *hara-kiri*, to be seriously injured, to fall and die together or to be killed outright

堪忍替人

Kannin hito ni kawaru

PATIENCE AND ADOPTING THE VIEWPOINT OF OTHERS

Observe things from the viewpoint of the enemy and consider carefully whether you should show tolerance or not. This also applies when you give someone advice.

夭死遁習

Yōshi nogareru narai

AVOIDING A PREMATURE DEATH

Yōshi means 'sudden death'. This can be delivered by drowning, burning, sword-fighting, strokes and disease. Keep in mind that all health problems can be pre-empted. Headaches, chest pains, nausea, a faint pulse, having cold breath, having urine and spittle with no bubbles, lack of sparkle in the eyes – these things should all be noticed.

The above twenty-three points are about *kenka, uchihatashi, seppuku* and killing at the request of the lord. With the nine secret traditions, this adds up to thirty-two points in total.

The following points are about revenge as well as capturing; the ideogram for revenge, 讐, has been put at the top. There are twenty points and seven points on secret traditions which adds up to a total of twenty-seven points.

Kataki

ARTICLES ON REVENGE

讐討欲出離主之事

Katakiuchi idento hosshite shu wo hanaruru no koto

LEAVING YOUR LORD TO DEPART FOR REVENGE

If a parent or a brother is killed by another *samurai*, then it is a fundamental principle that you kill the opponent in revenge – there are things to keep in mind on such killings. If you report to your lord to inform him that you shall be engaging in revenge and he, after consideration, asks you to postpone, it will make it difficult for you to undertake such a venture. Therefore, you should instead send a report to your commanding officer and leave immediately. The report should say:

> *My parent has lost his life by [insert name] and therefore I am going to strike him down. Please convey the circumstances fully to our lord and ask for his generous understanding.*

The wording does not have to follow a fixed pattern, but may vary according to your own style. For example, it might say:

> *I happen to know the location of my enemy and thus I present this letter in my own poor writing.*

This can be done in various ways. Also, for your close friends and relatives you should compose a memo or statement saying:

For the above reasons I will report back when I have successfully made the kill and returned.

You can have your servant deliver it to them after you have left. If you cannot find your enemy it cannot be helped, but if you *do not* target the enemy of your parents or brothers and *do not* try to kill them, you are simply not a *bushi*.

讐討ニ出心得之事
Katakiuchi ni deru kokoroe no koto
POINTS ABOUT JOURNEYS OF VENGEANCE

Samurai should have a detailed knowledge of their own arts, especially when they need to take revenge upon an enemy. It is dangerous not to be acquainted with *hyōdō* – the way of the soldier.[154] This includes:

- *kenjutsu* 剣術 – swordsmanship
- *iai* 居合 – quick-drawing of a blade
- *torite* 取手 – capturing
- *hayamichi* 早道 – fast travel

These are all essential and required elements.

Make sure to wear *kusari-katabira* chain mail and do not let it 'leave your skin'. *Kikomi* chain mail is discussed in detail in the scroll *Heigu Yōhō*.

As well as the above, continually hone yourself in the following areas:

- saving money to use when in a period as a *rōnin*
- *bōkei* 謀計 – plans and tactics
- *kanja no hō* 間者ノ法 – the way of the spy
- *shinobi no hō* 忍ノ法 – the way of the *shinobi*

讐持使者心得之事
Katakimochi shisha kokoroe no koto
POINTS ABOUT MESSENGERS WHO ARE ON MISSIONS OF VENGEANCE

---

154 兵道 'soldier-path' – in this context, the military training of the *samurai*.

Someone once asked:

> *Imagine you are targeting an enemy and do not have enough savings in reserve and thus face hunger and you have to find a temporary patron to serve. If your new patron sends you out as a messenger and you come across your enemy on the way, should you kill the enemy or fulfil the mission as a messenger? It can be disloyal for samurai to fail to continue to serve as a messenger, even if serving a temporary lord. However, if you do not strike down your enemy, you will miss a chance to settle a feud which may have lasted years. Therefore, which of these duties should be dropped?*

The master replied:

> *While this scenario is not impossible, it is highly unlikely. However, if it does happen in this way, then follow the original objective. You have left a generational lord to fulfil a filial debt over loyalty, all to avenge your father. Therefore, it is difficult to sacrifice filial devotion for the sake of loyalty to a temporary lord. Though loyalty should be more important than fidelity, the latter cannot be thrown away, even if dying of hunger in order to kill the enemy of your father. Having a temporary lord is a measure in your tactics and this lord was taken as a part of the requirements of your plan, so it is acceptable to stick to your original aim. In older days someone once joined the service of the enemy he intended to kill. Although it is a disloyalty to kill your lord, vengeance is considered an acceptable motive. However, you cannot forget the debt you owe to your temporary lord, so leave a letter stating that you came across your enemy and that you have acted accordingly, or even ask a close friend to pass the writing to the lord at a later point. Remember, though, that this situation is very rare.*

讐討可断品之事

Katakiuchi kotowaru beki shina no koto

THINGS THAT SHOULD BE REPORTED WHEN ON A QUEST OF VENGEANCE

If you come across your enemy, it goes without saying that if you are on a mountain pass or in a field you should just strike and leave. Even if in a residential area or such, just strike the enemy immediately *without* reporting to the head of the village or to the local governor. It is normally obligatory to report to the local office, but what if the enemy flees while you are reporting? Just strike as soon as you find him. You will never manage to kill him if you are slack-minded enough to think that you should make reports to the local office first. If you are questioned later and the issue of your having attacked without reporting correctly is brought up, simply say:

> I have just arrived and I was on my way to report to the local office, but while on the way I chanced upon my enemy and could not just leave the matter alone, so I killed him. This is why my report was delayed.

If you are accused of not reporting the matter, then there is nothing you can do about it. However, having tracked your enemy down, you should not let him escape through fear of being accused.

讐討助太刀之事

Katakiuchi sukedachi no koto

LENDING AID IN REVENGE

It is standard to give a coup de grâce when the enemy has been struck, but if you are to decapitate them then a coup de grâce is not required. If someone offers to perform as *sukedachi* – assistant to the killing – you should move towards them and decline, even if it is a colleague. If passing by and you happen to see an act of vengeance taking place, and gates have been secured to the front or to the rear, stopping the enemy from fleeing, then just continue to observe. If you notice that the man taking revenge is a *samurai* and if the combat is intense and *katanas* have been broken asunder and if the man taking revenge asks to borrow your *katana*, draw your sword and pass it to him. Also, say: 'I have noticed that you are fighting with earnest and I am impressed. If you get tired then I will become your *sukedachi*.'

After making this offer, you should remain there. When the combat has finished and the person returns your sword, say: 'Please keep it and wear it, even though it may be a humble blade, as I see that you do not have a replacement.'

In this case do not take back your sword. This is unlikely to happen, but I have mentioned it so that you are aware of it. If the person targeted for revenge asks you to perform as a *sukedachi*, then do not agree. Say to him: 'Sir, it is not appropriate for someone who has been targeted to ask for assistance.'

These points apply to an encounter where the combatants are strangers to you. You should not fight for a man who has been targeted, as it is against filial devotion.

敵討他国司頼事

Katakiuchi hoka no kokushi wo tanomu koto

GAINING AID FROM A PROVINCIAL GOVERNOR AFTER AN ACT OF VENGEANCE

If you successfully kill your target and seek employment with another clan, using your achievement of this act of vengeance as an example of your value, then in most cases you will not be hired, even if the combat was outstanding. This is because a *samurai* killing his enemy is not an unusual occurrence. If you wish to serve a provincial governor but think you may be rejected, you should say:

> I [insert name] killed the enemy of my parent in [insert place] and
> have moved from there. As I have long since been a rōnin, and as
> I have fallen into poverty, if I am given shelter and kindness, my
> appreciation will be vast and I will devote myself to you.

If you are offered a position you should accept it, but if you are not offered one make sure to talk about yourself in only a light manner. If you and your achievement then impresses your prospective employer and you are considered an earnest person, then he may decide to hire you and keep you within the clan. If you are asked of the salary you require, simply say, 'To be retained is my only hope.' Do not discuss an amount of fief and rice.[155] As revenge is not a rare occurrence for *samurai*, it is ill-mannered to place vanity in this act.[156]

入國讐討之事

Kuni ni iru katakiuchi no koto

THOSE WHO ESCAPE TO YOUR PROVINCE HAVING EXACTED REVENGE IN ANOTHER PROVINCE

If someone has killed his target and seeks shelter in your province, even if there is no position for him in the clan you must still not let him be killed, no matter how many are in pursuit. This is the jurisdiction of the provincial governor. If the provincial governor does not know of the man's presence, sometimes his death cannot be avoided, but otherwise it is not allowed for anyone to kill someone who has come to your area hoping to serve in your province. If it is decided not to retain him, then escort him with officials or captains through your province. If someone has fled [from your province] to another province after a revenge killing, taking advantage of the above principle, know that there are ways you should keep in mind to kill or capture him.

走込者心得之事

Hashirikomimono kokoroe no koto

POINTS ABOUT THOSE WHO SEEK SANCTUARY

A person who has killed his enemy or someone against whom he holds a grudge may be chased and therefore seek sanctuary. As it is a principle for a *samurai* to give shelter in such cases, shelter must be given. However, there are traps you should be aware of. Some people may falsely claim to have killed someone in order to ward off hunger or to receive a gift of money; there have even been cases where they turned out to be thieves – therefore, be sure to examine the situation. Find ways to identify impostors after hiring them, such as observing how they conduct themselves in the master–retainer relationship.

---

155 知 *chigyō* – land rights.
156 i.e. a *samurai* should not self-promote the success of his vengeance killing.

走込者抱様之事

Hashirikomi mono kakaeyō no koto

HOW TO RETAIN THOSE WHO SEEK SANCTUARY

As this situation may arise suddenly, it is often the case you have no idea how to actually deal with it. The first thing to do when someone seeks sanctuary is to ask him to talk about his situation and the specifics of their grudge. If he appears to be telling the truth, say the following: 'You have done well. Therefore, do not worry for I will provide shelter.' You may decide to take charge of his long and short swords. Sometimes it may be better to give the man gold and silver and let him escape through the rear gate. It may also be the case that one of your servants is attacked and injured by a pursuer, who may attack from an area near a neighbour's house and may chase the servant back into your grounds in order to get to the man seeking sanctuary.[157] Sometimes the sanctuary seeker's long and short swords should not be confiscated – this will all depend on the situation. Make sure to instruct the gatekeepers and servants to inform anyone who arrives in pursuit that no one seeking sanctuary has entered your residence. If the gatekeepers or servants become flustered and confess that the sanctuary seeker is in fact within, and if the pursuers accuse you of harbouring their target, taking your gatekeeper's words as evidence, say the following: 'As a *samurai* family we do not give shelter. These words from such a low class man cannot be used as evidence.' If you say this in a gentle manner, they should not insist that you show them the inside of your complex. However, if they still demand to come in to investigate, then it becomes a situation where you can definitely enter into combat with them.

科人抱可出事

Toganin kakae derubeki koto

SHELTERING AND HELPING CRIMINALS FLEE

If you are asked for help by a *samurai* who has set himself against someone above him or entered into a duel with another *samurai* serving the same clan,

---

157 A pursuer may target a servant of the *samurai* who is providing sanctuary and attack him as he passes a nearby house. This way the attacking *samurai* can look as if he is giving chase for a supposed foul deed by the servant and push right through the gate with the actual intention of killing the sanctuary seeker.

know that he has broken official laws and so it will be difficult to offer him shelter. However, if you wish to give him at least some form of aid, simply let him flee to another province before you receive any official orders to detain him. If you delay your decision to let him escape, it may become too late. Instead you may have to say to him the following:

> Although I intended to let you flee by any means that you could, officials have arrived to arrest you. Therefore, I have no choice but to hand you over to them, as this is the order of the lord.

By saying this you can convince him of your good intent before passing him over to the officials. If you have previously confiscated his long and short swords, you should *not* return them. However, sometimes you *should* let him wear his swords with the intention that he will die by the sword – as always, everything depends on the situation. All this applies to *samurai* from other provinces, but if someone from your own clan finds himself in this situation, it may be appropriate to present a request to the officials to save his life.

他国之走込者之事
Takoku no hashirikomimono no koto
CONCERNING SANCTUARY SEEKERS FROM OTHER PROVINCES

If you shelter a sanctuary seeker from another province who is being pursued, report to your captain or the officials in charge and tell them of the circumstances, saying the following:

> As the man has put trust in me and has come from another province, I have given him shelter; this is a principle of the *samurai*. Those others who have come from his province are insisting on a transfer of custody, which is why I am referring to a higher authority. While I am not a man of any consequence, this man still came to me in good faith and therefore it is difficult for me to simply hand him over. If those who are in pursuit insist upon their capture by any and all means, I shall enter into combat, so please consult our lord about this issue.

In most cases the authorities will declare that the man has their official protection. Make sure to present full information in a written report to these authorities, including the family name of the *samurai*, the name of the *samurai* who was killed, their previous master and any other details needed.

走込者糺ス似者事

Hashirikomimono nisemono wo tadasu koto

DETECTING A BOGUS SANCTUARY SEEKER

If a sanctuary seeker appears dubious, first remove his long and short swords and ask in detail about his situation, the clan in which he served and also question him about which members of that clan he was acquainted with – check this against your knowledge of the *samurai* there. After this, say the following: 'I do not doubt you, but I will still need to send someone to verify what you have told me.' If he turns pale, this will add to your suspicions. At this point, press him in a strict manner, saying: 'If you are telling the truth I will offer you shelter, but if I find you are lying then I will not let you go.' Telling him this will surely reveal whether he is being truthful or not. As well as the above, use your own strategies.

敵之頸持走込者之事

Teki no kubi wo motsu hashirikomimono no koto

FOR A SANCTUARY SEEKER WHO IS HOLDING THE DECAPITATED HEAD OF AN ENEMY

If a sanctuary seeker has killed his enemy and arrives with the decapitated head in his hand, the first thing to do is discover if the situation is true or false.[158] If the case is real then say:

> *I understand that the head you hold is evidence of the defeat of your enemy, and I am extremely impressed by it, but I am not happy for you to bring the head in here. Your date of departure from us is unknown, so I will stand as a witness to the fact that you did bring the head if I am needed to, but please now dispose of that head.*

---

158 虚実 *kyojitsu* – literally, 'substantial or insubstantial'.

It is best to state the above to ensure he throws the head away. It is not appropriate to allow the head to be kept and thrown away at a later point.

取者緩急之事

Torimono kankyū no koto

CAPTURING PEOPLE QUICKLY OR SLOWLY

Uchimono – killing at the lord's order – is a suitable punishment for someone who has killed another person or has robbed gold and silver and is holed up in a house, forest or abandoned home. It is also an appropriate way to deal with someone who has committed a crime against the laws of the lord and fled to another province.

However, *uchimono* will not always be necessary. There is also *torimono*, which involves capturing someone who has barricaded himself within a place. It may be that they are insane. In all cases of *torimono*, do not kill the target but detain him and keep him alive. Be aware that a *samurai* should be captured quickly, while farmers, craftsmen and merchants should be flushed out over an extended period. This is the ancient teaching of *kankyū* – 'with haste or by patience'.[159]

捕者心得之事

Torimono kokoroe no koto

POINTS ABOUT CAPTURING CRIMINALS

Capturing farmers, craftsmen and merchants is straightforward, but there are many teachings on the capture of *samurai* and others if they are defending themselves with bladed and projectile weapons, such as bows and muskets. Know that various plans and measures need to be deployed, such as:

- the throwing of hot water or fire
- putting ash into a musket and shooting it at them
- using body armour
- using the *tsukubō*, *sasumata* and *kumade* pole-arms[160] along with the traditional grappling hook

---

159 緩急 *kankyū* – *kan* is 'to take time' over a matter while *kyū* is 'to engage with speed'.

160 These are three varieties of pole-arms used in capture operations. In order, they are: U-shaped サスマタ, barbed 突棒 and raked 熊手.

You should be flexible according to the situation.

飛道具持退者之事

Tobidōgu mochi shirizoku mono no koto

CONCERNING PEOPLE WITHDRAWING WITH PROJECTILE WEAPONS

When pursing someone who is retreating along a street in full view, be aware that he may sometimes stand and prepare to fire a projectile weapon. If this happens, move on him without hesitation and at speed to make the capture. Remember that you will only be struck by a projectile weapon if you hesitate. Retain a firm mind and know that it is a disgrace and slight against *samurai* ethics to fail to make the capture. There is a clear and definite difference between your bravery and his cowardice. Because of the above way, know that you will not be hit in most cases. Also remember that after a musket has been shot there is a pause while it is being reloaded with the next round. If you don't understand this you will be one who 'fears the fuse of an unloaded musket or an arrow which is broken' – a term used to describe a cowardly pursuer. Instead, 'let your mind escape the forest of thorns'.

籠者捕様之事

Komorimono toraeyō no koto

CAPTURING THOSE WHO ARE BARRICADED WITHIN

If a thief or murderer is holed up in a house and has a blade to defend himself, there are various weapons you can use to capture him. However, circumstances will vary and sometimes you may not have any specialized weapons or tools available – if this is the case, then know that there is a mindset for such situations. First, bear in mind that if the killer or robber has set himself up defensively inside a house, it means he is fully aware that he has committed a harmful act and is in fear of his pursuers and will try to evade them and survive, even if just for a moment longer. For such cowardly people, saying the right words can sometimes make the capture easier – this may involve deceiving them, coaxing them or even threatening them in an aggressive way. However, if your plan overreaches itself and goes off course you will not gain any benefit. In our school we go directly to the destination, without hesitation, and capture the target by adapting our tactics to the circumstances. Generally, those who retreat and defend themselves within a building lack courage. If they did have courage and understood that there was no escape, they would come out to fight or cut open their own guts. If they do come out to fight there are certain points to bear in mind, for this shows they are courageous fighters. They are called *hisshi no mono* – those who are determined to die.

追逃心得之事

Nigeru wo ou kokoroe no koto

POINTS ABOUT PURSUING SOMEONE WHO IS FLEEING

If you are walking along a narrow alley or the like and you happen upon a criminal who is being pursued and the pursuers order you to make the capture, do not block his path – this is because the criminal will fight like a 'cornered soldier'. In this situation, the teaching is to pretend not to hear the order, allow the criminal to pass and then capture him from the rear.

成黨家屋籠之事

Tō wo nashi kaoku ni komoru koto

THOSE WHO FORM GROUPS TO DEFEND THEMSELVES WITHIN A HOUSE

It is not difficult to capture or attack those people who are defending a residence, etc., when they are in number and forming a large group. If the enemy are large in number then you should also have a large number and protect yourself appropriately, have the correct equipment and join in combat. If they have secured the gate you should break down the *nagaya* buildings on either side of the gatehouse,[161] but if they have secured both the main gate and the *nagaya* then have your people cross over the wall and then enter the *nagaya* to fight those within. Sometimes you should just break through the gate and demolish the house or make an incendiary attack; there are countless ways to achieve this. Not every teaching of *kyojitsu* within our school can be recorded here.[162]

---

161 長屋 *nagaya* – a long building built into the wall adjacent to a gatehouse.
162 The implication here is that *kyojitsu* – the substantial and the insubstantial – encompasses every conceivable way to achieve the goal.

取者縄掛様之事

Torimono nawa kakeyō no koto

HOW TO BIND A CRIMINAL WITH ROPE

Each school has its own way to use the quick-rope[163] or other equipment for securing prisoners. It is difficult to initially bind someone by using a hook and regular rope, so first bind with the quick-rope and then later bind him with regular rope. In some cases people have tried to bind with normal rope from the beginning and have been unsuccessful.

Δ Tradition says:

Below are traditions on the above twenty points. They are called *hiden* – secret traditions – and you should understand and take them for what they are. The following traditions are for revenge and capturing.

取者大小用捨

Torimono daishō yōsha

CONSIDERATION ON THE USE OF LONG AND SHORT SWORDS WHILE CAPTURING

If there is someone who must be captured alive, remove your long and short swords and have a retainer look after them so that you can take hold of a weapon such as the *hananeji*,[164] then you should jump in[165] and capture him. However, if the person is a townsman or farmer you should wear your swords because such people do not have the heart for sword-fighting and are likely to become scared when they see yours. When dealing with a *samurai* do not go in wearing swords. This is so that the person is not cut while being captured.[166] Whether you should wear swords or not depends on the situation.

---

163 早縄 *hayanawa* – a thin cord used to ensnare a prisoner.
164 鼻捻 *hananeji* – originally a loop of cord on the end of a stick. It was used to twist around the nose of a horse to keep control of it, but is also adapted to use for binding criminals. The version used for capturing criminals is generally stout and robust and consists of a short staff with a loop for placing over a body part, although variations exist.
165 The term used is *tobi-iru* 飛入, 'to spring in'.
166 The translation of this point is based mainly on the Koga transcription.

逃者向品

Nigerumono mukau shina

WHEN THOSE YOU ARE CHASING SUDDENLY STOP AND TURN

If you chase straight after the enemy, he may suddenly turn back on you, making you run into him. Therefore, give chase so that you come up alongside your target.

逃込者心得

Nigekomimono kokoroe

POINTS ABOUT SANCTUARY SEEKERS

Whoever you are chasing, if the person runs into another's gateway then run in after them and kill them without regard for any others there. If you first ask for permission to go in and so on, the situation will become complicated – especially if the authorities get involved.

走込者君命借時

Hashirikomimono kunmei kariru toki

WHEN AN ORDER FROM THE LORD IS INVOKED TO TRY TO CAPTURE A SANCTUARY SEEKER

If you are sheltering a sanctuary seeker, sometimes his pursuers will come to your door and invoke an order from the lord saying that he be handed over. In these situations consider whether they are telling the truth or a falsehood. If the lord has given such an order, the pursuers will move through your gate without hesitation and will decisively capture their target. However, if it is a personal matter and they do not have authorization they will waver in intention and will hesitate when moving through your gate. Also, listen to their speech to identify the truth.

一気捕物

Ikki no torimono

CAPTURING IN THE INSTANT

Without wavering, jump in and capture your target. Retain a normal mindset even when dealing with those who are insane and be without hesitation.[167] There

---

167 Do not overthink or overestimate the enemy and do not allow fear to creep in through internal debate. Act decisively and with bravery.

is no particular reason for concern. Be aware that if you have 'two thoughts and double beats'[168] then you will fail to make the capture.

乳切木飛鐵

Chigiriki tobigane

THE *CHIGIRIKI* OR THE *TOBIGANE* TOOL[169]

This is a ball upon a chain and is sometimes attached to a staff, which is called a *chigiriki-zue*. This should be thrown over the enemy.

早縄鉤心

Hayanawa kōshin

THE HOOK AND QUICK-ROPE

Attach the kind of hook used for fishing to a quick-rope and hook the enemy with it. As this is painful, the enemy can easily be pulled around by his hand.[170] The hook can be inserted into his mouth or one of his ears.

The above twenty points are about revenge and capturing. With the seven additional secret traditions, this adds up to twenty-seven points in total.

The following are points to keep in mind on messengers, investigations and lawsuits. The ideogram for accusations, 訟, has been put at the start of these ten points. There are a further six points, which adds up to sixteen points in total.

---

168 二念二気 *ninen-niki* – literally, 'two thoughts and two *chi*' – this means to think twice or to hesitate.
169 A tool that consists of a staff and chain with a metal ball attached to the end.
170 This could be either the hand or the arm.

Shō

ARTICLES ON ACCUSATIONS

使者心得之事

Shisha kokoroe no koto

POINTS ABOUT ACTING AS A MESSENGER

It is normal practice for *samurai* to receive an order from the lord to serve as a messenger. The first thing to keep in mind when visiting another clan is to present the letter or the message from your lord faithfully, without additions or subtractions. This way should be followed even by lower people, but especially by *samurai* – even the slightest inaccuracy may become a matter of *kyojitsu*,[171] or of disloyalty.[172] While with the other clan, do not attend to any personal matters; a *samurai* should never mix personal matters with official duties. If you make an unscheduled call while on messenger duty, if your servant is ill-mannered or does something which wrongs someone, it is considered as extreme disloyalty towards your lord. Any unexpected and undesirable issues that arise while you are carrying out the orders of the lord are inexcusable. For unexpected or undesirable things that happen to you while serving as a messenger there are things you should be aware of [as explained in the following points].

---

171 i.e. hidden implications.

172 A lord receiving a message from another lord will consider the hidden political implications. Therefore, if a *samurai* adds to or subtracts from a message there may be unintended consequences.

使者喧嘩可慎事

Shisha kenka tsutsushimu beki koto

MESSENGERS SHOULD ABSTAIN FROM COMBAT

When acting as a messenger, you and your servants should abstain from arguments and sword-fighting in the streets. The orders of the lord are important and therefore you should make sure that no trouble arises; this includes things such as *uchihatashi* – combat to satisfy your own grudges. If anyone slights you, remember that you can deal with him afterwards. First, fulfil the orders of the lord, even if you are suffering disgrace. When you return you can make a proper judgement of the situation. This is the principle of *buyū* – the courage of the *samurai* and of they who cherish their lord.

使者刀被盗事

Shisha katana nusumaruru koto

WHEN YOU HAVE YOUR *KATANA* STOLEN WHILE ON MESSENGER DUTY

When you are delivering a message, your *katana* is passed to a retainer at the entrance, as you must give the message wearing no other weapon but your *wakizashi*. Remember to instruct your servants not to conduct themselves in an ill-mannered way at this time. Be aware that one of your servants may steal your *katana* and flee. This will not happen if you hire servants with care, but is harder to avoid when you are serving in Edo, because there you may have to employ wandering servants.[173] If you do have your *katana* stolen, do not create a fuss but inform the entrance keeper as follows:

> *I cannot find the servant who is guarding my* katana. *It is possible that he became sick and has returned. However, I am having trouble because I do not have a sword to wear for my return journey. Although I am hesitant to ask this of you, I wish to borrow a* katana *for my return.*

---

173 渡り奉公人 *watari hōkōnin* – servants who wander from master to master.

You should then just return with the borrowed sword. This situation is the result of not correctly judging someone when you hired them, but this does *not* cast any form of dishonour on you. However, do not return without a *katana* because this *is* a dishonour. While this may be a rare event I have still recorded it here as such a case may cause you temporary difficulties. Apply this way of thinking to other cases.

主君詞可重事

Shukun no kotoba omonjiru beki koto
RESPECT THE WORDS OF YOUR LORD

When making a judgement on a matter, correctly evaluate that which is loyal and that which is disloyal. Concerning disloyalty, those who have some military achievements will still be useless if they have a disloyal mind.

In older days there was a *samurai* called Tsukuda Mataemon, who would always announce to others: 'If a lord meets his subjects and says unreasonable things, no one should contradict him.' When he was serving Gamō Ujisato of Aizu, he went to battle in Ōshu. Now, Ujisato would move around the huts at night observing his army, and on one occasion the enemy made a night raid which was successfully repelled. The next morning, when there was a meeting to discuss the raid of the previous night, Ujisato said: 'Tsukuda is well prepared at all times and performs with excellence in the vanguard, but it appears that he became flustered as he stabbed his spear without unsheathing it.'

Tsukuda answered: 'That is correct, my lord. I did this because clouds were gathering in the evening and therefore I used my rainproof sheath and moved out with it still on and as the raid was harsh I just fought on with the sheath still attached.'

This impressed Ujisato much. Even if it was cloudy, there was no way that anyone would have kept a rainproof sheath on his weapon. Tsukuda simply took the lord's words as they were given. These words by Tsukuda were golden as he managed to maintain his own reputation without contradicting the lord, which would have been disloyal. If there is something immoral in the will of the lord, you should plead against it. If the lord does not take heed of your words, plead a second and a third time, but if he still does not listen to you then resolve to die alongside him – this is the path of the *samurai*. In ancient times, when loyalty was extreme, it was recorded in the *Taiheiki* war chronicle that Yakushiji Jirō Kaneyoshi pleaded with Moronao several times. He failed to sway his lord, so he decided to become a monk and was mocked for this act; know that this ridicule was justified. Keep an accurate judgement on what is truly loyalty and what is disloyalty and become determined to die. This is the root of courage for the *samurai*.

訴訟依怙有間敷事

Soshō eko arumajiki koto

TO BE IMPARTIAL IN THE SETTLEMENT OF DISPUTES

When settling disputes among lower people, favouritism plays no part in the way of *samurai*. Be aware that due to personal preferences you will sometimes feel pity for someone you favour and have a bias against the other. Or you will think ill of someone if they are unknown to you, especially if they have an unsavoury face. Once in ancient times an experienced magistrate listened to the claims of two people behind a screen to avoid being unintentionally unfair to one of them on account of their appearance. Someone once said: 'If you always remember you are a *samurai* you will not show favouritism.' However, stupidity often prevails and officials may forget this precept.

奉行役人心得之事

Bugyō yakunin kokoroe no koto

THINGS MAGISTRATES AND OFFICIALS SHOULD KEEP IN MIND

Those officials who listen to disputes are called *bugyō* – magistrates – and such a station should be taken up by *samurai* who have the appropriate abilities. The office cannot be performed by those without intelligence or virtue. People of a base quality will try to influence magistrates and officials using gold and silver or by entertaining them or by other unrighteous ways. This is commonly called *mainai* – bribery. It goes without saying that *samurai* should not be biased. Those magistrates and officials who do not follow the correct path do not deserve the offices they hold. Such untalented people take advantage of the orders of their lord to elevate themselves, and then exploit their position to throw their weight around. Generally, those who are unaware of what is right and wrong and are without proper judgement cannot achieve honour and fame through excellence. Only those who can execute *budō* and have restraint should become magistrates and officials.

聞訴訟肝要之事
Soshō wo kiku kan'yō no koto
ESSENTIAL CONSIDERATIONS WHEN HEARING A DISPUTE

If you do not pay equal attention to each party in a dispute, you cannot make a correct judgement. As the proverb says, 'Do not give judgement having listened to only one side.' Furthermore, when listening to two people, it is common to believe the first one you hear and not the second. To avoid this problem, there is a way of testing people by asking them about a truth you already know.[174]

法式可心得事
Hōshiki kokoroeru beki koto
LAWS THAT SHOULD BE KEPT IN MIND

When examining a case, remember that each clan has its own set of laws and those who go against these laws are judged to be criminals, while those who stay within the laws are judged to be righteous. Therefore, when in temporary lodgings, *samurai* should learn about the laws of that area and take care not to break them. However, the orders of your lord always take priority.

喜怒不移面事
Kido omote ni utsusazaru koto
TO WITHHOLD JOY AND ANGER FROM YOUR FACE

When listening to an examination to decide the right and wrong of a matter, know that unrighteousness should be punished and righteousness should be honoured. If you do not have a proper judgement of who is right or wrong, you may show a gentle face when joy is in your heart and when you become angry you may speak roughly and stare intensely – this is not considered *samurai* behaviour. Since ancient times it has been said that, 'The Way is to not display

---

174 i.e. ask questions that you know the answer to and observe which person lies.

anger.' If you allow your mind to be as it wishes, it is against the Way and is considered to show a lack of bravery and wisdom. Sometimes, if any bravery exists at all it is only foolhardiness and is considered wrong. There are teachings on benevolence, righteousness and foolhardiness.

奉行忠義心得事

Bugyō chūgi kokoroeru koto

A MAGISTRATE SHOULD KEEP LOYALTY IN MIND

Normally, magistrates and other officials carry out their duties in keeping with the established ways of the clan. However, if you, as an official, need to change the normal way of doing things, you should carefully weigh up the new approach in terms of loyalty and righteousness. If it accords with loyalty and functions well within the administration, then make the change with purpose and confidence. Be aware that you should set aside your own interests but *never* forget loyalty. This is because magistrates, in particular, are the model to which everyone else aspires.

Δ Tradition says:

The following six traditions are about the above ten points. They should be kept in mind and understood for what they are. They are the traditions on the points about messengers and the examination of disputes and lawsuits.

本末分明

Honmatsu bunmei[175]

DISTINGUISHING BETWEEN ESSENCE AND PERIPHERY

Discern that which is the central core in all matters and know it well. Do not confuse the way of reason and the way without reason – these can often be intertwined. Understand that which is essential and that which is peripheral and give priority to the essential.

---

175 本末 *honmatsu* – this can also be translated as 'cause and effect', 'the core and the external', 'the trunk and the branches', 'importance and non-importance' or 'substance and its shadow'.

與利道理之別
Ri wo ataeru dori no betsu
THE DIFFERENCE BETWEEN CONTRIVED LOGIC AND RIGHTEOUSNESS

Eyes and ears – the young monk is the apprentice and the old monk is the master.[176]

役人目付之品
Yakunin metsuke no shina
CONCERNING OFFICIALS AND INSPECTORS

When giving evidence to an official or inspector, be it about yourself or another person, speak with your mind fully engaged and make sure the information you give reflects the overall circumstances and will not contradict something that may be said later.

貴人賤人之品
Kijin senjin no shina
THE DIFFERENCE BETWEEN THE PRIVILEGED AND THE HUMBLE

Be aware that, although all people think in essentially the same way, there are different ways of talking to people of high and low status.

口上專要
Kōjō senyō
THE ESSENCE OF DELIVERING A MESSAGE

A spoken message can easily be misinterpreted, so first of all give a summary of the message, describing its essence, and then go in the details section by section.

双論不奪
Sōron ubawarezu
PROTECTING YOUR ARGUMENT

---

176 A reference to a teaching concerning the identification of truth and falsehood, the full description of which is found in the *Shōninki* manual.

As soon as someone gives an opinion, another person may try to pass it off as his own. This is commonly called *shiriuma ni noru* – to mount the same horse. Therefore, a *samurai* should state only seven out of the ten points that are in his mind and leave the remaining three unspoken. This is called *ubawarezu no wakimae* – defending against those who steal your argument.

The above ten points plus six traditions add up to a total of sixteen points. These are teachings that officials should keep in mind, including teachings on disputes and lawsuits.

The following thirteen points are about the strong and the weak, victory in battle and departing for war. The ideogram for strong, 強, has been put at the top. There are also a further eight traditions, adding up to twenty-one points in total.

Kyō

ARTICLES ON STRENGTH

勝負強弱之事

Shōbu kyōjaku no koto

STRENGTH AND WEAKNESS IN BATTLE

In all contests, not only military ones, there is a difference between being strong or weak and being victorious or defeated. Sometimes the winner may be weak, while the loser is strong. Those who die may be honoured, while those who have survived can be shamed. It is a question of who is loyal and righteous and who is disloyal and unrighteous. To die showing loyalty to your lord is honourable, while to obstinately cling to life is disloyal and shameful. If you remain righteous but are defeated one hundred times in one hundred battles, how can this be called weak? Know that if you are unrighteous and gain victory one thousand times then this is not the way of the *samurai*.

Being strong or weak in battle fully depends on loyalty and disloyalty and righteousness and unrighteousness. Dedicate yourself completely to this.

計謀勝ル力量事

Keibō rikiryō masaru koto

STRATEGY OUTDOES PHYSICAL STRENGTH

Physical strength depends upon the nature a person is born with; some have it and others do not. Some can carry twenty or thirty *kan* in weight, while others can carry only five or ten *kan*. This fact of life must simply be accepted – you cannot make yourself stronger through force of will. However, physical strength does not serve loyalty and in days of old there were cases where people of immense physical strength were nonetheless weak in loyalty or righteousness. Today those who gain achievement on the path of loyalty often outshine those who have only physical strength. If you gain benefit through strategy and direct or indirect tactics, people will admire you as long as these tactics are born out of the righteousness found in your loyalty. However, if someone gains victory, even over one hundred people, by means solely of physical strength backed up by disloyal and unrighteous strategies, how can such a person be admired? Be aware that loyal strategy excels physical strength.

与力者勝負心得之事

Rikisha to shōbu kokoroe no koto

FIGHTING SOMEONE OF SUPERIOR PHYSICAL STRENGTH

If you are fighting someone who is physically more powerful than you, use swordsmanship when you are up close, and projectile weapons when you are at a distance. Above all, do not grapple with someone of such physical strength – this would be like using fire to fight water. Knowing this is a military skill.

對得道具勝負之事

Edōgu ni taishi shōbu no koto

FIGHTING AGAINST SOMEONE WITH HIS FAVOURED WEAPON

Generally, it is difficult to gain a victory over someone using a certain art that he has mastered. If the opponent has exquisite mastery in swordsmanship, then secure your victory with projectile weapons. Keep this mental attitude in mind; it is called *shōbu keisaku no narai* – the teachings of the tactics of victory.

兵具嗜専要之事

Heigu tashinami senyō no koto

ALWAYS BE PREPARED WITH MILITARY TOOLS

As mentioned previously, *samurai* should not forget about war even in times of peace. Keep in mind that you should never be lacking in the realm of military equipment and weapons. *Samurai* who lack the proper attitude and the necessary military equipment and skills are like farmers who have forgotten how to farm, craftsmen who know nothing of iron squares and merchants who have lost the art of calculation. This can be called *tōshoku* – to steal one's salary.

戦国雑談心得事
Sengoku zatsudan kokoroe no koto
CASUAL TALK ABOUT TIMES OF WAR

Samurai without dedication to the Way during peacetime do not understand military skills (*gunjutsu*) or the military way (*gundō*). When preparing for war comes up in casual conversation, these people tend to betray their ignorance of the subject. They are like lumberjacks who talk about the sea or fishermen who talk of the mountains. Keep in mind that a *samurai* should not discuss matters he does not understand.

陣觸心得之事
Jinbure kokoroe no koto
POINTS ABOUT ORDERS FOR WAR

Wars can have various different causes. They may be sparked off by a riot, for example, or by a quarrel between two provincial governors, or by the occupation and barricading of a castle by a person who holds a grudge against his lord. There are many ancient cases recorded of each of these types of situation. When war does break out, the lord will issue *jinbure* – orders for war. First tell your men what needs to be done immediately and what can be done later, then make your departure through the gate. Further details are in the scroll *Ippei Yōkō*.

出陣心得之事
Shutsujin kokoroe no koto
POINTS ABOUT DEPARTING FOR WAR

When given an order to march to war as mentioned above, you may be unsure what to take with you or what instructions to give to the servants who are coming with you, and so on. This is because you are not constantly dedicated to the military way. However, all *samurai* groups will receive orders from their captains. It is not acceptable to fail to leave for war because of a lack of weapons, armour, people or horses. *Samurai* must be prepared at all times – study the path of warfare and take care to maintain stocks of military equipment. These points should be kept in mind concerning departure for war.

俄出陣心得之事

Niwakani shutsujin kokoroe no koto

POINTS ABOUT IMMEDIATE DEPARTURE FOR WAR

Sometimes the lord is ordered to depart for war at short notice and you may need to set off in two or three days, which may leave no time to question anyone.[177] In these situations those who are not prepared will come unstuck. No matter how urgent the case is, when moving to war with haste, move lightly, as if you were preparing for a journey during normal times. Details on tools and so on are given in the scroll *Heigu Yōhō* – this information should constantly be checked and given continual attention.

軍行不替常事

Gunkō tsune ni kaezaru koto

THERE IS NO CHANGE FROM THE NORM WHEN DEPARTING FOR WAR

People consider war to be very different from normal times and there are many tales of upheaval and the various ways that life changes. However, nothing should differ from normal times. For those who are determined and prepared, should there be any change when going to war? They are called soldiers and *bushi* because there is no difference for them between war and peace. Some may even venture the opinion that warfare is not the path of a *samurai*. Keep in mind that, be it in times of peace or times of war, *samurai* should be prepared for war and not forget *heidō* – the way of the soldier.

出陣帰陣之事

Shutsujin kijin no koto

LEAVING FOR AND RETURNING FROM WAR

Each *samurai* school has its own established ways to leave for and return from war. In our school details are given in the scrolls *Ippei Yōkō* and *Gunbai*

---

177 Meaning that if a *samurai* is unprepared in matters of war, he will not have time to ask the many questions on protocol that may arise.

Yōhō, and so the subject is not discussed here. You should refer back to these documents, study them diligently and keep them in mind.

着具心得之事
Chakugu kokoroe no koto
POINTS ABOUT DONNING ARMOUR

Many people who are not prepared do not know how to put on armour. Here is a summary of the task:

The first step
- *hadagi* 膚着 – under-kimono
- *momohiki* 股引 – light trousers
- *habaki* 脛巾 – gaiters
- *waranjigake* 草鞋掛 – foot covering
- *waranji* 草鞋 – straw sandals

The traditions for these are in the scroll *Heigu Yōhō*.

The second step
- *suneate* 脛當 – greaves

Use the traditional method for tying the strings.

The third step
- *haidate* 佩楯 – thigh protectors
- *gusoku* 具足 – full cuirass[178]

These are fully secured by the *kurijime*-cords. The main outer *obi*-belt should also be put on at this point.[179]

The fourth step
- *kurijime* 繰縮 – armour-securing cords

The measurements for these are in the scroll *Heigu Yōhō*.

---

178 The original simply states *gusoku* and *haidate* together.

179 Steps three to five concentrate on securing the armour and are done at almost the same time, so are not as distinct as the process in the text makes them appear.

The fifth step
- *uwaobi* 上帯 – outer obi

The measurements for this are in the scroll *Heigu Yōhō*.

The sixth step
- *kabuto shita* 兜下 – padded cap
- *hachimaki* 鉢巻 – headband

The measurement and fastening are done in the traditional way.

The seventh step
- *hōate* 頬當 – faceguard

Details are in the scroll *Heigu Yōhō*.

The eighth step
- *kabuto* 兜 – helmet
- *shinobi-no-o* 忍ノ緒 – helmet cords

Details are in the scroll *Heigu Yōhō*.

The ninth step
- *koshiate* 腰當 – sword clasp

There are traditions for this.

The tenth step
- *ōgi* 扇 – fan

Details are in the scroll *Ippei Yōkō*, but illustrations are in a different scroll.

The eleventh step
- *sashimono* 指物 – banner

This should be put outside the gate. There are traditions about how to place and secure it.

The twelfth step
- *saihai* 采拝 – war baton

The illustrations and traditions for this are in another writing.

These are called *tō-ryū jūni yoroi* – the twelve parts of armour of our school. There are other teachings in addition to the above. Remember that items should be donned from the lower to the upper. There are more details which have not been recorded here and they are found in the scrolls *Heigu Yōhō* and *Ippei Yōkō*.

軍学不可怠慢事

Gungaku taiman subekarazaru koto

HAVE NO NEGLIGENCE IN MILITARY STUDIES

Samurai are not permitted to be lax in their military studies at any time. To reinforce this point, a golden saying from an ancient warrior has been recorded here.

Honda Heihachirō Yasutoshi was a retainer of Shinkun.[180] Once he saw his son practising with a spear, upon which he chastised him by saying:

> *Those* samurai *who clash with spears during battle are low ranking. High-ranking* samurai[181] *have to manoeuvre large bodies of people, thus spear-fighting is not a task they should engage in. From the first time I engaged in battle, I wished less for glory with the spear and was more focused on the manoeuvring of my troops. Any* samurai *who commands people with a war baton should think more of the larger goals than his own petty achievements.* Samurai *should nonetheless train themselves in* gunjutsu – *military skills – including spear-fighting and so on. To be clear, spear-fighting, swordsmanship, archery, horse-riding and so on are arts that cannot be mastered without effort. However, war is an art that cannot be mastered without constantly conducting it. Keep this in mind. This is even more so for my sons, for they should not devote themselves to the spear or the like.*

---

180 Tokugawa Ieyasu.
181 *Shōshin* and *taishin*, low- and high-ranking *samurai*.

In Chu[182] there was an excellent swordsman and a retainer reported his expertise to King Xiang. The king said:

> That is an art of fighting only one enemy. I will study how to defeat tens of thousands of enemies.

True to his word, he attained great achievements through the ability to manoeuvre vast armies. There are countless stories like this. *Samurai* should always keep in mind the military path. A commander-in-chief needs to know how to position his troops correctly so that they are ready for situations like the first clash of spears or musket-fighting. This is not like the knowledge passed on from father to son.[183] This is the learning to which *samurai* should dedicate themselves.

Δ Tradition says:
The traditions for the above thirteen[184] points follow below. They should be kept in mind and understood as they are said. They include teachings on the different meanings of strong and weak, contests[185] and preparing for war.

勝負一騎合
Shōbu ikki ai
CONTESTS AND SINGLE COMBAT
When in single combat, attack from a lower position. At night it is even more desirable to position yourself lower. An opponent who attacks you from a higher position tends to make mistakes. For example, if he attempts to strike you with his sword as soon as he has drawn it, he may misjudge the distance.

---

182 An ancient Chinese state.
183 Meaning that warfare is an extremely high-level skill that requires actual experience.
184 The original manual states that there are only twelve.
185 勝負 *shōbu* – two or more factions standing against each other.

刀抜卜不抜心

Katana nuku to nukazaru kokoro

THE MINDSET OF WHETHER TO DRAW YOUR SWORD OR NOT

Drawing your sword is weak, while not drawing is strong. Those who have a courageous mind will not draw without care.

鑓之心持

Yari no kokoromochi

THE HEART BEHIND THE SPEAR

At night, sweep the spear horizontally and when you hit something, pull back and stab. When in a thicket or forest, do not stab using a cross-shaped spear, instead you should thrust with the butt of the spear. For this situation there are things to be kept in mind about the butt of the spear. The mind should be fully aware of the use of weapons.

陣觸軽進

Jinbure keishin

MARCHING LIGHTLY WHEN ORDERED TO DEPART FOR WAR

When you are ordered to march to war, you have not got time for meticulous preparations. You just need to go. Rushing off to war is expensive, so make sure you have enough gold and silver in reserve at all times.

祖名告妻

Somei tsuma ni tsugu

INFORM YOUR WIFE OF YOUR ANCESTRY

Make sure your wife understands that your ancestry obliges you to leave immediately for battle and to be prepared to sacrifice your life for the lord. This will mean that in an emergency she will know what to do and will carry out the appropriate tasks.

剛臆中志

Gōoku chūshi

THE MINDSET THAT LIES BETWEEN BRAVERY AND COWARDICE

To have too much courage can be as detrimental to a *samurai* as to have too little. In times gone by, Yoritomo taught Noriyori and Yoshitsune about advancing and retreating and bravery and cowardice by using a thick bronze cauldron. This mindset is called *chūshi* – the middle mind. This means to be neither too brave nor too cowardly.

平世蓄粮

Heize rō wo takuwaeru

STORING UP FOOD IN TIMES OF PEACE

Prepare dried rice and soy pulp each year. Be aware that stockpiling food is an essential part of preparing for emergencies.

平世蓄人

Heize hito wo takuwaeru

KEEPING PEOPLE IN RESERVE FOR TIMES OF PEACE

Also keep extra people in reserve. Choose appropriate people, give them gold and silver and have them promise that they will perform as your servants if an emergency arises. Lower people will feel indebted to you and will not break their promise and will come in times of need. This is called *hito wo takuwaeru no nari* – the teaching of keeping people in reserve.

The thirteen points and the eight traditions add up to twenty-one points in total. These are concerned with the teachings of strength and weakness, contests and preparations for war.

There have been 290 articles up to this point, following on from the twelve tools of virtue, which were listed at the start. These articles run from the heading *Heika Jōdan Mokuroku* and end here.

Ippei Yōkō

IMPORTANT POINTS FOR THE INDEPENDENT SOLDIER

発端
Hottan

INTRODUCTION

This document records every aspect of soldiery, from the departure for war up until a triumphant return, including: advancing as a force, marching, camp construction, advance and retreat, the different kinds of language to be used, personal exploits, the eight most prestigious achievements, blunders and the difference between bravery and cowardice. Above all, *samurai* should place loyalty before survival and welcome a death that is for the sake of righteousness. This holds true from the *shushō* commander-in-chief to the *heisotsu* ordinary soldiers, although specific considerations differ greatly by rank. According to Sun Tzu's Five Constant Factors and Seven Considerations, as well as the guideline for generals contained within the *Three Strategies of Huáng Shígōng*, a general's tactics should be guided by the benefits of heaven and of earth and the harmony of man, whereas common vassals need not concern themselves with these matters. An independent soldier should concentrate on mastering the following points:

- unsheathing their weapon in battle
- holding a steady gaze
- bearing arms
- not becoming disheartened if injured
- fighting with fury
- competing to be the first

The purpose of this entire scroll is to transmit a methodology for mounted warriors and soldiers. Therefore, it is entitled *Ippei Yōkō* 一兵要功 – 'Important Points for the Independent Soldier'.

First we will examine the significance of the four ideograms that make up the name of the scroll.

POINTS ON THE IDEOGRAM 一
Commentator one

The *on* reading[1] is *itsu*. The *kun* reading[2] can be *katsu* or *hitotsu*. According to the document *Zihui*,[3] Fu Xi studied *bagua* – the eight hexagrams of divination – and gave the ideogram 一 primary position. Also, know that the meaning of the ideogram is 'one' and it is the first of the *yō* numbers.[4]

Commentator two

The meaning can be either 'a beginning' or 'a single person'. The Japanese reading is *katsu*. In this context the ideogram plays on the word *katsu*, which means 'to have victory over an enemy'.

POINTS ON THE IDEOGRAM 兵
Commentator one

The *on* reading can be *hei* or *hyō*. The *kun* reading is *tsuwamono*. According to the document *Zihui*, the pronunciation of *hyō* consists of the initial section of *ho* 補 and the final section of *myō* 明, which together make a homophone of *hyō* 冰. The meaning is 戒器 – weapon.

According to the document *Shi Ben*,[5] *hei* weapons are made of iron and there are five kinds:

- *kyū* 弓 – bow
- *shu* 殳 – spear with a spiked collar
- *bō* 矛 – spear
- *ka* 戈 – halberd with a horizontal blade
- *geki* 戟 – halberd with a horizontal blade and spearhead

---

1   Mock-Chinese reading based on sound and pronunciation.
2   Japanese reading based on the meaning held in the ideogram.
3   A Chinese dictionary edited by Mei Yingzuo and published in 1615.
4   Odd numbers.
5   A record of history prior to the Qin Dynasty.

Swords are called *tanpei*, which means 'short weapons'.

The ideogram 兵 has the two pronunciations of *hei* 敝 and *hyō* 氷, but both have the same meaning [of 'soldier' or 'weapon']. The usage of these ideograms should follow the way they have been used over their long history.

In the *Six Secret Teachings* scroll within the 'Civil Teachings' chapter, article twelve, 'The Way of the Military', it states:

> *Kings of old considered weapons to be implements of evil that were*
> *to be used only when no alternative could be found.*

Drawings of the five weapons can be found in the document *Wu Jing Kai Zong*.[6] In our country this document should be used. Weapons include:

- *yumi* 弓 – bows
- *ya* 矢 – arrows
- *yari* 鎗 – spears
- *naginata* 長刀 – halberds
- *tachi* 太刀 – great swords
- *katana* 刀 – long swords
- *wakazashi* 脇指 – short swords

It is solely *samurai* who conduct war (the aim of which is to settle the realm and preserve good governance). Therefore, in wartime *samurai* are referred to as *hei* – soldiers. In Sun Tzu's volume of the *Seven Chinese Military Classics*, in the chapter 'Initial Plans' the annotation states that *hei* means 'weapons'. However, the term was extended to also mean 'soldiers', because they are the people who use weapons.

Commentator two

Samurai carry the 'five weapons', therefore the military name for them is *hei*.

---

6   A military reference book written by Huang Xian Chen during the Ming Dynasty and published in Japan as the *Bukei Kaisō* in 1661. It provides extensive discussions on Sun Tzu and other military tacticians.

POINTS ON THE IDEOGRAM 要

The *on* reading is *yō*. The *kun* reading is *kaname*. According to the document *Zihui*, the pronunciation consists of the initial segment for *yi* 一 and the final segment for *shō* 笑 – thus combined, they become *yō*.

Meanings include:

- *sūyō* 樞要 – importance or principle
- *yōkai* 要會 – a key point

Xuanzang gained prestige for the passage from the *Xiao Jing* document[7] that reads: 'The late emperor possessed the ultimate virtue and *yōdō* – the path of principle.'[8] According to the annotations of the *Xiao Jing* document, this ideogram means 'to go deeply into a truth'.

POINTS ON THE IDEOGRAM 功

Commentator one

The *on* reading is *kō*. The *kun* reading is *isawoshi*. According to the document *Zihui*, the pronunciation consists of the initial segment of *ko* 古 and the final segment of *kō* 紅, which is a homophone of *kō* 公. The meaning is 勲 – 'achievement'.

The *Setsumon* text[9] states that 功 is defined as 'to establish a state with great effort'.

Commentator two

The ideogram 功 is included [in the title of the scroll] because for every single soldier 'achievement' is of fundamental importance. However, soldiers also serve with dedication, within the rules and according to their rank and position.

---

7   Known in English as the *Classic of Filial Piety* (c400 BC).

8   This is an example of the ideogram in use.

9   *Setsumon* 説文解字 is the Japanese name for the *Shuowen Jiezi*, a second-century Chinese dictionary.

This is why this ideogram is used. Know that the *Ippei Yōkō* document explains in full the way of achievement, something which should be mastered. Know that a soldier who gains such achievements may attain the level of general.

CHAPTER ONE

CATEGORIES OF *SAMURAI*

An *ippei* is an independent *samurai* who belongs to a unit.[10] This excludes:

- *shō* 将 – generals
- *bugyō* 奉行 – commanders
- *kashira* 頭 – captains
- *yakunin* 役人 – officials

There are also other types of independent *samurai*, who can be classified as:

- *ikko* 一己 – independents
- *ikki* 一騎 – single mounted riders[11]
- *ippo* 一歩 – soldiers on foot

Furthermore, the following are general terms for rank-and-file soldiers:

- *shisotsu* 士卒 – soldiers
- *heisotsu* 兵卒 – soldiers
- *shosotsu* 諸卒 – various soldiers
- *heishū* 兵衆 – soldiers
- *hosotsu* 歩卒 – soldiers on foot

Within the above types there are differences between upper and lower ranks. Generals, commanders and captains should know and use the different types.

---

10 An *ippei* generally had his own income, lands and servants. Although independent, he would fight in a unit if required to serve his lord.

11 This term can sometimes refer to a soldier on foot.

MILITARY UNITS

The following terms are used to refer to military units of different sizes:

- *go* 伍 – five people
- *ichijū* 一什 – ten people
- *ittai* 一隊 – fifteen people
- *ikkō* 一甲 – twenty-five people
- *issotsu* 一卒 – 100 people
- *ichiryo* 一旅 – 500 people
- *issui* 一帥 – 2,500 people
- *ichigun* 一軍 – 12,500 people, and this makes a single army
- *sangun* 三軍 – three armies – is a combination of three *ichigun*, i.e. 37,500 people.

According to the *Wei Liaozi* scroll:

- A unit of fifty people is called a *shoku* 屬
- A unit of 100 people is called a *ryo* 閭
- A unit of 1,000 people is called a *sotsu* 卒

There should be one general for every 10,000 people.

In an army, an *itte* single formation is led by a general, while a *kumi* group is led by a *kashira* captain. Remember, the general's task is to give orders and control all and everyone even to the lowest – they govern all actions.

Soldiers have to devote themselves to the primary skills of swordsmanship, archery and horse-riding and always be prepared with weapons and gear. To hone themselves in these skills and to fulfil achievements of bravery is considered a matter of principle. *Samurai* who aspire to the rank of general should pursue and fully know these aims.

Commentator one

Concerning all terms that discuss the idea of *ippei*, consult the writings of old and understand that they all refer to independent soldiers:

- *go* 伍 – five people
- *ichijū* 一什 – ten people

- *ittai* 一隊 – fifteen people
- *ikkō* 一甲 – twenty-five people
- *issotsu* 一卒 – 100 people
- *ichiryo* 一旅 – 500 people
- *issui* 一帥 – 2,500 people

One annotation of the *Wei Liaozi* scroll of the *Seven Chinese Military Classics* states, 'Everyone should be responsible for each other.' To be 'responsible' means to be answerable if anyone in the unit violates an order or commits an offence. This holds true from five people to ten, 100, 1,000 or even to 10,000. Discipline should be strictly maintained so that all of the units remain undisturbed and in formation. For this reason these names were given.

There is one general for a *bannin* – an army of 10,000 men. *Bannin* here is an abbreviated form of the full army of 12,500. Also, one common saying states, '10,000 people have one general.'

The word *itte* means 'single formation', while a *hito-kumi* is a sub-group within a single formation. They are similar but have a minor difference. They are directed by generals and captains.

The first priority for independent soldiers is to pursue the paths of swordsmanship, archery and horse-riding and to reach the deepest understanding of them. They must train themselves and become skilled in these paths. Bravery, achievements and fame cannot be gained without these skills. Therefore, consider these areas as your main arts. Concerning the use of military equipment, you should consider each item separately. This cannot be done without *tanren* – strict training – during normal times. The alternative reading for *tanren* is *kitae neru*, which means 'to train and refine', just like tempering iron or degumming silk. Without training or refining, you will not discover the benefits of anything. A sword made of raw iron cannot cut bones and silk clothes that are not made correctly cannot warm the skin. That is why iron is forged to allow it to cut bones and silk is degummed so that it is gentle on the skin. There are numerous examples, both from Japan and China, of those who reached a deep understanding of such skills and became generals. Emperor Gaozu of Han was of low rank but became the founder of an empire that lasted for four hundred years.

Toyotomi Hideyoshi was born of the people in Bishū but assumed the reins of the country, rose to the top and became known as *kanpaku* – supreme minister – a fact that is well known to people. To learn for one hundred days is called *tan*, while to execute training for one thousand days is called *ren*.

Commentator two

Every name for *ippei* can be found within old records and there is a distinction between high and low ranks.

Higher-ranking soldiers:

- *ippei* 一兵
- *ikki* 一騎
- *ikko* 一己
- *shisotsu* 士卒

The above, plus others, are mounted *samurai*.

Lower-ranking soldiers:

- *hosotsu* 歩卒
- *shosotsu* 諸卒
- *heishū* 兵衆
- *ippo* 一歩

The above are soldiers on foot.

Categories of general, commander and captain include:

- *samurai-daishō* 士大将 – commander of a *samurai* group
- *hata-bugyō* 旗奉行 – commander of the flags
- *mono-gashira* 物頭 – various captains
- *kachi-gashira* 歩行頭 – captain of the foot soldiers

Details about the above positions are in the scroll *Heieki Yōhō*.

Even if the lord does not behave as a lord, a retainer must always behave as a retainer.

The use of the number five is based on the Five Elements, which is the foundation of the universe and nature.

CONCERNING THE TERM *TAI*

Although *tai* literally means a group of fifteen people, it is now used more generally to denote a group of soldiers placed into a formation. There are three different kinds of *tai*:[12]

- *shōtai* – twenty-five to thirty people
- *chūtai* – fifty to seventy people
- *daitai* – 100 people

CONCERNING THE DEVELOPMENT OF BRAVERY

It is the role of generals and commanders to give orders, but an army's success and achievement will depend on the determination of each individual. Consider, how can those who were born into a *samurai* family do without courage?

You should cherish lower people. If you treat peasants and merchants appropriately and maintain the correct distinction between the two, they will develop bravery.

There are different kinds of bravery. Sometimes people who excel in skills and are quick in fighting are not, in truth, brave, but yet their matchless and speedy skills may give them the momentum they need to defeat an enemy in combat. Likewise, some generals who do not have superb bravery but fully comprehend the path of war and who have an innate talent in the realm of tactics may win every battle they enter, gaining momentum from their repeated victories. People think these men are brave. However, they will show cowardly behaviour when they are in a perilous situation and death seems inevitable. They will give people the impression that they are brave by using brave words in unthreatening situations, but when the situation is dire their brave talk will dry up.

---

12 The numbers are not always divisible by fifteen because of differences in army setup between China, where the term originated, and Japan.

BEING PREPARED

Military equipment should always be selected carefully and prepared in accordance with your status. If there is something lacking in equipment that has been prepared for war, then it is because of a failure in its preparation during times of peace. Those who experience this are known as *yudan-mono* – people of negligence. Those who lack nothing are considered to be well-prepared and determined *samurai*.

Commentator one

It is essential to be prepared at all times in everything. Speaking figuratively, it can be said that when it is raining think ahead to dry weather, and when there is a drought think ahead to rainy days. The *Yulizi* collection[13] states: 'When in a drought think of preparing a ship, and when in a heatwave, think of preparing furs.' This is a golden saying.

ORDERS FOR WAR I

Before a battle commences there will be *jinbure* – orders for war. At these times all essential instructions will be given by the captain. For other issues that you need to be aware of, it is important to ask those people of the older generation who have already achieved great feats.

Commentator two

Since we are now in a period of more than one hundred years of peace,[14] no one has any direct military experience. Any battle will be the first for everyone involved, both old and young. Therefore, for such information it is best to consult *gunshi* – tacticians.

---

13 A Chinese collection of fables written by Liu Ji in the fourteenth century.
14 This means that commentator two must have been writing no earlier than 1700.

ORDERS FOR WAR II

Orders for war are sometimes given well in advance – normally thirty days, a hundred days or even a year before the war. However, sometimes they are issued urgently, at the very moment of an emergency arising. If you are never negligent, then your departure will never be delayed.

Commentator one

Be aware that orders for war are sometimes given one year or half a year before a war, otherwise it can be a short period such as half a month or even ten days before. There are few old men with military experiences these days, so it is essential to ask *gunjutsu-shi* – master tacticians – for information. Since this peaceful reign has lasted quite a long period, for both old and young warriors it will be their first battle.

Commentator two

As for emergencies, *samurai* must not forget war, even when the country is stable and at peace.

According to the *Methods of Sima* [from the *Seven Chinese Military Classics*]:

> If a state is vast, but people are belligerent, disaster will arrive without fail. If a country is at peace and its people forget warfare, they will surely be in danger.

CHAPTER TWO

Before going to war you should examine your equipment and check it against the following lists.

兵具ノ目録

Heigu no mokuroku

LIST OF MILITARY GEAR

- *kabuto* 甲 – helmet (plus *kabutodate* 甲立 – helmet stand)
- *hako* 箱 – box
- *gusoku* 具足 – armour (plus *hitsu* 櫃 – armour container)

The following tools are accessories for the above.

六具

Rikugu

THE SIX TOOLS

- *kote* 小手 – gauntlets
- *yugote* 弓小手 – archer's sleeve
- *haidate* 佩楯 – thigh protectors
- *suneate* 脛當 – greaves
- *kutsu* 沓 – footwear
- *nodowa* 喉輪 – throat protector

Also included [among the *rikugu*] are:
- *wakibiki* 脇引 – side protectors
- *koshiate* 腰當 – sword clasp
- *ukezutsu* 請筒 – banner cylinder

- *sashimono* 指物 – banner
- *shitagi* 下着 – undershirt (different kinds for summer and winter)

Other items include:
- *kikomi* 着籠 – chain mail
- *momohiki* 股引 – light trousers
- *kyahan* 脚絆 – gaiters
- *hadaobi* 膚帯 – loincloth
- *waranji-gake* 草鞋懸 – foot coverings (plus *waranji* 草鞋 – straw sandals)
- *tachi no udenuki* 太刀ノ腕抜 – looped sword cord (plus *hikihada* 引膚 – scabbard bag)[15]
- *bajō-yugake* 馬上決袷 – archer's gloves for horse-riding
- *sashimono-dake* 指物竹 – bamboo banner pole
- *dōkataginu* 胴肩衣 – sleeveless jacket (plus *haori* 羽織 – jacket; and *komonobaori* 小者羽織 – sleeveless jacket)
- *mizunomi* 水呑 – flask
- *koshioke* 腰桶 – waist container
- *yari* 鑓 – spear (plus *yari-yasume* 鑓休 – spear rest)
- *koyakakigami* 小屋柿紙 – paper for constructing huts (plus *kanzeaya* 観世綺 – patterned material)
- *kansenrō* 貫銭縷 – string for securing coins together[16]
- *hosobiki* 細引 – thin rope (plus *kaginawa* 鍵縄 – grappling hook)
- *yamagatana* 山刀 – hunting knife[17]
- *kama* 鎌 – sickle
- *nata* 鉈 – hatchet
- *nokogiri* 鋸 – saw
- *kiri* 錐 – drill
- *tettsui* 鉄鎚 – iron hammer
- *kugi* 釘 – nails
- *hasami* 鋏 – scissors

---

15 The Koga transcription lists the name as *oshihada* 押膚.

16 Coins with holes in the centre were secured with string. This item only appears in the Koga version.

17 Literally, 'mountain blade'. This item appears only in the Koga transcription.

- *kumade* 熊手 – rake
- *suki* 鍬 – spade
- *karasuki* 唐鍬 – thick spade
- *irekonabe* 入子鍋 – set of cooking pans with the smaller fitting into the larger
- *maku* 幕 – a set of curtains (plus *kui* 杭 – poles)
- *mononuibari* 物縫針 – sewing needles (plus *ito* 糸 – thread)
- *kasa* 笠 – straw hats
- *ogi* 扇 – folding fans
- *sodetōyu* 袖湯油[18] – oiled-paper raincoat
- *muchi* 鞭 – riding crop
- *taimatsu* 炬 – torches
- *hinawa* 火縄 – fuses
- *dōnohi* 胴ノ火 – body warmers
- *hiuchi* 火打 – flint and steel (plus *tsukegi*[19] 付木 – spills)
- *noroshi* 狼煙 – fire signals
- *chōchin* 挑燈 – lanterns
- *rōsoku* 蝋燭 – candles
- *hoshizakana* 干魚 – dried fish
- *katsuobushi* 鰹節 – dried bonito for making broth
- *miso* 味噌 – soup bean paste
- *shio* 鹽 – salt
- *umeboshi* 梅干 – salted plum

You should also take other foods that can be preserved for extended periods. The ones listed above are just examples.

---

18 The Koga transcription uses the ideograms 袖桐油.
19 In the Koga transcription this is referred to as *iōgi* – 'sulphur wood'.

馬道具

Umadōgu

LIST OF EQUIPMENT FOR HORSES

- *umayamaku* 馬屋幕 – stable curtains (plus *tsunagikui* 繋杭 – stakes for horses)
- *kura abumi* 鞍鐙 – saddle and stirrups
- *chikaragawa* 力皮 – stirrup leathers
- *harubi* 腹帯 – saddle girth
- *tazuna* 手綱 – reins
- *kutsuwa* 轡 – bit (plus *tabi hanagawa* 旅鼻皮 – nose bands for travel)
- *zōmuchi* 雑鞭 – basic riding crop (plus *hananeji* 鼻捻 – nose twister)
- *hishaku* 柄杓 – ladle
- *asagutsu* 浅履 – jute footwear
- *kebiki* 計曳 – pliers
- *uma-abumi* 馬鐙 – horse stirrups
- *hitaigake* 額掛 – forehead cover for horses
- *habaki* 脛巾 – greaves
- *kayu-bukuro* 粥袋 – feedbag

The above equipment is used for horses. Use any tool that is found to be beneficial. Also, prepare a *kuragatame* – saddle-securing tool – and other such equipment.

None of the above items needs to be resplendent. Military equipment should be compact and have quality enough to fulfil its purpose. Kusunoki's tradition says:

> *Do not favour a masterpiece* tachi *great sword, but instead prefer those that cut through bone. Concerning armour, do not favour resplendent types but instead prefer those with hard breastplate bands. Horses should be chosen not for their height but for their legs and power. A* tachi *great sword should be two* shaku, *three or five* sun *in length. A horse of three* sun[20] *and seven or eight years of age should be used.*

---

20 Horses are measured by how many *sun* in height they are over the four *shaku* mark. Therefore, a horse of three *sun* actually measures four *shaku* and three *sun* in height.

Commentator one
Concerning accessories

Some of the above items should be kept in a container for armour. Also, keep gold leaf in the amour box. If you look pale during the campaign, ingest the gold leaf every morning and evening to make yourself look healthier.

Concerning *kutsu* – footwear

This means to prepare the following items, among others:

- *waranjigake* 草鞋カケ – foot coverings
- *yukigutsu* 雪沓 – snowshoes
- *tsunanuki* ツナヌキ – shoes for snow and ice made of cattle leather with iron studs for grip

Concerning the *sashimonodake* – bamboo banner pole

Follow the oral traditions.

Concerning the *komono baori* – sleeveless jacket

This is used for identification.

Concerning the *kuragatame* – saddle-securing tool

There is a secret version of this tool in our school. There are various methods for using this tool which differ slightly from one school to another.

None of your equipment should be resplendent. The equipment mentioned here is military and horse equipment. Armour that is too glorious stands out and thus invites an unnecessary death in battle. In ancient times Minamoto no Yoriyoshi prohibited resplendent armour, believing it to be unlucky. This is found in the *Taiheiki* war chronicle. Military gear should be complete, but it is better that it is not too decorative.

According to the tradition of Kusunoki:

> with one tachi great sword valued at one hundred kan, it is difficult to defend against a hundred enemies; however, a hundred great swords each valued at one kan will defend against a hundred

enemies. Therefore, obtaining a hundred great swords valued at one
kan is better than having a single one valued at one hundred kan.

It is said old horses of seven or eight years will know the path ahead well. The
Jōsuiki[21] document contains an episode in which Yoshitsune used an old horse
to find a path in the snow.

Commentator two

Lists are useful not only when preparing to set out for war but also for any
form of journey. If you check your equipment off against the lists, you need
not worry that you will forget anything as the lists will account for everything.

Although the list in the text is called the *rikugu* – six tools – it contains
eleven items, and should be understood simply as 'things you should be
equipped with'.[22]

[The following should also be added to the list of tools:]

- *hachimaki* 鉢巻 – headband
- *shinobi-no-o* 忍ノ緒 – helmet cord
- *kurijime-no-o* 繰締ノ緒 – body-armour fasteners
- *uwaobi* 上帯 – outer belt
- *koshiate-no-o* 腰當ノ緒 – sword-clasp cords
- *hikae-no-o* 扣之緒 – banner-pole cord

Concerning *kikomi* – chainmail

Use one with the family crest upon it.

Concerning *bajōyugake* – archer's gloves

These are used when shooting from horseback.

---

21 盛衰記 *Genpei Jōsuiki*, a war chronicle concerned with the rise and fall of the Taira and
Minamoto clans written around or between the Kamakura period and the period of the
Northern and Southern dynasties.

22 The term *rikugu* translates to mean literally 'six tools', however, this is simply a saying
which should be understood as 'equipment needed'. This term has been translated
throughout Natori-Ryū documents as 'six tools'.

Concerning the *udenuki* – looped sword cord

The three benefits of the looped sword cord are:

- to prevent dropping a sword during combat
- for a better appearance as a warrior
- to enable you to hold the strap in your mouth when on horseback

Concerning the *dōkataginu* – sleeveless jacket

This has broad ties just like a *haori* jacket, but the collar is different. It is put on *under* the *obi* belt. The pattern can be any that you like. It has no sleeves but has a family crest upon the back and slits to aid in horse-riding.

Concerning the *yamagatana* – hunting knife

This is also called a *kaifu*.

Concerning *kumade* – rakes

Rakes are used for capturing and also for water-borne warfare.

Concerning *maku* – curtains

A set of curtains contains two curtains. One set of curtain poles contains eight poles. The length should be more than eight *shaku*. They have hooks on the top.

Concerning the *iōgi* – fire starter

This is also called a *tsuketake* and is a bamboo splint with sulphur put on it.

The list in the text are things that have been carried during war since ancient times, and therefore have been recorded here.

Concerning *umaya-maku* – stable curtains

These are also called *uma-nouren* – horse curtains. One curtain is six *shaku* five *sun* by five or six *shaku*. There are oral traditions for this.

Concerning *tsunagikui* – poles for securing horses

These should be about three *shaku* long and have a ring fixed to them.

Concerning the *hananeji* – nose twister

This should be two *shaku* in length. It should be hollowed out so that it can hold water. It is desirable to make it out of bamboo.

Before carrying a sword, even if it is one which has been passed down for generations, make sure to test it. Even a top-quality sword will become dull over time, and while it may have served its predecessor well, that does not mean it will serve you the same. Fujiwara Nobuyori acquired a treasure sword, but the sword was blunt and he was killed as a result. Minamoto no Yorimasa is said to have cut a rock in two just as if cutting a clump of mud. Taira no Nobunaga[23] took the sword of Imagawa Yoshimoto and tested it before wearing it. Later it was given to Oda Nobutada, who also tested it, in Gifu, before wearing it.

As stated in the text above, a *tachi* great sword should be between two *shaku* three *sun* and two *shaku* five *sun*.

Horses between four *shaku* one *sun* and four *shaku* three *sun* in height are called *san* サン, while those above four *shaku* three *sun* are called *ki* キ. 'A horse of three *sun*' is actually four *shaku* and three *sun* in height. The method of measurement is to place a weighted string across the horse's shoulders.

23　Also known as Oda Nobunaga.

CHAPTER THREE

戦馬之事

Senba no koto

THE WAR HORSE

Undisciplined horses should be avoided. Remember that Wu Qi said that a horse is more likely to be injured near the start of a war than the end. Military horses should be appropriate to your own ability and you should not ride a horse that you cannot control with ease.

Those horses of a violent temper and which gallop at high speed and cannot stand being in the presence of other horses should not be used in ambushes. However, these horses can be used for other purposes.

Choose fast, strong and robust horses for mounted scouting or when you need to break an enemy formation. Also, use these types of horses for the notification of emergencies. Nothing is as important for a state as its ability to win battles and a key factor in deciding its military success is the quality of its horses. A horse can save a *samurai's* life and therefore we should care for them as we would care for ourselves.

Commentator one

A 'war horse' means a horse which a *samurai* rides and which is not a packhorse.

The 'Managing Troops' chapter by Wu Qi states:

> *Normally, horses are injured not towards the end of a war but at the start of one. Similarly, they may become injured not through starvation but through overfeeding.*

A horse that is suitable for your strength and that you can control freely should be used. It is detrimental to use a horse you cannot control well. However, there are cases where strong and weak horses can be used appropriately, so do not hold rigidly to this principle. In all cases, only ride horses you can control properly. Generally, if you use a strong horse for *jōkan*, it will keep energy in reserve. Even so, it is not beneficial to use a horse you cannot control freely, therefore use one suitable for your strength and ability. There have been many examples where those who rode unsuitable horses suffered defeat. At the battle of Ishibashiyama, Sanada Yoichi Yoshisada was killed by Matano Gorō because he was riding a strong horse after he had been weakened by a bout of illness. This episode is found in the *Jōsuiki*.

There are many examples of a horse saving a *samurai*'s life. During the battle of Minatogawa of Sesshū, Oyamada Tarō Takaie offered his horse to Nitta Yoshisada and thus saved him from imminent danger. Even though this came about because of the earnest loyalty that Takaie had, it was made possible by the use of a horse. How could Nitta have survived without the horse? This is found in the *Taiheiki* chronicle. You should take care of horses as you would take care of yourself; that is, you should not leave everything to your servants, but make sure your servants feed them, wash them with hot water, observe them and give them care.

In the chapter 'Managing Troops' Wu Qi states:

> *A stable should be clean and comfortable. Horses should be fed with appropriate grass and water. Feeding should leave them neither too hungry nor too full. In winter, they should have warm stables and during summer, cool ones. Their manes and hair should be trimmed and their hooves properly cared for.*

INAPPROPRIATE HORSES FOR MILITARY SERVICE

The following types of horse are considered unsuitable:

- *nige* 二毛 – dual-coloured[24]
- *ashige* 葦毛 – grey-coloured
- *ippaku* 一白 – those with white hooves at the front
- *nihaku* 二白 – those with white hooves at the rear
- *ihaijiro* 位牌白 – those with a white forehead, where the white runs down the centre of the face to the upper lip
- *goshi no uma* 五歯ノ馬 – the 'five-toothed' horse
- *yome-no-fushijiro* 夜目ノ節白 – those with white patches that can be seen at night

In addition to the above, those with wounds over hair whorls should be avoided. Some older schools used to allocate horses to riders based on the colour of the horse. It is also said that if a horse has been in a funeral parade then it should not be used – there is a way to discover if this is so. Those horses with a 'face of death' should be avoided. According to tradition, a horse with the 'face of death' has stiff ears and a white film that covers half of each eye. There are also oral traditions for the tail and the horse's breath.

Commentator one

Military horses are horses to be used for riding by *samurai*.

The description 'dual-coloured' does not refer to horses that are generally white and dappled all over. However, it does include horses that have patches on the rump. Those horses are called *nige-jiri* ('dual-coloured buttocks') and are regarded as inappropriate because *nige* sounds similar to *nigeru*, which means 'fleeing'. *Ashi* 葦, from the name *ashige*, has a similar pronunciation to *ashi* 悪シ, which means 'bad'.

Ippaku refers to horses with white front hooves, whereas *nihaku* refers to those with white rear hooves. In general, white hooves are soft and easily damaged. Skilled horsemen do not avoid horses with white patches from the

---

24　These horses were avoided by *samurai* because the word for 'dual-coloured' – *nige* 二毛 – sounds similar to the verb *nigeru* 逃, which means 'to flee'.

knees to hooves, but if the hooves themselves are white then this makes the horse unsuited to battle.

Ihaijiro horses are disliked because their description contains the word *ihai*, which is a Buddhist death tablet. These horses have white patches from the forehead to the lips, and the lips are white or pale pink. *Ihaijiro* horses may also be called *ōjaku*. Generally, white horses have reddish skin when they are born, while horses of other colours have blackish skin at birth. This is true not only for horses but for other animals. In China, there are horses called *tekiro*.[25] According to the document *Sesetsu Shingo*,[26] Yu Liang owned a *tekiro* horse and he was advised to sell it on. Liang answered: 'If I sell it, there will be someone who would surely buy it, but as this is a horse that will be detrimental to its owner, and as this issue is of concern to me, then under no circumstances should I pass it on to someone else.'

Five-toothed horses are disliked since they are said to bite people. They have one tooth in the centre and two on either side, which adds up to five teeth. Horses that have three teeth on one side and two on the other side are not said to be five-toothed horses even though they, too, have five teeth.

Yome-no-fushijiro horses have white skin growths around the lower leg. Horses with white knees are considered bad for riding at night, as they will stand out and make you an easy target for the enemy. A saying goes:

夜眼照一丈

At night they can be seen from one jō.

'One *jō*' here is the same as the length of a roll of cloth.[27]

In general, horses have a part called a *yome* – skin growth – which is on the vein above the knee. This is why the knees are called *yome-no-fushi*. In ancient times, there were cases where one army released a dual-coloured horse and drove it across to the opposing army in order to bring misfortune to the enemy. In such cases, it was customary to cut some of the horse's tail hair

25 Horses with white patches from the forehead to the lips.
26 世説新語 – 'A New Account of the Tales of the World'.
27 The commentator is stating that the *jō* used here is not the standard length of his time, but an earlier, longer measurement.

and discard it, brand the horse's forehead, attach an *oharaitaima* talisman[28] and send the horse back. This action should be led by a *gunbaisha* adviser. Alternatively, one theory states that the tail clippings should be offered to a 'divine horse'.[29]

One of Yoshitsune's military poems says:

敵よりも二毛なる馬の来る時は尾が毛を切て神に手向よ
When a dual-coloured horse comes over from the enemy,
some of its tail hair should be cut and offered to the gods.

Concerning unlucky hair whorls

Every horse has hair whorls. There are numerous kinds, some of which are lucky, while others are half-lucky or unlucky. The unlucky whorls are called *kekizu*. You should obtain teachings on this.

Concerning whether a horse's hair colour is compatible with its rider

There are ten colours of horse hair and they are associated with the Five Elements. Know the creative and destructive cycles that correspond with the element of the rider.

The associations [for horses] are:

Wood
- *aoge* 青毛 – bluish black
- *ashige* 芦毛 – grey

Fire
- *kurige* 栗毛 – chestnut
- *hibarige* 雲雀毛 – yellowish dapple with blackish mane and tail

Earth
- *kage* 鹿毛 – bay
- *kasuge* 糟毛 – roan

---

28 Talismans given out at the Grand Shrine of Ise to avert disaster.
29 *Shinba* or *jimme* – a horse offered to the gods at a shrine.

In this context, *kasuge* is actually *ao-kasuge*, which is bluish grey with white mixed in. For other kinds of *kasuge*, the name of the colour mixed in is placed before the word *kasuge* and is classified by the colour added. The term *kasuge* without any other named colour is always considered as bluish.

Metal

- *tsukige* 鴇毛 – palomino
- *kawarage* 河原毛 – buckskin

Water

- *kuroge* 黒毛 – black
- *same* 鮫 – the base colour including white

Same should be classified by the base coat colour. When a base colour is specified, the name of the colour is placed before the word *same*. The base *same* is a blackish 'double dilute'. Types of *same* are specified by adding the base colour before the word *same*.

Concerning horses used for funerals

Such horses usually have marks on the tongue from where it has been bound. Those horses should not be used for war. Tradition says that if a horse neighs at a funeral, it will take other people to the afterlife with the dead person. Therefore, funeral horses have their tongues bound with thin cord or their reins to prevent them from neighing. Horses are simple and innocent by nature so they will not forget such a painful experience and if they are to be used for night attacks or the like, they will have doubt and fear and will resist being bound in the same manner and they will not serve correctly when haste is required.

Horses with a 'face of death' have stiff ear bases and they have a white film over the eyes. When handled they have tails in poor condition and lack strength – they move as if they were pulling casks wrapped in straw mats. They breathe hard through the nose, their breathing is shallow and short and has no warmth to it.

Commentator two

Sometimes defeat may be brought about because horses become surprised by war cries or large numbers of people.

There are five faults with horses:

- biting and champing
- bucking
- fidgeting
- refusing to move
- bolting

Nige horses have dual colours and *ippaku* have white left hooves.[30]
Five-toothed horses have five front teeth, while most horses have six.
Each school has its own traditions on hair whorls. Study the traditions of each school. The ten colours of horse hair are divided according to the Five Elements. Inquire within a horse-riding school for such details. An old poem says:

芦青木栗毛雲雀火鹿粕土月瓦金黒二毛八水

Grey and bluish black are of wood; chestnut and yellowish dapple
with blackish mane and tail are of fire; bay and roan are of earth;
palomino and buckskin are of metal; and black and same[31] are of water.

Some horses may have wounds on their hair whorls, which may have been caused by burning in an attempt to cover up unlucky whorls. These horses are called *kizu* – wounded.

---

30 Commentators one and two differ on this point. The first commentator states that *ippaku* horses have white front legs, while the second commentator states that the whiteness is on the left fore leg and left hind leg.

31 The Koga transcription quotes *nige* here. But in the text it states that *same* is of water. Therefore this is most likely a transcription error. It has been corrected here.

CHAPTER FOUR

下人召連ル次第ノ事

Genin meshitsureru shidai no koto

HIRING SERVANTS TO TAKE TO WAR

When hiring *wakatō* young assistants and *komono* servants, retain those from an enemy province, but only after examining them in detail. Servants with inside knowledge of the enemy province can be invaluable. However, there are important factors concerning these people. Also, *kawaramono* outcasts should be avoided and there are ways to discover if they are in fact outcasts.

Commentator one

When hiring servants to take to war, there are certain traps to avoid. Although those from other provinces are convenient and good as guides to their provinces, you need to make sure they are not spies sent from the enemy. Spies tend to be *samurai* who have been chosen for their particular intelligence and bravery, and ability to speak fluently and think on their feet. They normally disguise themselves as servants in order to infiltrate. No matter how much they try to behave just like a member of the lower class, their true qualities will show through at times. Keep your eyes peeled for these tell-tale signs. Basically, servants cannot speak properly and they act with a 'rustic attitude'. No matter how well pretenders try to imitate this, if you observe them closely enough they will end up revealing their true *samurai* identity.

As well as spies, you also need to watch out for outcasts. There are certain ways to identify them. For example, if they reside alongside normal people the smoke from their morning and evening cooking does not rise upwards, but hangs lower at floor level. Also, they cannot hold two different thoughts in their mind at the same time but have to deal with each of them one after the other.

These two things have been commonly said since days of old. If you suspect someone to be an outcast, you should not hire him. Not only are outcasts extremely ignorant and stupid, but they are so cowardly that they will be useless in battle. In the customs of our country, it is shunned to eat from the same fire as an outcast because our country is a holy land. Since outcasts do not associate with normal people, they do not understand basic common issues and certainly know nothing of quality. They are similar to the lowest members of the lower class, but outcasts are particularly stupid and vile. Knowing that many people are needed in times of war, outcasts may think they can find employment by hiding their identities. Judge potential servants extremely carefully and do not hire any you suspect to be outcasts.

Commentator two
Although servants from other provinces are convenient and good as guides for their areas, bear in mind that they may be spies sent from the enemy. Be careful and confirm if this is the case. Details of these matters are transmitted in the scrolls *Shinobi no Maki*, the *Shōninki* and so on.

SPEAKING TO YOUR SERVANTS BEFORE DEPARTING FOR WAR
When you inform your servants that an order for war gives a specific date for departure, remind them that your fief was given by the lord, that their bodies and lives are maintained through this, and that repayment can be given during battle. If they forget this relationship and flee, leaving the lord's service, then make sure that they understand it is equivalent to living as cattle or a horse. Also, tell them that if this happens they will be searched for across all the lands and then executed, and that if they have fathers, mothers and children, that they too will face this punishment. In addition, say this to them:

> When we are in the upcoming battle, if you attend me well
> when I engage the enemy in combat or if I have pinned him to
> the ground and I am trying to decapitate him and you assist

*me by slashing at him or killing and decapitating him with me,
attaining achievements for yourself, then I will promote you and
you will receive a fief. Servants can become* samurai *and a fief
will be given according to the achievement attained. However, do
not complain or spread rumour if the adjudication seems unfair
to you. Give me an oath swearing that you shall not break our
bond on this matter.*

If you have three *samurai* retainers, they should make the following pledge
together:

*If two of us flee but one of us remains then all of our properties,
including our wives, children, parents and brothers, are to be given
to servants and slaves. Also, our paddy fields, houses and property
will be given to any of the servants who did not flee.*

They are to write the above with their seal and signature here.

Tradition says to use the 'two forms of death' to convince all that they should
not flee. These are:
- *gishi* 義死 – death in righteousness
- *zanshi* 慚死 – death in shame

Commentator one

This point is about what you should tell your servants before departing for
war. It also applies to all other situations. Be they *samurai* or lower people,
inform your retainers about battle and impress on them that they must not
be cowards and must not flee. As the saying goes: 'There are no weak soldiers
under a strong general.' Even a master with only a few servants must show
proper leadership.

The second paragraph, on upcoming battles, contains what you should tell
your servants. Always make it clear to them that going to war is a fundamental
duty for those who serve a *samurai* family. You should emphasize to them

that war is a great opportunity, and that even servants, if they carry out an outstanding feat, may be promoted to *samurai* – this has happened in many cases. Not only for their master's sake, but also for their own advancement, they should try to be noted for their achievements.

To encourage your servants you should praise them for:

- unselfish diligence in service
- capability
- honesty
- intelligence
- anything else that they excel at

Benevolence, righteousness and courage are virtues too profound to instil in lower people, but you can rouse their spirits by showing them encouragement.

Further teachings on how to manage your servants can be found in the *Kōketsu* scroll.

Commentator two

Lower people tend to be ignorant, so give them careful instructions that they can easily understand. The important points in managing servants are transmitted in the *Kōketsu* scroll.

The ideogram 義 for *gi*, meaning 'righteous', is used in *giri* – moral obligation. If a servant dies for his master, it will be seen as *gishi*, a righteous death; while if he dies as a wandering servant, having left his master, it will be seen as *zanshi*, a shameful death. Explain this to them repeatedly.

The motivations behind service to a master can be divided into three levels:

- *jō* 上 (upper level) – virtue and that which is owed to the master
- *chū* 中 (middle level) – personal honour and reputation
- *ge* 下 (lower level) – personal desires and benefits

CONCERNING OATHS

Prior to departing for war have your servants sign a joint pledge,[32] which should say the following:

> *Whether advancing or retreating, we shall not flee. We will follow*
> *our master's orders and endure every hardship until our return. If*
> *our master engages in battle we shall never leave his side or escape.*
> *We will not break the above promises.*

Be aware there are different ways to write an oath properly depending on which Buddhist sect your servants belong to. For example, if they belong to the Hokke-shū,[33] have the names of the thirty gods from their pantheon written on the oath. If they are from the Ikkō sect then have them write the phrase:

一代之後生可無仕

If my oath be broken I shall not enter into the afterlife.

Commentator one

In the foreign country [of China], *kishōmon* pledges are called *yakumei*. As is written in the ninth scroll of the *Taiheiki* chronicle, oaths are made in turbulent times. This practice came to our country from China, where the king used to gather feudal lords and make sacrifices and have the lords sign an oath of loyalty. The *kishōmon* of our day derives from this tradition.

For devotees of the Hokke-shū sect, have them write the following:

三十番神ノ御罸可蒙

If my oath be broken I shall receive punishment from the thirty gods.

For devotees of the Ikkō sect, have them write:

32　連判之起請文 *renpan no kishōmon* – a document or written oath signed by multiple people.

33　法華宗 – also known as the Nichiren sect.

一代ノ後世無可仕

If my oath be broken I shall not enter into the afterlife.

The crux of the oath should be whatever that sect values most. Lower people are ignorant and unenlightened so that they worship and stand in awe of the gods. Therefore, as well as the above examples, there are other holy gods called *ikumusubinokami* (gods of creation) and *ubusunagami* (gods of homeland). Each person has his own deity to worship according to his religion or sect. Therefore, add a general statement that the punishment for breaking the oath shall be meted out according to the deities each person believes in.

In our country, there are various kinds of written oath to the gods. Here is an example of the *shichimai-gishō* – the seven-sheet oath.

Shichisha kishōmon
Seven oaths from seven shrines given with due respect
Sheet one

- [contents of the oath]
- [contents of the oath]
- [contents of the oath]

Though the above pledges may be hard to keep, if I infringe or violate them in any way I shall receive divine punishment from the lord of heaven,[34] the Four Guardians of Taishakuten[35] and all major and minor gods from more than sixty provinces from all over Japan, especially Atago Daigongen.[36] This includes all equivalent gods and attendant gods. In witness whereof I hereto set my hand and seal to this *kishōmon*.

> Name – position – personal seal
> Year – month – day [apply blood from the left ring finger here]

> To [insert name]

---

34 暁天帝 *Gyōtentei.*

35 帝釈四大天王 *Taishaku Yondai Tennō.* Taishakuten is the Lord of the Centre and he governs the guardians of the four cardinal points, who are Jikokuten, Zōchōten, Kōmokuten and Tamokuten.

36 愛宕大権現 – the Great Manifestation of Atago.

Sheet two

For breaking this oath, made under the protection of the Daigosan temple, know that punishment shall come from the Sanbōin and the Godaidō.[37] In witness whereof I hereto set my hand and seal to this *kishōmon*.

> Name – position – personal seal
> Year – month – day [apply blood from the right ring finger here]

> To [insert name]

Sheet three

For breaking this oath above, from this sheet I will receive punishments from Fuji Daigongen.[38] In witness whereof I hereto set my hand and seal to this *kishōmon*.

> Name – position – personal seal
> Year – month – day [apply blood from the tongue here]

> To [insert name]

Sheet four

For breaking this oath above, from this sheet I will receive punishments from Ōmine Daigongen.[39] In witness whereof I hereto set my hand and seal to this *kishōmon*.

> Name – position – personal seal
> Year – month – day [apply blood from the nape of the neck here]

> To [insert name]

---

37 The Sanbōin is the main building in the Daigoji temple complex in Kyōto, and the Godaidōis a hall in Matsushima which houses statues of the Five Great Wisdom Kings.

38 富士大権現 – the Great Manifestation of Mount Fuji.

39 大峯大権現 – the Great Manifestation of Mount Ōmine.

Sheet five

For breaking this oath above, from this sheet I will receive punishments from Hachiman Daibosatsu.[40] In witness whereof I hereto set my hand and seal to this *kishōmon*.

> Name – position – personal seal
> Year – month – day [apply blood from the left foot here]

> To [insert name]

Sheet six

For breaking this oath above, from this sheet I will receive punishments from the god representing the Jūra[41] for that day and also the *happō-yū*.[42] In witness whereof I hereto set my hand and seal to this *kishōmon*.

> Name – position – personal seal
> Year – month – day [apply blood from the right foot here]

> To [insert name]

Sheet seven

For breaking this oath above, from this sheet I shall receive difficulties and agonies from the Buddha of the [Konpon] Chūdō[43] in Ōmi province, which shall last through the afterlife no matter how long. In witness whereof I hereto set my hand and seal to this *kishōmon*.

> Name – position – personal seal
> Year – month – day [apply blood from the left and right palms here]

40　八幡大菩薩 – the Great Bodhisattava Hachiman.
41　十羅 – the Ten Demon Daughters.
42　八方遊 – a period of time (the god will change accordingly).
43　[根本] 中堂 – the main temple in the Hieizan complex in Ōmi.

To [insert name]

The above is an example of the seven-sheet pledge. The manners concerning the paper to be used or how to write it are found in the oral traditions. Also ask for details from calligraphers.

A *kishōmon* pledge contains the phrase, 'In witness whereof I hereto set my hand and seal to this *kishōmon*.' It also has a blood seal at the end and is written on *goō* paper.[44]

A *shinmon* pledge contains the phrase, 'In witness whereof I hereto set my hand and seal to this *shinmon*,' has a blood seal at the end and is written on normal paper.

A *seimon* oath uses normal writing paper and has no blood seal, and is also called a *seishi*.

Commentator two

Umashiuchi-no-sukune[45] slandered his brother Takeuchi Daijin. The emperor had the brothers endure trial by boiling water to determine which of them was in the right and which was in the wrong. It was discovered that Umashiuchi-no-sukune was in the wrong and thus the emperor punished him. This is the origin of *yugishō* – trial by boiling water.

A *shinmon* pledge should be made before the gods, while a *kishōmon* pledge can be made before the lord.[46] Both types of pledge should be written on a *kumano gofu* talisman.

---

44 A type of paper with holy images printed on it
45 A legendary character appearing in the *Kojiki* (Records of Ancient Matters), and the *Nihonshoki* (Chronicles of Japan).
46 Most likely not directly in front of him, but pledging to his authority.

CHAPTER FIVE

If treated with true trust, people will have a sense of shame. Those people who are evil and have no mercy are called *hyōbyōhei*.[47] Such people do not fear their superiors and ignore any orders given to them. Mindset should be the same for your superiors and your inferiors. Do not think little of the inferior only because they do not have fear of their superiors.

The *Analects* say:

> *If you attempt to smash the strong with a sword, the blade will break. However, soft rain dropping from the eaves can destroy a stone.*

The weak and lower can attain achievement. It is said that if you do not show enough kindness to people, they will not feel indebted enough to die for you. Those who are ready to die will surely be able to attain achievements. If you have a selfish and evil mind and try to drive your men recklessly to their death, or if you suddenly and unexpectedly try to be kind, your men will sprout fear within their minds and will not truly obey you. This holds true at all times and you should be fully aware of it.

Systems of reward and punishment should be made clear. There are five ways of punishing and four ways of rewarding – these come from ancient times. Originating in ancient China, the five levels of punishment are called the *gokei*:[48]

- *boku* 墨 – tattooing the forehead
- *bi* 劓 – cutting off the nose

---

47 Non-existing ideogram. Possibly 豹々兵 – literally 'leopard solider' or 'savage soldier', however, maybe a transcription error and should read 狗々兵 – *kukuhei*, which means 'dog soldier' or someone who relies only on brute courage.

48 五刑 – these should be considered as Chinese.

- *hi* 刖 – slicing the tendon of the leg
- *kyū* 宮 – castration
- *taiheki* 大辟 – killing by banishment to a remote and desolate place or to sea or to a steep area[49]

The four rewards are called the *shishō*:
- *haku* 帛 – silk fabric ('giving colours')
- *ei* 盈 – a higher position
- *chō* [archaic ideogram] – financial reward[50]
- *kyoku* 昴 – village and land

With the above systems in mind, punish and reward according to each specific case. Generally, rewards can be given quickly, while punishments should be decided only after careful investigation.

Commentator one

Human beings of all stations are born through heaven's will. Therefore, according to Mencius, even those who are evil or ignorant still contain the following:
- *sokuin no kokoro* 惻隠心 – compassion
- *shūo no kokoro* 羞悪心 – a sense of shame and dislike of injustice
- *jijō no kokoro* 辞譲心 – modesty
- *zehi no kokoro* 是非心 – correct judgement

These are called the *shitan* – the four principles.

The loyalty your servants show to you comes from the kindness you show to them. Therefore, if you reward and look after your people with a fair mind, know that because they have the above four principles within their nature, they will feel grateful to you. This is because benevolence, righteousness, courtesy and wisdom are triggered by the above principles. If servants live an

---

49 To send people into an isolated destination to die, to an island in the sea or adrift at sea.

50 Treasure, property and financial benefit – *u* in the Koga transcription and *chō* in the Tōkyō version. Both of these are made up of archaic ideograms.

unrighteous and evil life, this is their master's fault. A master should treat his servants with a great amount of benevolence and affection. That being said, to show *only* generosity will bring about harm. Buddhism teaches us to pay resentment with kindness, but in *samurai* households such an attitude is not advisable. On the other hand, if a master is always harsh and intimidating towards his servants, they will be afraid of him but they will not be obedient to him below the surface. Instead they will behave immorally and disloyally, they will disobey their master's orders and they may flee, leaving their master in danger.

Therefore, you should follow *the middle way*. Have your servants understand that you are usually kind and merciful, but that if they ever do anything inconsiderate you will be firm, speak in extremely strong language and drive home reason in such a way that they will fear you and feel remorse for their wrongdoings. Make sure that they respect orders, show utmost courtesy to you when receiving your kindness, and work for you with respect and self-sacrifice. Be fully aware that all of this will happen if you and your servants have the same intention. It is said that cold and hot, joy and sorrow are the same for everyone, be they noble or humble. Therefore, how can you allow your servants to live in discomfort while you are indulging in comfort? This is not the path of a master.

According to the *Seven Chinese Military Classics*, 'The weak can defeat the strong.' This principle can be applied to everything, especially warfare.

People who appreciate their master's kindness will not hesitate to die for him. Kindness from masters includes:

- speaking to servants with kindness
- making them happy
- showing deep compassion
- giving rewards

In ancient times, an emperor in the era of Engi[51] wore less clothing on cold nights to remind himself of the suffering of his people – *this* is the path of a king. Although this could also be seen as a tactical move, even if viewed in a different light the effect remains the same.

---

51 Alternative name for Emperor Daigo (884–930 BC).

In the *Upper Strategy of the Three Strategies*, it says: 'When payment is generous, righteous officers will disregard death.'

There are traditions about the above points.

Those who are given favour and salaries during normal times will, of course, be ready to die. If a master who has only two or three existing servants has to hire more people when going to war, then the new recruits will not have been given such favour or monetary reward – therefore, how could it be possible for them to readily die? There are three teachings in our school to make those who have recently been hired feel indebted. These are transmitted in the scroll *Kōketsu* as secret traditions. In olden days, Akechi Hyūga-no-kami Mitsuhide killed Lord Naifu Nobunaga,[52] despite having received favour from Nobunaga. Even though the favour was minor, Mitsuhide should have repaid it, rather than killing Nobunaga for strategic gain. No righteousness can be found in his conduct.

Zanzai – decapitation – is the Japanese form of one of the five punishments. However, here in Japan we do also cut off the nose.

Concerning the four rewards
In Japan these include giving official rank in the imperial court. For *samurai* families, reward can be an increase in fief, or the offer of a better position.

Concerning the first punishment of tattooing the forehead
This is to inscribe an ideogram on the forehead and put black ink in it.

Concerning cutting off of the nose
This is to cut off the nose to mark people as criminals.

Concerning the cutting of tendons of the legs
To cut the tendons is another way to mark people as criminals.

Concerning the castration of men and the imprisonment of women
These are punishments for lewdness.

---

52 Oda Nobunaga, who held the office of *naifu* 内府, or imperial minister.

Concerning the death penalty

Shikei – the death penalty – is the gravest punishment and is given to those who have committed severe offences.

According to the annotations of the *Xiao Jing*,[53] in ancient times corporal punishments were used. Emperor Wen of the Han Dynasty of ancient China abolished them for the first time. Instead of cutting the tendon of the left leg, 500 lashes were given. Instead of the cutting of the nose, 300 lashes. However, many soldiers were killed by these punishments, so Emperor Jing of the Han Dynasty reduced the number of lashes from 500 to 300, 300 to 200, etc.

The number of offences covered by each punishment:

- 1,000 offences punishable by tattooing
- 1,000 offences punishable by the cutting off of the nose
- 500 offences punishable by cutting the tendons
- 300 offences punishable by castration
- 200 offences punishable by death

Thus the five punishments cover a total of 3,000 offences.

The above are the *gokei*, which is our way of using punishment as a deterrent.

Concerning the four rewards

The Upper Strategy says: 'When granting monetary reward to the capable do not begrudge the expense or delay the award. Only then will your subordinates unite to conquer the enemy.'

In the *Setsumon* dictionary,[54] the entry for 'silk fabric' refers to the ceremonial silk cloth which was made into *nishiki* – gold brocade. Certain colours of silk were given as rewards. The entry on 'giving colours' details the appropriate colours to be used. These are listed below.

Seishoku – correct colours:

- blue
- yellow

---

53 The Classic of Filial Piety.
54 説文解字 *Shuowen Jiezi*, a second-century Chinese dictionary.

- red
- white
- black

Kanshoku – intermediate colours:
- green
- deep red
- deep blue
- purple
- pale blue

Saishoku – pale colours:[55]
These pale colours do not stand out in people's sight, also starving people eat grass and therefore these colours represent being ill. Zhui Xi's commentaries state that 'men are pleased with the colours worn by women'. Commentaries on the *Shān Hǎi Jīng* say that 'women produce colours'. Such colours should be used for a *kosode-kimono*.

Concerning reward by position
The ideogram *ei* 盈 means 'sunrise' and 'to be full of light'.

Concerning the third and fourth rewards
Generally, these kinds of reward have to be given based on assumption alone.[56] The *Analects* say: 'Rewards should be given even when there is doubt, but punishments should be withheld if there is any doubt.'

Commentator two
Concerning the four rewards
The first reward is to be given coloured clothing. In Japan this means to be given seasonal clothing by the court. The second reward is normally to be given

---

55 Literally, the 'colour of grasses'.
56 i.e. do not worry too much about proving an individual's achievement, but just give the reward freely.

the position of Second Rank[57] by the court, although *samurai* may be appointed to other positions.

Whether retainers obey or disobey depends on the mind of the general. If the lord is on a righteous path, shows consistency in his rewards and punishments, and behaves in the way he expects others to behave, then his retainers and soldiers will obey him faithfully. If he is unrighteous and does not have a proper sense of right and wrong, his retainers and soldiers will hold grudges against him and become estranged. Building harmony is of the greatest importance.

---

57   二位 – an official rank given by the court.

CHAPTER SIX

Social standing has no bearing on the true nature of a person, or his inner heart. Therefore, the essence of a person cannot be judged from his level of privilege. Be sincere and keep this principle in mind.

Also, the importance of plots in military strategy has been stated many times. One example of basic tactics that has been passed down involves having your servants find a divine talisman from a shrine.

Commentator one
Heaven distributes good and bad character throughout society, making no distinction between noble and humble. That which is substantial is a person's true nature and this holds true for everyone, be they good or evil, noble or humble. The ideogram for substantial, 實, is a key concept for beginners. There is no one who does not have *honshō* – original nature; however, the seven emotions can overturn the mind and cause a person to stray from his nature.

An old poem says:

> 萍をかき分け見れバ月の影ここに有とは誰かしるべき
> *Moving aside the duckweeds, the reflection of the moon is revealed.*
> *Who would have known it was there all along?*

You should be fully aware of these matters, which are normally taught by Confucian scholars.

Concerning the tactic of having your servants find talismans
Place talismans of protection against being hit by arrows and so on within armour containers so that your servants will find them – this will give them

courage. Lower people are ignorant and usually have faith in Buddha and the gods, so they will not suspect your ruse. This is a tactic to be used.

Commentator two
Concerning the word 'plot'[58]

The word *keibō* – plot – comprises two sections:

Kei 計

According to Sun Tzu, the seven *kei* are considerations to be made during warfare. They are:

- Which of the two sovereigns has moral justification on his side?
- Which of the two generals has more ability?
- With whom lie the advantages derived from heaven and earth?
- In which army is discipline more rigorously enforced?
- Which army is stronger?
- In which army are the officers and men more highly trained?
- Which army rewards and punishes more fairly?

Bō 謀

Bō means having the flexibility to adapt your plans to the situation – for example, to conduct night raids, sudden attacks or other tactics to counter tactical alterations made by the enemy.

CONCERNING CYLINDER BASKETS AND MEDICINE

When departing for battle, prepare all things, including equipment. Construct a cylinder basket and place half-lids at both ends. Insert the previously listed tools in this and have medicine for both humans and horses prepared.

Commentator one

The cylinder basket is about the right size for one person to hide in. Therefore, if an enemy *kanja* or *shinobi* has infiltrated and is hiding, the general will give

---

58 計謀 *keibō*.

an order to search all of the baskets. They are of this size so that not too many tools are carried. The description of cylinder baskets are described in detail in the scroll *Heigu Yōhō*.

Commentator two
Concerning medicine for horses and humans
This includes food-poisoning remedies, wound balms and hunger pills. Also, medicines for ease of breathing or damaged hoofs should be carried. Some of these can be given to both humans and horses.

CONCERNING FOOD RATIONS FOR PEOPLE
Rations for both people and horses will be provided by the general – these will be roughly in proportion to the size of their respective fiefs. While the size will normally be based on the number of people in your retinue, this may not always be the case and may differ between clans. If you take many servants, it is your responsibility to prepare rations for them.

Rations for the emperor
one *shō* and two *gō* of food – 84,000 grains of rice
Rations for *samurai*
six *gō* of food – 42,000 grains of rice
Rations for farmers
three *gō* of food – 21,000 grains of rice
Rations for merchants
five *gō* of food – 35,000 grains of rice
Rations for craftsmen
five *gō* of food – 35,000 grains of rice

Concerning the above, understand that as one full day only has twelve [Japanese] hours, these amounts are more than enough.

Commentator one

You should always carry extra rations for your own troops. This is so that you will have enough to cater for any new recruits you might hire during the campaign, who will not be included within the calculations for food distribution by size of fief. Therefore, be prepared with the extra amount required. You do not know what situations may arise and rations may become scarce – always be aware of this.

The above text describes the old way of distributing rations, but it is done differently nowadays. The number of rice grains is specified to make it clear that none of the rations should be wasted, but instead should be highly valued. Each general has his own way of distributing rations. If too much is given out in one go, some people may indulge themselves, or waste the rice in making alcohol or even throw it away. Rations are the most valuable military resource; therefore, rice should not be distributed abundantly. On the other hand, if too little rice is given out, the soldiers will starve. Make sure that the amount to be distributed should be appropriate and not so much that it will encourage waste or misuse. In ancient times, Nitta Yoshisada distributed ten days' rations at a time with a daily allowance of two *shō* for each general and one *shō* for each *samurai*. Kusunoki Masashige distributed three days' rations at a time, nine *gō* each day for each *samurai*: three *gō* for breakfast, three *gō* for lunch and three *gō* for supper. If any was left over, it served as a late-night meal. Each general has a different way. Be prepared so that there will be no problems, no matter what type of situation arises. Estimates depend on the situation and only the outline is given here.

RATIONS FOR A HORSE FOR A SINGLE DAY

For horses which are ridden use either of the following:
- three *shō* of soya beans
- one *shō* or five *gō* of rice

For workhorses use either of the following:

- two *shō* of soya beans
- five *gō* of rice

Commentator one

If rice is used as rations for horses, it is given by sprinkling it on top of horse feed – therefore, it is called *furigome* – sprinkle rice. It is known that rice makes horses strong.

CONCERNING WATER RATIONS

Water for each person per day:

- one *shō*

Use these rules of thumb to make your preparations for horse and water rations, but know that each school has small variations on these measurements. the above come from an older school.

Commentator one

When digging wells, remember that each well will supply around fifty people. It all depends how much water wells up. There are traditions on how to dig wells in 'The principles of building huts and castles'.

According to an old school, the following is also needed (amounts are per person per day):

- two *gō* of *miso*
- one *gō* of salt

CHAPTER SEVEN

戦場ノ言葉好嫌ノ事

Senjō no kotoba kōken no koto

POSITIVE AND NEGATIVE MILITARY TERMS

The six commanders create and announce new terms every day, but the words that are recorded here have been used since ancient times. They are called *ikusa-kotoba* – military terms.

Commentator one

Here 'new terms' means passwords. These are created and announced by the six commanders each day and each night.

The six commanders comprise:

- two *ikusa bugyō* – war commanders
- two *yari bugyō* – spear commanders
- two *hata bugyō* – flag commanders

The military terms mentioned here are those words that have been used since ancient times and are associated with various military weapons and tools. When these words are used at normal times, consider whether they are auspicious or inauspicious and choose them appropriately.

Commentator two

The terms listed here are those that have been used since old times, so be aware that some are different from those used today.

征伐
SEIBATSU

This is an expedition led by the *seii-taishōgun* when an *inzen* order is given by a retired emperor, sending the *shōgun* to war.

Commentator one

The word *inzen* denotes letters issued from the *sentō* – the residence of a retired emperor. Letters issued by the present emperor are called *chokusen*.

Commentator two

Once, Minamoto Yoritomo, acting upon an *inzen* order given by Shirakawa Jōkō, the retired emperor, engaged in *tsuitō* – the destruction of a king's army – then brought about the annihilation of Kiso no Yoshinaka, after which he engaged in another *tsuitō* war, which destroyed the entire Heike family. In recognition of these achievements, he was given the position of *seii-taishōgun*. He also became *sōtsuibushi* military commander for the sixty-six provinces of Japan. As *samurai* power grew throughout the country, every lord followed him. Consequently, the imperial court grew weaker day by day and eventually the whole country was governed by the *buke* – *samurai* families.

追討
TSUITŌ

This is a term used to describe one king destroying the army of another king who is of equal status.

Commentator one

Examples of the destroying of a king's army by another of equal status are the Hōgen Rebellion [of 1156], the Heiji Rebellion [of 1160] and the Kenmu Restoration [of 1336].

発向

HAKKŌ

This is a term used for when the *seii* goes to war himself.

Commentator one

Here *seii* is an abbreviation for *seii-taishōgun*.

Commentator two

From Yamato Takeru[59] to Sakanoue no Tamuramaro the position of *seii* was called *seii-shōgun*. At the time of the rebellion of Taira no Masakado, Fujiwara Tadabumi[60] was designated as the first *seii-taishōgun*. His brother Tadanobu was sent to war against Taira no Masakado as deputy *shōgun* along with Minamoto no Tsunemoto. After that, the position of *seii* was discontinued for a long period.

進發

SHINPATSU

This is a term meaning to venture out and destroy a distant province in response to a *rinji* – an order from the emperor. This written order is carried with a *hinohata* – flag of the sun.

Commentator one

If a *rinji* order is given, it always makes the mission a *shinpatsu*, even if it is not led by the *shōgun* but by someone else.

Commentator two

When the court sends its army on an expedition, it gives the army flags of the sun and moon to carry on the mission. These are made of gold brocade with gold and silver embroidery and carry images of the sun and the moon. A *ryōji* is an order from a prince, while a *rinji* is an order from the emperor. The Book

---

59 A legendary prince who appears in the *Kojiki* and *Nihonshoki* chronicles.
60 Also known as Sangi Uemon-no-Kami.

of Rites says: 'A king's words are like a thread, and once uttered they are as thick and as straight as [tight] cord.'

退治
TAIJI

This term refers to the subjugation of someone within your own province. This can also be called *seitō*. Other kinds of departure for war are called *shutsujin* – moving out to war.

Commentator one

Taiji are those cases where lords of countries or provinces defeat retainers within their own domains. That is, to defeat families or retainers that have engaged in betrayal. All other kinds of departure for war are called *shutsujin*, be they major or minor conflicts.

院宣
INZEN

This is an order from a retired emperor and bears a seal.

Commentator one

An *inzen* will have a seal.

勅使
CHOKUSHI

This is an imperial messenger. He will carry a flag of the sun to identify him.

天書
TENSHO

This is a document issued by a *sesshō* regent[61] while a *migyōsho* is a document issued by the *sadaijin*, who is the Minister of the Left, or the *udaijin*, the Minister of the Right, or even by the *shōgun* himself.

Commentator one

A *tensho* is issued by a regent in lieu of a *chokumei*, which is an order issued by the emperor. If the emperor is young or female, a regent is appointed. All the terms such as *tenki*[62] and *tenpai*[63] relate specifically to the emperor.

御教書
MIGYŌSHO

This is a document given by the Minister of the Left or the Minister of the Right or even the *shōgun*.

Commentator one

A document from the *shōgun* is called a *migyōsho*. The term originates with Sir Rokuon-in Yoshimitsu, who was the third Ashikaga *shōgun* after Ashikaga Takauji. He was also called Sir Muromachi as he lived in a palace in Muromachi. Members of the Ashikaga family were designated as *daijō-daijin* – chancellors of the realm – and were of the first rank[64] and regarded as on a par with a regent family. From that time on, the term *kubō-ke* was applied to the family of the *shōgun* and the *migyōsho* document entered into use. When a *migyōsho* is issued, the *kanrei* deputies issue the required documents according to the order given. Signatories do not write their personal names on the documents, but instead give their official positions with a written seal below.

---

61 摂政 – a regent to an emperor.
62 天気 – the state of mind of the emperor.
63 天盃 – a *sake* cup given by the emperor.
64 正一位 *sho ichii* – a rank given by the court. First rank is the top rank and equates to prime minister.

The *migyōsho* is no longer in use. Apart from the above, such documents as the *kudashigaki* and *segyō* were issued by the *kubō*, the family of the *shōgun*. These have also been discontinued.

御書
GOSHO

This is a document from court nobles or a *daimyō*.

Commentator one

A *gosho* is a document from a *seiga* family[65] or an aristocratic family of a rank just below *seiga*. Today it can also be given by a provincial lord or *daimyō*. These documents are issued by *bugyō* commanders upon an order from the lord, while a document issued by a *rōjū* senior councillor upon the order of the emperor is called a *hōsho*.

奉書
HŌSHO

This is a formal document to be circulated in a province and should be written on *origami* – formal and official folded paper.

Commentator two

A *hōsho* is a document issued by a *bugyō* commander upon an order given by the *shōgun*. Alternatively, it can be issued by a *rōjū* senior councillor upon an order from the *shōgun*.

---

65   A high-ranking family whose members qualify to serve as ministers.

CHAPTER EIGHT

山城

YAMA-JIRO

Commentator one

A mountain castle. There is a list of various kinds of mountain castles, each defined by its shape. This is called *yasoyama* – literally, 'many mountains'. Details are in the *Shirotori* scroll.

平山城

HIRAYAMA-JIRO

This is a castle built on the plains, yet with mountains to the side(s).

平城

HIRA-JIRO

This is a castle on a plain.

掻上

KAKIAGE

Even the smallest *shiro* castle has bells and drums to give signals. A *kakiage* is a type of castle that does not have bells and drums.

Commentator two

Kakiage-jiro is a name given to small castles. The normal criteria for castle layout are not followed, but it has earthworks and moats with exterior fences of bush-wood. *Kakiage* means 'to dig earth and stone and to build up'. The following are all forms of *kakiage*:

- *kaname no chi* 要ノ地 – strategic points
- *eiheki* 営壁 – walled places
- *gunrui* 軍塁 – military earthworks

付城
TSUKE-JIRO

This is a castle that is built close to an enemy castle.

Commentator two

Tsuke-jiro can be large or small. They are crude constructions built quickly so that troops do not have to be stationed in the open.

出城
DEJIRO

This is a separate fortification to the front of a main castle.

境目ノ城
SAKAIME-NO-SHIRO

This is a castle built on the boundary between the enemy province and your own province.

Commentator one

One example of a *sakaime-no-shiro* – castle on a boundary – is Kawanakajima castle in Shinshū.

Commentator two

These castles are used to defend against a neighbouring province. Castle layout and use of natural fortification should be planned according to the topography of the area.

籠城
RŌJŌ

This term means to bring your people into the cover of the castle and wait for the enemy to advance.

守城
MORI-JIRO

To defend your castle during normal times.

Commentator one

There are differences between *mori-jiro* and *rōjō*.

前ノケタシ
MAE NO KEDASHI

This is the area to the front of the castle.

後ノケタシ

USHIRO NO KEDASHI

This is the area to the rear of the castle.

The above two terms are also used for a battle camp.

Commentator one

Mae no kedashi and *ushiro no kedashi* have been recorded here because they are names of certain areas of castles. Other parts are listed below.

PARTS OF A CASTLE

A castle consists of:

- *tenshu* 天守 – keep
- *honmaru* 本丸 – main enclosure
- *ninomaru* 二ノ丸 – second enclosure
- *sannomaru* 三ノ丸 – third enclosure
- *sōkuruwa* 惣郭 – outer wall

Apart from the above, other terms used include:

- *nishi-no-maru* 西ノ丸 – west enclosure
- *higashi-no-maru* 東ノ丸 – east enclosure
- *kita-no-maru* 北ノ丸 – north enclosure
- *minami-no-maru* 南ノ丸 – south enclosure

The terms used will depend on the layout of the castle.

Other areas of a castle include:

- *umadashi kuruwa* 馬出郭 – enclosed gateway
- *yagura* 矢倉 – turrets

These terms can be understood by listening to what others have said. Details are given in the *Jōsei Jōkan* – the upper scroll of Jōsei – and in the 'Jōdai' chapter of the scroll *Heieki Yōhō*.

Commentator two

In the first month of Tenshō 4 (1576), Oda Nobunaga had a castle built on Mount Kuwayama in Gōshū. It was completed in the fourth month and in the seventh month the castle tower was erected. The castle tower had double stone walls of twelve *ken* in height and ran a length of twenty *ken* from south to north and seventeen *ken* east to west. Seven stone walls ringed the castle tower. This is the most exquisite keep of all Japanese castles.

A small ring-like layout is desirable for castles and this is the basic principle of castle construction. Therefore, enclosures are called *maru* – rings.[66] The form of a ring revolves and has no end. The entire ground inside the castle gate is called the *sōkuruwa*.

The terms *honmaru*, *ninomaru* and *sannomaru* – the main, second and third enclosures – have been in use since ancient times. Furthermore, there is also the *shōryūkuruwa* – the rising dragon enclosure.

Emperor Jimmu, who was the first emperor and the descendent of a god, built the first castle in our country, at Kashiharanomiya. He ordered officials from various provinces to build this capital.

The *Setsumon*[67] says that castles are to be filled with people and that once a castle is built it should not be destroyed.

Maru – defensive rings – are inner enclosures, while the *kuruwa* are the outer walls which surround the *maru*.

Major castles proper have east, west, south and north enclosures, while smaller castles tend to have only east and west enclosures.

The *umadashi* is a small enclosure just outside a castle gate and defends the gate itself. Soldiers use this enclosure to advance out of the castle.

---

66 Each area is called a *maru* 丸 and these concentric areas are divided by walls and moats.
67 説文解字 *Shuowen Jiezi*.

CAPTURING AN ENEMY CASTLE

Terms for capture:

- Use *semeotosu* to capture a *yama-jiro* – mountain castle
- Use *kuzusu* to capture a *hira-jiro* – castle on a plain
- Use *nottoru* to capture a *fukenuma* – castle in a deep marsh

Commentator one

The following are all *ikusa-kotoba* – military terms.

御陣城

GO-JINJŌ

This is a position taken up in the mountains by a lord.

Commentator one

The way of taking such a position is described in detail in the chapter 'The ways of constructing camp huts'.

御陣場

GO-JINBA

This is a position taken up for a single night by a lord.

御陣所

GO-JINSHO

This is a position taken up for multiple days by a lord.

御旗本
O-HATAMOTO

This is where the *taishō* lord-commander has set up his position. The entire area is called either *go-jinchū* or *go-jinsho*.

御本陣
GO-HONJIN

This is the place where the lord stays in a battle camp.

御宿陣
GO-SHUKUJIN

This is a term used for when the lord stays in a town residence.

御進發
GO-SHINPATSU

This is to move out to war on an arranged date for battle. It is also called *go-hakkō*.

Commentator one

Shinpatsu means to venture out carrying war curtains to far lands with the aim of destroying rebels after a *rinji* or *inzen* order has been given. Details are found in the *Shokugen Shōsetsu*.

御出張
GO-SHUCCHŌ

This is to advance towards the enemy from a battle camp.

Commentator one

Be aware that the explanations listed up until this point should not be considered as definitive. Do not use terms which will make people uncomfortable or will be considered ill-fated. Up until now military terms have been given. The rest of this chapter consists of a list of terms for war curtains.

幕之事

Maku no Koto

WAR CURTAINS[68]

The following are curtains used for war.

幔幕

MANMAKU

This is the war curtain constructed for the lord-commander.

Commentator one

Curtains are an essential tool for military families and details are in another writing. A *manmaku* curtain is made of stitched pieces of cloth. The fabric used is satin or satin with raised patterns.

幕

MAKU

This means war curtains erected by various *samurai*.

---

68 The translation 'war curtains' has been applied to those curtains that are clearly used in battle. Others have been termed simply 'curtains'.

Commentator one

The curtains mentioned here are all war curtains. There are certain ways of creating them. There are curtains of *in* and *yō*. Details are in the scroll *Maku no Maki*.

仕寄幕

SHIYORI-MAKU

These are war curtains constructed on a battlefield when undertaking siege warfare.

Commentator one

Shiyori-maku are used for arrow or musket shooting when conducting a siege. There is a set way to create them, which is transmitted separately.

POINTS CONCERNING THE PARTS OF A CURTAIN

War curtains have five parts, each of which has a different name:

- *ten* 天 – top section
- *ai* 相 – second section
- *fū* 風 – third section
- *nami* 浪 – fourth section
- *shiba* 芝 – fifth section

In addition, there are *monomi*, which are the observation holes.

雑幕
ZŌMAKU
These are curtains which are set up for flower viewing and such activities and are also called *keshō no maku*.

Commentator two
When making *zōmaku* there are no set rules for the size, colour or type of cloth.

幕一重
MAKU-HITOKASANE
One set of curtains means a 'pair of war curtains' while *katashi* is a single war curtain. These are called *in-yō no maku* – *yin* and *yang* curtains. Details are given in the scroll *Maku no Maki*.

Commentator two
A *yō no maku* – *yang* curtain – has twenty-eight loops, which represent the twenty-eight lunar mansions. The *in no maku* – *yin* curtain – has thirty-six loops, which represent the thirty-six animals.[69] Both outline and details are transmitted in the scroll *Maku no Maki*. There is also a traditional way called *in-yō ittai no maku*, which is a curtain with elements of both *in* and *yō*.

THE FIVE SECTIONS OF A WAR CURTAIN
The cloth of a war curtain can be divided into five sections:
- *tenno* 天布
- *aino* 相布
- *fūtei* 風躰

---

69 Three animals are designated as belonging to each of the Twelve Earthly Branches, adding up to thirty-six in total.

8

- *namiyosei* 浪寄
- *shibauchi* 芝打

Commentator two
The five sections of cloth represent the Five Elements.

菊トヂ
KIKUTOJI
These are the leather sections at the viewing holes within the war curtain.

コマリ
KOMARI
This is the cord used to raise the war curtain.

Commentator one
The *komari* cord is made of twisted paper, just like a woman's hair cord.[70]

TERMINOLOGY USED IN THE HANDLING OF WAR CURTAINS
Use the term *utsu* for the raising of allied war curtains, while *hiku* refers to the enemy raising their war curtains.

Kachioku means to lower curtains. The term *hazusu* should be avoided.

Hashirakasu is the raising of war curtains on ships. *Kakou* is used for raising curtains of a viewing area. *Haru* 張 is used for raising funeral curtains.

Osamuru is the lowering of a curtain, but do not use the term *tatamu*. *Shiboru* is used for the action of lifting a curtain [that has already been constructed].

---

70 モトユヒ *motoyui* – a strong tie for women's hair.

Commentator one

One important tradition says that war curtains should not have arrow ports. Consider those terms after *utsu* and *hiku* as *ikusa-kotoba* – military terms – concerning war curtains.[71]

From *hashirakasu* onwards, the listed terms relate to curtains of peacetime. The terms *osameru* and *shiboru* should always be used, for both wartime and peacetime curtains.

Commentator two

The *tenno* section of the cloth has viewing holes called *nichi* and *getsu* – sun and moon. Viewing holes are on the seam between the first and second cloths. Each is one *shaku* and three *sun* in length.

The above are terms used for curtains. From the point referring to ship curtains onwards, the terms listed are for use during peacetime. The following are military terms relating to weapons.

This is the end of terms for curtains.

---

71 Here *ikusa-kotoba* refers to auspicious and inauspicious words which should or should not be used on a military campaign.

CHAPTER NINE

COUNTING IN THE LANGUAGE OF WAR

Hitofuri is used to count *drawn* swords, while *hitokoshi* is used to count swords in other cases.

Commentator one

From this above point on until the end of this section, consider these to be military words associated with military gear.

Commentator two

For one *katana*, the term *hitokoshi* – a single blade at the waist – is used. If a pair of swords is worn, the term *sashisoeru* – to wear in supplement – is used.

SHIELDS AND BOW STRINGS

Tsuku is the term for a shield; alternatively, *kubaru* can sometimes be used. When you are in the *koguchiba*, the outer entrance of a castle, and you inform your men to loosen their bow strings, you should use the term *yasumeru* – literally, 'to rest' – but do not use the word *hazusu*, which means 'to remove'.

Commentator one

Tsuku is used for one or two shields, while *kubaru* refers to a larger number. *Hazusu* should be avoided as it is the word of a coward.

CASTLE GATES

The main castle gate is called the *ōte* or the *ōte no kidoguchi*, while the rear gate is called the *karamete* or the *karamete no kidoguchi*. Castle entrances have to be strong and therefore the ideogram for tiger, 虎, is used.[72] During a battle against the Heike family, Kabano Noriyori was designated as the commander of the *ōte* gate while Kurō Yoshitsune was the commander of the *karamete* gate.

There is sometimes a sign at the front of a castle to ensure that people dismount from their horses at that point. A sign saying *gejō* prohibits vehicles from passing that point. The size and the methods of writing these signs are transmitted in calligraphy schools. Certain Chinese writings such as the *Que li zhi* record that signs for dismounting were put in front of ancestral mausoleums. Therefore, similar signs are also put up in front of shrines and temples in Japan.

ARROWS AND BOW STRINGS

- *hito-koshi* 一腰 – a bundle of twenty-one arrows.
- *wa* 把 – a bundle of fifty-one arrows.
- *hito-oke* 一桶 – a unit of twelve bow strings
- *hito-hari* 一張 – a unit of seven bow strings.

Commentator two

The term *koshi* – waist – is used because the bundle was put on the waist of an archer.

The *hitosuji-honya* is your primary arrow; it has your name and position written within the fletching. This can also be called the *tai no ya* – the arrow of the body. It remains even after you die. There are things to be orally transmitted on this subject.

---

72 The term *koguchiba* used above this point literally means 'the tiger's mouth'.

ARCHER'S GLOVES

A *yugake ichigu* is a pair of archer's gloves, consisting of the *oshite*, the glove for the left hand, and the *katte*, the glove for the right hand.

Commentator one

The *yugake ichigu* can also be called the *shura-yugake* – the gloves of hell.

In war [during the 'ceremony of resounding bowstrings'], strike the bowstring only once. Striking three times should be avoided.

Commentator one

The reason for not striking the bowstrings three times is that the term for this, *miuchi*, is pronounced in a similar way to the term for to be struck, *mi wo utsu*.

Commentator two

The term *hitotsu*, meaning once, is preferred in conjunction with the above terms, because it can be also read as *katsu* – victory.

The term *susumu* – to advance – should be used to indicate the movement of flags when an army departs for war.

The term *shiboru* should be used to describe the rolling of a flag around a pole. From ancient times it is a tradition to roll flags in front of a shrine dedicated to Hachiman, the god of war.

Commentator one

According to ancient custom and manners, flags should be rolled around their poles in front of the gates of Hachiman shrines. This is because the ideogram for man, 幡, is the same ideogram as that for flag. Hachiman is the foremost military god, thus respect should be shown.

Commentator two

Hata wo maku – to roll flags – means to surrender [so therefore should be avoided].

Hipparu is used to indicate that the enemy has raised its flags while *uchitateru* should be used for the raising of your own flags.

Avoid the term *kiru* – to cut – when discussing the making of banner poles. Use *karu* – to hunt – instead. Also, the term *horu* – to dig – can be used.

The terms above are used to dispel the enemy and bring victory to your side.

Ichi-ryō is used to count suits of armour while *hito-hachi* is used to count helmets.

Commentator one

Ichi-ryō is used only for body armour.

Hito-hane should be avoided when referring to a single helmet because the pronunciation of *hane* is the same as for *haneru* – to decapitate. Therefore, *hito-hachi* or *hito-kashira* is used instead.

Commentator two

The term *issō* is used to count the armour of a lord, while *hitotsu* or *futatsu* can be used for the armour of common *samurai*.

SOUNDS IN BATTLE

Inanaku or *isamu* should be used to describe the neigh of a horse from the allied force while *naku* is used for the neigh of an enemy horse.

Ikiou should be used for the vocal cry of cattle within the allied force. *Hoyuru* should be used for the cry of enemy cattle.

Tatsuru should be used for when allies are blowing conch shells while *fuku* is used for the blowing of an enemy conch shell.

Ikute is used when counting formations on the allied side while *ikukire* is used when counting formations on the enemy side.

Uttedetaru is used when your allies advance and attack, while *hikidashitaru* is used for the enemy attack.

Teki ni kirasete or *tsukasete* are used to describe being injured by the enemy, while *kitte* and *tsukite* are used to describe injuring the enemy.

Togetaru is used to describe an ally being killed in battle. *Shitaru* should not be used to describe death in battle.

From Yoshitsune's war poems:

討死ヲシタルト云ハ尾篭也タヽ遂タリト云ベカリシヲ
To say shitaru, '*killed in war*', *is inappropriate.*
Togetaru, '*a death achieved in battle*', *is the preferred term.*

The term *kiwamuru* is used to describe military achievements. To describe higher achievements, *hitokasaue* or *futakasaue* should be used. *Ichibai* and *nibai* should be avoided when describing military achievements.

Commentator two

The sound *bai* is reminiscent of *hai*, as heard in *haigun* – defeat, and is thus disliked.

The term *modoru* should be used when discussing a return voyage by ship, while *kaeru* should be avoided in this context.

Fune-wake is used when talking about ship formation, while *fune-wari* should not be used.

For other nautical terms, ask a sailor.

Commentator one

Nautical terms are known to ship's crews. For further details, discuss this with them.

Commentator two

Fune-wake is also inappropriate, thus *fune-kubari* can be used instead.

Kubi-ikka represents two decapitated heads.
Kubi-ichida means eight decapitated heads.
Kubi-issha means fifty decapitated heads.

Commentator one

The term *issha*, meaning 'one cart', comes from a custom of the Tang Dynasty where heads were loaded on carts. It is said that this custom was also sometimes followed in our country in ancient times.

Commentator two

In our country there are ancient accounts of heads being carried on a cart. The head of Shōnagon Shinzei[73] was carried in this manner.

The weight of a decapitated human head is about one *kan* and 300 *momme*.[74] A person weighs almost the same as one [sixty-kilogram] sack of rice, and fifty heads was considered a suitable number to carry on one cart. To take and carry decapitated heads is considered the same as capturing a person's body itself.

There is a difference in the way the terms *hajimuru* and *awasu* are used in relation to the starting of spear fights. *Hajimuru* is used for the first battle of the day, while a term ending in *awasu* is used to refer to an individual spear fight.

---

73   Also known as Fujiwara no Michinori.
74   Equal to 4.8 kilograms.

Kubi-taimen indicates an allied general's inspection of the head of an enemy general while *jikken* is used for the inspection of the heads of lesser soldiers.

Commentator one
The *jikken* head inspection is an old custom no longer in use.

Commentator two
The *jikken* is an ancient custom and if done wrongly it can be unlucky for the lord-commander. Head inspections should be supervised by a *gunbaisha*. Details are written in the scroll *Gunbai no Maki*. A *jikken* can alternatively be called a *kenbutsu*.

獄門之事
Gokumon no Koto
GIBBETED HEADS
One of the following woods should be used for a low gibbet – one that comes below eye level:

- cedar
- *sawara* cypress[75]
- chestnut

Heads should be washed before they are gibbeted.
The heads of thieves should be gibbeted up high.
The term *hyakugōgake* – lily gibbet – means to gibbet a head by ramming it on an eight-*sun* nail. To gibbet a head by securing it by the top knot is called *hiroigake* – the lifted gibbet. An identifying tag should be placed through the left earlobe and the tag itself should be four *sun* in length.

---

75 *Chamaecyparis pisifera.*

Commentator one

Gokumon, meaning prison gate, is the name given to the gibbeting of heads in front of prisons. The practice is also called *kyōken* or *kyōshu*. The term *kyōshu* originated around the era of the Yellow Emperor in ancient China. In ancient Japan, the first aristocrat – i.e. a member of the third rank of the imperial court or higher – to have his head gibbeted was Taira no Munemori, who suffered this fate during the Yōwa period (1181–1182).

Commentator two

There are set ways for gibbeting heads. Those of lower people should be gibbeted high, while those of *samurai* should be gibbeted low. The purpose of the act is to notify people of the offender's name and to disgrace his family. The heads of thieves should be raised high in order to expose their faces.

In ancient times in our country, it was a principle not to gibbet the head of an aristocrat of the third rank or higher. During the rebellion of Fujiwara Emi no Oshikatsu [in 764[76]], Prince Shōtoku had a soldier named Iware decapitate Oshikatsu's head in the province of Ōmi and presented it to the court in Kyōto; however, it was not gibbeted. Fujiwara no Nobuyori was accused of being felonious [and beheaded], but his head was also not gibbeted. Therefore, it was inappropriate to parade the aforementioned Taira – who was of the position of *naidaijin*[77] – and his son through the streets of Kyōto and for them to beheaded and gibbeted.

According to the *Mōkan*, the term *kyō* represents a punishment that is intended to degrade a person's reputation.

断陣
DANJIN

This is a term for carrying out the punishment of prisoners.

---

76 There is an error here, as Prince Shōtoku (572–622) died more than a century before this rebellion.

77 An official just below the rank of the Minister of the Left and the Minister of the Right.

Commentator two

This means taking a prisoner for his punishment, particularly someone who is sentenced to perform *seppuku* or who is taken bound with rope to be executed.

斬罪
ZANZAI

This means beheading a *samurai* in a graveyard.

切腹
SEPPUKU

This means a *samurai* cutting open his own abdomen.

Commentator two

It is said that the first example of *seppuku* was carried out by Tosa-no-bō Shōshun (1141–1185), who was made to perform the act at Rokujōgawara in Kyōto. Details on how to station the people on the parade to the execution are given in another writing.

Ageru is used for war cries given by the allied forces, while *tachikiru* is used for war cries given by the enemy.

Mawasu is used to describe constructing allied huts or fences, while *hiku* is the equivalent term for the enemy's constructions.

An *uma no hito-ashi*[78] is the stride of a horse – it is six *ken* long.

---

78 This may refer to one of the following: a double step (e.g., left and then right), a complete step cycle, or the area that a human or horse occupies. Therefore two understandings can be taken from this: the distance travelled per complete cycle of steps or the area that the subject takes up.

Commentator two

The step of a human is one *ken*, while a horse's is about six times longer. Taking the two attending grooms into account [and adding one *ken* for each groom], one step is eight *ken* in total. This is used in *musha kotoba* – language for warriors – when on a campaign.

The statement that the step of the human is one *ken* is found in the classic *Methods of the Sima*. According to this writing, the step of one leg is called a *ki* and is three *shaku* long, while one cycle of steps with both legs is called a *ho* and is six *shaku* [which equals one *ken*]. The *Annotated Rites of Zhou* says six *shaku* makes one *ho*.

CHAPTER TEN

烽燧
HŌSUI

This is a field signal fire and is also called *noroshi* – wolf smoke. In Japan it can be called *tobuhi no nomori* – the 'flame keeper's fire of speed'.[79] In ancient times these signal fires were used in a place called Kasugano.

Commentator one

Field signals are found in the *Records of the Great Historian* and the *Book of Han*. In ancient Japan, these field signals are referred to as *tobuhi*, as seen in the poem below, and those who were in charge of such positions were named as *nomori*. The term *tobuhi no nomori* is also found in the *Kokin Wakashū* – a collection of Japanese poems of ancient and modern times:

> 春日野の飛火の野守出てみよ今幾日ありて若菜つみてん
> *Keeper of the fire signal of Kasugano, venture out and see how many more days*
> *it will be before we can gather wild green grasses.*

Commentator two

According to the document *Noroshi* [illegible text], signal fires have wolves' dung within them to make the smoke ascend straight without any tilting, even in wind.

Hō from *hōsui* stands for watch fires. *Sui* from *hōsui* here represents fire signals. An annotation of the *Book of Han* says that during the day they are called *hansui* and at night they are called *kyohō*.

---

79 飛火ノ野守 – the ideogram for 'flying' can mean to fly in or through the air. In this context it means to transmit signals at speed.

間者

KANJA

This means spy and has a similar meaning to *shinobi no mono*. It is considered to be equivalent with *Kōka-mono* (man of Kōka) and *Higo-mono* (man of Higo).

Commentator one

Kan is found in the chapter 'The Use of Spies' in Sun Tzu's *Art of War*, it occurs in the *gokan* – the five types of spy:

- *kyō* 郷 – local
- *shi* 死 – doomed
- *han* 反 – converted
- *nai* 内 – internal
- *sei* 生 – surviving

Details are given in the above mentioned writing.

There is a type of *kan* called *dakkō-kan* which was used by Kusunoki Masashige. *Kanja* and *shinobi* are similar in various aspects but differ slightly in mindset. Our school has secret traditions on the excellent methods of *shinobi heijutsu* – the military skills of the *shinobi*. Masashige often used these skills. In the Genryaku period (1184–1185), as described in the *Genpei Jōsuiki* scrolls,[80] Yoshitsune used Ise no Saburō Yoshimori as a *kanja* spy.

Generally, if an ignorant person uses *shinobi* skills he will be detected, which will make it difficult to defeat an enemy. Those who engage in *shinobi* activities should be carefully selected. They exist in the districts of Kōka, Iga and Ōmi and are thus named after those places. They are also called *uramagure* – those who blend in behind the scenes; and sometimes, *sonae no hashikuzushi* – those who break down formations.

---

80 A version of the *Heike Monogatari*, famous war stories written in the twelfth century.

見崩レ

MIKUZURE

This term is used in war to mean a formation that collapses without fighting at the sight of an enemy attack.

裏崩

URAKUZURE

This term is for when people within your own army and to the rear break formation, even if the enemy is at a distance.

友崩

TOMOKUZURE

This term is for when troops break formation when they mistake approaching allies as an enemy.

Commentator two

The above three issues all happen in an army led by an ignorant general. Be aware that they happen because the formation is not under appropriate control and the *samurai* and soldiers are not in good harmony.

直甲

JIKA-KABUTO

This term is used for a group of *musha*-warriors made up entirely of *samurai*.

Commentator one

Jika-kabuto is used for a group that consists only of *samurai*.

混甲

MAJIRI-KABUTO

This term is used for mixed troops.

Commentator one

Majiri-kabuto is used for a mixed group of *samurai* and *zōhyō* – lower soldiers.

歩行武者

KACHI-MUSHA

This represents anyone who is wearing armour, including archers, musketeers, foot-soldiers, banner-men, spearmen, etc.

徒膚武者

SUHADA-MUSHA

This term is for warriors who return to the fight without armour. In a lengthy campaign in which there have been only close combats between *ashigaru*, and *samurai* who move around to fight and are injured only upon the shoulder [or other such light injuries], some may wish to venture out to war again before the injury recovers or go back to battle without armour on. In this case they must inform the captain or commander of their intention; only then can they set out without armour on.

Commentator one

You need to notify your commander before you become a *suhada* – warrior without armour. If such a warrior appears on the side of the enemy, kill them without fail because they are proper *samurai*.

頭棒武者

TŌBŌ-MUSHA

This term is used for those who wear armour but do not have a banner; it can also be written as 統羽亡. If they stand out from the other soldiers, this probably means that they have a high rank, such as *samurai-daishō* or *kashira* – captain. If your side cannot win the battle, then at least pursue a man such as this and take his head, even if it is an *oikubi* – a head taken in retreat.

青歯者

AOBAMONO

This is a term used for a person who has never worn armour; examples are *wakatō*, *chūgen* and *komono*. The word *arashiko* has the same meaning.

Commentator one

Aoba was originally written as 白歯 and means 'one with white teeth'. The ideogram 白 is read as *ao*; this is because 白馬ノ節 is read as *aouma no sechi*. *Aouma no sechi* is a ceremony held on the seventh day of the first month. In this ceremony the emperor views horses from the Council Hall in the Imperial Palace. *Aobamono* came from an old custom where all aristocrats and *samurai* who were given official rank [by the court] had blackened teeth, while lower people did not, leaving them with white teeth. Taira no Atsumori, who was also known as Mukandayū, meaning 'he without rank', had light makeup and blackened teeth. This meant that Kumagai Naozane realized that he was in fact of noble stock [and not a common soldier] and thus killed him. This episode is found in the *Heike Monogatari*.

Commentator two

Also those *samurai* who are of the fifth rank or lower in the court are called *aoba-zamurai*.

假リ武者

KARI-MUSHA

This term is used for temporary combatants, which can include *rōnin*, messengers from other forces, people from a neighbouring province and reinforcements. Their flags, helmet crests and banners should differ from those of your own forces. The various *samurai* of your own side need to know how these warriors are dressed. In battle put these people in the vanguard and make sure they know the passwords and have identifying marks on their sleeves.

Commentator two

According to Kōshū-Ryū, these warriors should be placed in the vanguard. This is done in case they betray you or attack your allies. The same precaution applies to enemy warriors who have surrendered.

CHAPTER ELEVEN

旗指物之事

Hata sashimono no koto

BANNERS AND FLAGS

The three main types of flag are:

- *matoi* 圓居 – carried at the front of a procession
- *umajirushi* 馬印 – carried close to the lord-commander
- *hata* 旗 – carried at various positions within the formation

Further details are given in the scroll *Heigu Yōhō*.

Commentator one

The name *matoi* originally comes from the 'gathering' of an entire army. *Umajirushi* flags differ from clan to clan.

Commentator two

There is something called a *ko-matoi* – a smaller *matoi* – which is carried by close retainers of the lord.

The *matoi* should be:

- at the front of the army when advancing
- moved to the sides when in battle
- used to rally a scattered army

If there are two *matoi*, one should be larger than the other. The larger one should be used as above and the smaller one should be carried by the *hatamoto* command group.

TYPES OF BANNERS

The main types of banner are:

- *fukinuki* 吹貫
- *hankō* ハンカウ
- *giragira* キラキラ
- *nobusuma* ノブスマ
- *baren* バレン
- *irokogata* イロコカタ
- *etsuru* エツル
- *habiki* ハビキ
- *tsuetsuki* ツエツキ
- *shide* シデ
- *maneki* マネキ
- *shaguma* 赤熊
- *kurokuma* 黒熊[81]
- *shirokuma* 白熊
- *shihan* 四半
- *shinai* シナヒ
- *orikake-shinai* 折掛シナヒ
- *fukinagashi* 吹ナカシ
- *tanzaku* 短冊
- *kamuro* 禿

There are differences between *hata*, which are flags, and *nobori*, which are slim banners.

There are other flags and banners in addition to the ones listed above. For example, there is a set of banners called the *jūgo no sashimono* – the 'fifteen banners'. Further details are given in a different scroll.

---

81   This banner appears only in the Koga transcription.

Commentator one

Here the term *hata* refers to an individual flag for each troop.[82] For *sashimono* – banners – details are in the writing *Sashimonoshū*: a compendium of banners.

Flags of old times used a horizontal pole and were called *tenagabata*. In this respect they were like *hata*, whereas *nobori* have loops that go through a vertical pole.

The 'fifteen banners' are not allowed to be carried without permission, thus they are also called *gomen no sashimono* – the permitted banners. Details are in the scroll *Heigu Yōhō*.

Commentator two

The size of the *umajirushi* varies from clan to clan. In the main there are two sizes, large and small. Large ones should be referred to as *o-umajirushi* and are used for the lord. Small ones are placed near the horses of ordinary *samurai* when they are in battle. Those versions in use now are three *ken* long; previously, they were three and a half *ken* in length.

An *umajirushi* is carried by a close retainer of the lord-commander.

Kin-tenmoku and *kin-no-gohei* are the types of *umajirushi* standard used in Kishū province.[83]

タイマイノ鑓
TAIMAI NO YARI

This is a spear owned by a lord-commander or a captain. It has a *nashiji*-style lacquered handle.[84]

A warrior's outfit indicates his status, so he should avoid adding elaborate elements that are more befitting of a higher rank.

Warrior outfits are designated as follows:

- *horogake* 母衣掛 – includes arrow cape

---

82 One per *itte* 一手.

83 Kishū is the province where Natori-Ryū students served.

84 梨地 *nashiji* – a lacquered handle with gold embedded in the lacquer.

- *yamabushi* 山伏 – in the style of a yamabushi monk
- *karakake* 掛羅掛 – wearing a monk's apron[85]
- *haori-musha* 羽織武者 – includes haori jacket

Captains and above may wear certain kinds of outfit, in accordance with their personalities. These include the *haori* jacket, the *suhada-musha* (i.e. without armour), and the garb of the *samurai*-monk.

Commentator one

For details of the spear reserved for lord-commanders see the scroll *Heigu Yōhō*. Ordinary *samurai* are not allowed to carry such a spear without permission.

Horo – arrow capes – may be worn by the lord-commander and captains. Normal *samurai* are not allowed to wear them without permission.

The outfit of a *yamabushi* monk is allowed if the wearer has a certificate from the commissioners for *shugendō* practices of the Ōmine mountain range.

The *karakake* outfit may be worn by one who has entered a Zen sect and paid visits to a temple to study and attain enlightenment.

It is sometimes the case that *samurai*-monks, the lord-commander and injured warriors do not carry a banner or wear a helmet.

具足褒様

Gusoku no homeyō

THE WORDS USED TO COMPLIMENT ARMOUR

When complimenting someone's armour or helmet use descriptions such as:

- *isei aru* 威勢アル – full of spirit
- *susudoki* スストキ – sharp[86]
- *hanayaka* 声花 – splendid

---

85 掛絡掛 in the *Koga* transcription.

86 When used for a person this term has connotations of quick-wittedness. When used for an object it suggests 'coolness' or stylishness.

- *kekkō* ケツカウ – excellent

Do not describe it as *migoto* – spectacular – because this is the word used to compliment a good death in battle.

Commentator one

Do not compliment the armour of a nobleman as being *kekkō* – of an excellent standard. It should be taken for granted that his armour will be excellent. The word *migoto* is used to acclaim an honourable death, so it should be avoided when complimenting armour.

Commentator two

The word *kekkō* should not be used for aristocrats because it should be understood that aristocrats always have things that are of an excellent standard.

出陣之次第

Shutsujin no shidai

PREPARATIONS FOR WAR

When preparing to depart for battle, instruct the servants to return home so that they can inform their wives and children that they have been given orders for war and that they will soon be leaving. They should say goodbye and have no regrets, but they should not linger and they should make sure to put all their business in order.

Commentator one

Before departure, you should give your servants time off to say farewell to their wives and children. This way they will not feel regret and will be able to detach themselves from their family bonds. Make sure that everything is settled beforehand. This is important not only before departing for war, but also before any form of travel or venturing out. If issues are not settled until the day or the day before departure then they will not be settled at all. If they are not settled then you may forget or lose property and thus will not make good progress, whereas if your affairs are in good order then you can focus on your pre-departure celebration with a serene mind.

DIVINING YOUR AUSPICIOUS DIRECTION
Prior to departure, conduct a celebration for your venture in which you divine your *individual* auspicious direction, year, month, date and time. Your wife and children should not be present at this celebration.

Commentator one
Sometimes divination is done starting with the larger and moving to the smaller – for example, from the year to the month to the day to the hour. This is part of the art of a *tenmonsha* astrologist or a *gunbaisha*. Military establishments have teachings on how to [use divination to] avoid defeat and bring about victory.

The following are from Yoshitsune's war poems:

時取ハ味方よけれバ敵もよし只軍にハ方角を知れ
If an auspicious time is lucky for your side, it is also lucky for the enemy.
Simply understand the direction [in which you should advance] for war.

日取りとハ其家々に吉事あり扱ハてる日と風吹ぬ日と
Each establishment has its own customs for divining an auspicious day.
The most auspicious are sunny days and windless days.

Commentator two
You should perform this celebration on your own with a serene mind.

CHAPTER TWELVE

時取

Tokidori

DETERMINING AUSPICIOUS TIMES

天之十干

Ten no jikkan

THE TEN CELESTIAL STEMS

The Ten Celestial Stems are associated with the Five Elements as shown below:

- *kinoe* 甲 and *kinoto* 乙 – associated with Wood 木
- *hinoe* 丙 and *hinoto* 丁 – associated with Fire 火
- *tsuchinoe* 戊 and *tsuchinoto* 己 – associated with Earth 土
- *kanoe* 庚 and *kanoto* 辛 – associated with Metal 金
- *mizunoe* 壬 and *mizunoto* 癸 – associated with Water 水

地之十二支

Chi no jūnishi

THE TWELVE EARTHLY BRANCHES

The Twelve Earthly Branches are divided according to their associations with day or night and with the Five Elements.

Those of the day:

- *u* 卯 – hare
- *tatsu* 辰 – dragon
- *mi* 巳 – snake
- *uma* 午 – horse

- *hitsuji* 未 – ram
- *saru* 申 – monkey

Those of the night:
- *tori* 酉 – cockerel
- *inu* 戌 – dog
- *i* 亥 – boar
- *ne* 子 – rat
- *ushi* 丑 – ox
- *tora* 寅 – tiger

Those associated with Wood 木:
- *u* 卯 – hare
- *tatsu* 辰 – dragon
- *mi* 巳 – snake

Those associated with Metal 金:
- *tori* 酉 – cockerel
- *inu* 戌 – dog
- *i* 亥 – boar

Those associated with Fire 火:
- *uma* 午 – horse
- *hitsuji* 未 – ram
- *saru* 申 – monkey

Those associated with Water 水:
- *ne* 子 – rat
- *ushi* 丑 – ox
- *tora* 寅 – tiger

Commentator one

The Ten Celestial Stems are what enable the Five Elements to be allocated and controlled by heaven.

The Twelve Earthly Branches from hare to monkey are for the day and the ones from cockerel to tiger are for the night.

Of the Five Elements [but not including Earth], three branches are allocated to each [of the remaining four]. However, Earth has some influence over dragon, dog, ram and ox.

年之十二支[87]

Toshi no jūnishi

THE TWELVE EARTHLY BRANCHES OF THE YEAR [IN CONNECTION WITH THE I CHING]

The following are the Twelve Earthly Branches for the months of the year.

The first month of the year is the month of the tiger:
- 地 earth (upper trigram)
- 天 heaven (lower trigram)
- 泰 advancing (meaning)

The second month of the year is the month of the hare:
- 雷 thunder (upper trigram)
- 天 heaven (lower trigram)
- 大壯 great strength (meaning)

---

87   In the Koga transcription, this title is different 月之十二支.

The third month of the year is the month of the dragon:

- 澤 marsh (upper trigram)
- 天 heaven (lower trigram)
- 夬 eliminating (meaning)

The fourth month of the year is the month of the snake:[88]

- 乾 force (upper trigram)
- 為 heaven (lower trigram)
- 天 initiating (meaning)

The fifth month of the year is the month of the horse:

- 天 heaven (upper trigram)
- 風 wind (lower trigram)
- 姤 encountering (meaning)

The sixth month of the year is the month of the ram:

- 天 heaven (upper trigram)
- 山 mountain (lower trigram)
- 遯 retreating (meaning)

The seventh month of the year is the month of the monkey:

88　The order of this list is taken from the Koga transcription. The Tōkyō transcription is reversed, however but the meaning is the same.

- 天 heaven (upper trigram)
- 地 earth (lower trigram)
- 否 hindrance (meaning)

The eighth month of the year is the month of the cockerel:
- 風 wind (upper trigram)
- 地 earth (lower trigram)
- 観 watching (meaning)

The ninth month of the year is the month of the dog:
- 山 mountain (upper trigram)
- 地 earth (lower trigram)
- 剥 falling away (meaning)

The tenth month of the year is the month of the boar:[89]
- 坤 field (upper trigram)
- 為 earth (lower trigram)
- 地 responding (meaning)

The eleventh month of the year is the month of the rat:
- 地 earth (upper trigram)
- 雷 thunder (lower trigram)
- 復 turning back (meaning)

---

89 As previous note.

The twelfth month of the year is the month of the ox:

- 地 earth (upper trigram)
- 澤 marsh (lower trigram)
- 臨 approaching (meaning)

Commentator one

Here the Twelve Earthly Branches for the year are listed along with their associated *bagua* 卦 trigrams. The first month is the month of the tiger – it has been so since the period of the Zhou Dynasty. In the Xia Dynasty the first month was the month of rat.

THE *I CHING* TRIGRAMS IN RELATION TO THE MONTHS
The first month

坤 *Kon* represents 地 earth and 乾 *ken* represents 天 heaven. The trigram for 坤 *kon* is ☷, while the trigram for 乾 *ken* is ☰. Together they result in the hexagram 泰 *tai* – advancing.

The second month

震 *Shin* represents 雷 thunder and 乾 *ken* represents 天 heaven. The trigram for 震 *shin* is ☳, while the trigram for 乾 *ken* is ☰. Together they result in the hexagram 大壯 *daisō* – great strength.

The third month

兌 *Da* represents 沢 marsh and 乾 *ken* represents 天 heaven. The trigram for 兌 *da* is ☱, while the trigram for 乾 *ken* is ☰. Together they result in the hexagram 夬 *kai* – eliminating.

The fourth month

乾 *Ken* represents 天 heaven. The trigram for 乾 *ken* is ☰ and is doubled in this month. Together they represent 天 heaven.

The fifth month

乾 *Ken* represents 天 heaven and 巽 *son* represents 風 wind. The trigram for 乾 *ken* is ☰, while the trigram for 巽 *son* is ☴. Together they result in the hexagram 姤 *kō* – encountering.

The sixth month

乾 *Ken* represents 天 heaven and 艮 *gon* represents 山 mountain. The trigram for 乾 *ken* is ☰, while the trigram for 艮 *gon* is ☶. Together they result in the hexagram 遯 *ton* – retreating.

The seventh month

乾 *Ken* represents 天 heaven and 坤 *kon* represents 地 earth. The trigram for 乾 *ken* is ☰, while the trigram for 坤 *kon* is ☷. Together they result in the hexagram 否 *hi* – hindrance.

The eighth month

巽 *Son* represents 風 wind and 坤 *kon* represents 地 earth. The trigram for 巽 *son* is ☴, while the trigram for 坤 *kon* is ☷. Together they result in the hexagram 観 *kan* – watching.

The ninth month

艮 *Gon* represents 山 mountain and 坤 *kon* represents 地 earth. The trigram for 艮 *gon* is ☶, while the trigram for 坤 *kon* is ☷. Together they result in the hexagram 剥 *haku* – falling away.

The tenth month

坤 *Kon* represents 地 earth. The trigram for 坤 *kon* is ☷ and is doubled in this month. Together they represent 地 earth.

The eleventh month

坤 *Kon* represents 地 earth and 震 *shin* represents 雷 thunder. The trigram for 坤 kon is ☷, while the trigram for 雷 *rai*[90] is ☳. Together they result in the hexagram 復 *fuku* – turning back.

The twelfth month

坤 *Kon* represents 地 earth and 兌 *da* represents 澤 marsh. The trigram for 坤 kon is ☷, while the trigram for 兌 *da* is ☱. Together they result in the hexagram 臨 *rin* – approaching.

The above shows the system that controls the Twelve Earthly Branches across the twelve months. Consider the auspicious and inauspicious in everything, as all things are covered by this system of divination. The above list displays the divination and the earthly branch for each month. Divination should be mastered by studying the *I Ching*. The following are some basic trigrams from the *I Ching*. For further details study the *I Ching* itself and you will understand.

THE INDIVIDUAL TRIGRAMS

乾天
Heaven
☰

兌澤
Marsh
☱

離火
Fire
☲

---

90 The ideogram used above is 震.

震雷
Thunder

☳

巽風
Wind

☴

坎水
Water

☵

艮山
Mountain

☶

坤地
Earth

☷

LINES OF IN AND YŌ

陽
Yō

━━●

陰
In

━ ━●

A METHOD TO DETERMINE AUSPICIOUS DIRECTION

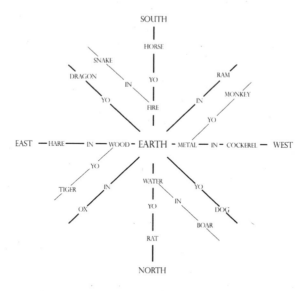

North

- is the element of *yō*
- is connected to Water
- is the direction of the rat
- the direction of the boar is of the element of *in* and is attached to north

South

- is the element of *yō*
- is connected to Fire
- is the direction of the horse
- the direction of the snake is of the element of *in* and is attached to south

West

- is of the element of *in*
- is connected to Metal
- is the direction of the cockerel
- the direction of the monkey is of the element of *yō* and is attached to west

East

- is of the element of *in*
- is connected to Wood
- is the direction of the hare
- the direction of the tiger is of the element of *yō* and is attached to the east

Centre

- is connected to Earth

Directions connected to the centre

- dragon, which is of the element of *yō*
- ox, which is of the element of *in*
- dog, which is of the element of *yō*
- ram, which is of the element of *in*

If you understand the concepts of *ko-kyo* and *ōsō* and their opposites, you will be able to divine for time and direction.

Commentator one

The directions consist of four cardinal points and a centre. Each one is connected to the Five Elements and the Twelve Earthly Branches. Both in Japan and China, military establishments use the directions of *ko* and *kyo*. They are used to establish auspicious and inauspicious years, months, days and hours.

It is said that *ko* will bring you defeat and that you will gain victory with *kyo*. Therefore, tradition says that if you stay in the direction of *ko* [facing *kyo*] and force the enemy in the direction of *kyo* [facing *ko*], you will win a great victory.

KO AND *KYO* DIRECTIONS
To discover the directions of *ko* and *kyo* for the year

If it is the year of the rat, the tenth position from the rat is cockerel, and the following two directions are dog and boar. These two will be *ko* and the opposite direction will be *kyo*.[91]

To discover the directions of *ko* and *kyo* for the month

If it is the first month of the year, the tenth direction from tiger is boar, and so the next months, rat and ox, will be *ko* and the opposite two will be *kyo*.[92]

The same method should be applied for all the four ways [i.e., the year, month, day and time]. For the day, start with the earthly branch of that day:

- from rat: dog and boar are *ko*; dragon and snake are *kyo*
- from ox: boar and rat are *ko*; snake and horse are *kyo*
- from tiger: rat and ox are *ko*; horse and ram are *kyo*
- from hare: ox and tiger are *ko*; ram and monkey are *kyo*
- from dragon: tiger and hare are *ko*; monkey and cockerel are *kyo*
- from snake: hare and dragon are *ko*; cockerel and dog are *kyo*
- from horse: dragon and snake are *ko*; dog and boar are *kyo*
- from ram: snake and horse are *ko*; boar and rat are *kyo*
- from monkey: horse and ram are *ko*; rat and ox are *kyo*
- from cockerel: ram and monkey are *ko*; ox and tiger are *kyo*
- from dog: monkey and cockerel are *ko*; tiger[93] and hare are *kyo*
- from boar: cockerel and dog are *ko*; hare and dragon are *kyo*

Use the same method to determine auspicious times.

According to the *Bubishi*:

- for an enemy above 100,000 in number, use the concept of *ko-kyo* for the year
- for an enemy above 10,000, use the concept of *ko-kyo* for the month
- for an enemy above 1,000, use the concept of *ko-kyo* for the day or time

---

91 The directions for *kyo* in this example are dragon and snake.
92 The directions for *kyo* in this example will be horse and ram.
93 The original states rat. It has been corrected here.

A theory from the *Taibaiyinjing* manual[94] holds that the earthly branch that corresponds with Taisaijin[95] and the one next to it are *ko* and the opposite two positions are *kyo*.

The *Bubishi* [illegible text] says that for the year, month, day and time the position for the god Taisaijin and the position before that will be *ko* and the positions directly opposite will be *kyo*. For example, if it is a year of rat, the boar and rat will be *ko* and the snake and horse will be *kyo*. For the other signs, the same principle should be applied.

THE CONCEPT OF ŌSŌ

Ōsō includes five phases:

- *ō* 王 – flourishing
- *sō* 相 – harmony
- *shi* 死 – death
- *shū* 囚 – capture
- *rō* 老 – hibernation

By using the above concept and allocating seasons to the phases, the strength of each season can be known:

- *Ō* and *sō* are strong phases
- *Shi* is a weak phase
- *Shū* is a weak phase but with a little strength within it
- *Rō* is a fatigued and tired phase

---

94   A Chinese military book of the eighth century.
95   Taisaijin is one of the Hasshojin – the Eight Commander Gods. They are the foundation of a divination system based in Onmyōdō. This god remains in the same direction as the earthly branch of that year. For example, if it is the year of the rat then the god Taisaijin will remain in the direction of the rat, which is north.

ŌSŌ ALLOCATIONS BY SEASON

Spring:

- *ō* – east
- *sō* – south
- *shi* – inter-cardinal points
- *shū* – west
- *rō* – north

Summer:

- *ō* – south
- *sō* – inter-cardinal points
- *shi* – west
- *shū* – north
- *rō* – east

In the *doyō* period:[96]

- *ō* – inter-cardinal points
- *sō* – west
- *shi* – north
- *shū* – east
- *rō* – south

Autumn:

- *ō* – west
- *sō* – north
- *shi* – east
- *shū* – south
- *rō* – inter-cardinal points

Winter:

- *ō* – north

---

96 There were four eighteen-day *doyō* periods each year. They divided the four seasons from each other.

- *sō* – east
- *shi* – south
- *shū* – inter-cardinal points
- *rō* – west

From these lists above you can discover the power of each season. The following is an example for spring:[97]

East [which is of Wood]. Everything will be in accord as spring is also associated with Wood. This is of the phase of *ō* – flourishing.

South [which is of Fire]. Spring is associated with Wood, and this is a relationship of generation. This is of the phase of *sō* – harmony.

Inter-cardinal points [which are of Earth]. Wood conflicts with Earth. This is of the phase of *shi* – death. The season overcomes the direction, because Wood overcomes Earth.

West [which is of Metal]. This will be conflicting with Wood. It is of the phase of *shū* – capture.

North [which is of Water]. This will be in generation. It is of the phase of *rō* – hibernation.

The rest can be deduced from the lists above.

There are many other theories about *ko-kyo* and *ōsō*, but they are not described here.

The following are the ways to apply *ko-kyo* and *ōsō* in our school.

The ideogram for *ko* 孤 can also be pronounced as *minashigo* – orphan – and therefore means 'fatherless'. If you match together the Ten Celestial Stems with the Twelve Earthly Branches, starting with the combination of *kinoe* and rat, then you will find that the last two earthly branches, dog and boar, are left without any celestial stems assigned to them. Therefore, the celestial stems of *kinoe* and *kinoto* – which are the 'fathers' to rat and ox – should be assigned and used a second time for the 'fatherless children' dog and boar. Consequently, the

---

97 This section explains how you can use the concept of *ōsō* to identify the most auspicious and inauspicious directions in each season. In the example, east is the most auspicious direction in spring.

signs dog and boar are designated to the concept of *ko* [because they do not have their own celestial stems].

For the celestial stems *hinoe, tsuchinoe, kanoe* and *mizunoe*, the direction of *kyo* is where the celestial stem and the earthly branch conflict with each other.

A phase of *ō* [which is a phase of flourishing power] occurs where an earthly branch and a celestial stem have a relationship of generation with each other.

A phase of *sō* [which is a phase of harmony] occurs where the celestial stem is of an element that corresponds to the element of the earthly branch. For example, *hinoe* and horse, which are both of Fire.

For divining the hour, use the celestial stem of that day.

You can divine for auspicious and inauspicious times and directions by considering the above concepts and their opposites.

首途ノ肴組之事

Kadoide no sakanagumi no koto

THE ARRANGEMENT OF CELEBRATION FOOD BEFORE DEPARTURE FOR WAR

On the day of departing for war perform this ritual celebration towards the east. A set meal should be presented on a *sanbō* or *ashiuchi* tray.

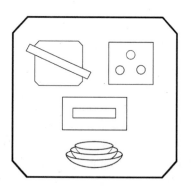

On the right are three *kachiguri* – chestnuts.
On the left is one or two slices of *uchiawabi* – abalone.

In the centre is a strip of *konbu* – kelp.

On the lower edge of the plate are three *sake* cups of unglazed pottery.

The method for eating the above

The first step:

Take up the abalone and say the following celebration:

打鮑

uchiawabi

Our allied forces will immediately defeat the enemy.[98]

Then drink some *sake*.

The second step:

Celebrate eating and then say:

勝栗

kachiguri

Our allied forces shall never fail to gain victory.[99]

The third step:

Concentrate intensely on the idea that a ritual celebration from a pure heart has been carried out and then drink *sake* in the style of *sansankudo* – the way of three cups.[100] Do not draw the *sake* cup towards your face. Then when the ritual is finished stand up first on the left foot and, when having stood up, throw the tray behind you and depart briskly.

---

98 There is a small play on words here: as well as being the first part of the word for abalone, *uchi* means 'to strike' and therefore 'to strike down the enemy'.

99 Another play on words: *kachi* means 'victory' and makes the chestnut a symbol for victory over the enemy.

100 Pouring three times for each of the three cups, which adds up to nine pours in total. Nine is the highest, and most important, *yō* number.

Commentator two

An *ashiuchi* tray can also be called an *ashiuchizen*. For aristocrats, the edge around the tray should be two *sun* in height.

'Celebrating towards the east' means to face the sun. When the sun comes around to the south [as it is no longer sunrise], then face the direction of dragon, snake or horse.

Konbu kelp specifically means *arame – Eisenia bicyclis*.

Uchiawabi – beaten abalone – is so called because the abalone is flattened on stone. When eating *uchiawabi*, start at the thinner end and work your way towards the wider end.

Hold the cup with the middle finger and the ring finger. As this is not as easy as the normal way of holding a cup, it will force you to keep your mind calm.

Concerning *sansankudo*, the nine pours of *sake*, the first three pours represent the three powers of:

- *ten* 天 – heaven
- *chi* 地 – earth
- *jin* 人 – man

The second three pours represent the three virtues of:

- *chi* 智 – wisdom
- *jin* 仁 – benevolence
- *yū* 勇 – courage

The last three pours represent the whole:

- *sho* 初 – beginning
- *chū* 中 – middle
- *shū* 終 – end

Have a server pour the *sake* three times in each cup. Just after it is poured the third time, drink it.

Do not bring the *sake* cup towards you, put your mouth to the cup to drink the *sake*. Then, when you stand up, stand up on the left leg because the left is *yō*; this is also called *kachiashi* – the winning leg. This is an old custom.

DEPARTING FOR WAR

During *shutsujin* – moving out to war – depart from the gate on horseback and do not have women in attendance or let them see you from the rear as you move away. Also, do not look back within the first one or two *chō* as this is extremely unlucky. It is also said that if you have concerns in mind you should retighten the saddle girth and your own *obi*-belt and then pat the horse with a riding crop – this is made from the nandina plant. Ride out and chant the following with clenched teeth:

十方世界魔利支天北斗大晨皆来守護急々如律令
Jippō sekai marishiten hokuto taishin kaiki shugo kyūkyūnyoritsuryō.

If you depart in this manner, ill fate will disappear and good luck will increase. Make sure to start your ride out when the horse is about to step forward with its front left leg.

Tradition says the above method is an ancient way. You do not always have to set out to war in this manner; it depends on the situation. That being said, when you deviate from this way, there are things that need to be considered.

Commentator one

Having women present when departing for war is to be avoided because the *chi* of *in* will mask the *chi* of *yō* and destroy it.[101]

Shiba Sakyō-dayū Ujitsune, when going to war to the west of Japan, took women to the war. This is criticized in the thirty-eighth volume of the *Taiheiki* with reference to the ancient episode of General Li of Baling.

The nandina tree [which is used as a riding crop] is of *yō* and its fruits look like fire.

Taishin-sei is the name connected to the constellation Ursa Major. Common folk do not worship *Taishin-sei* and it cannot be properly worshipped without

---

101 Women were considered to be of *in* while men were of *yō*, meaning that women will negate the masculinity of the war troop.

knowing the correct traditions of *ōboshi*. It is known that Yamamoto Kansuke used this at the battle of Toishi.

Only a person of great power and high virtue can go against such principles. Those who are inexperienced should follow ancient customs and there are things to keep in mind when using such principles, which shall be transmitted orally.

Commentator two

When departing for war, retighten the saddle girth and also retighten your own outer *obi*-belt. This is to refresh your mind.

A rod of the nandina plant is not for whipping a horse but is used for purifying your mind, as nandina is a wood which removes any impurities. It is of *yō*. The crop should be held with the right hand when the lord inspects decapitated heads. Also this wood is used when worshipping at a shrine.

One way to achieve harmony is to gather your people together and notify them of the rules. However, it is not practical to seek to achieve harmony only through rules. A general should know this and not dwell too much on rules because once your soldiers are united in harmony, principles will naturally become established. The essence of courtesy is to value harmony, which will lead to the awareness of principles and in the end such principles will penetrate everyone's mind.

A notable example of the tightening of the saddle girth came when Kajiwara Genta tightened his saddle girth while mounted at the battle of Minatogawa.

The spell given in the text above should be chanted by the lord-commander or another general, but should not be chanted by other people. Simply concentrate intensely on the idea of defeating the enemy. The word *jippō* in the chant means 'every inch and every direction of heaven and earth'.

Details on the nandina rod are given in the scroll *Muchi no Maki*.

Concerning the horse, use *kachiashi* – left leg first.

The nandina plant is of *yō* and bears red fruit like fire. This is considered as a rod to be used when worshipping at a shrine.

Chant the above spell with clenched teeth. There are thirty-two teeth in the mouth, but the number two is a number of *kyo* [which is negative]. Adding the clench makes thirty-three [which is positive].

The above are the procedures to be followed when an order for war is given. Do not violate such principles unless you have integrity. There are traditions called *muhō no tsutae* – traditions for being without principle – which are to be transmitted orally. Know that if you break any of the rules, you may have to justify yourself later on and do so without hesitation in speech. Sometimes judgement is required as to which of the rules to use or not. Shinkun, the Great Lord Tokugawa Ieyasu, once took a bath just before leaving for war and departed while still donning his armour.

CHAPTER THIRTEEN

When marching to a distant province there is no need to wear your armour; instead march forth in your *haori* jacket. However, at times you may have to don your armour and wear your jacket over it. Also, sometimes your armour will be in its container and should be carried behind you. Alternatively, it can be kept with the helmet container and both can be carried together. Have your spear carried on the right and your armour carried on the left; keep these two close at hand. The helmet may be carried on the *kabutodate* – helmet stand.

Commentator one

Even while marching over a long distance, always keep your spear and armour close by in case of emergency. It is deemed a grave dishonour not to have them at hand when such a time arises, and if this happens you will gain a reputation for unpreparedness. Unpredictable situations do not happen when you anticipate them but only when you do not.

Commentator two

In the 'Substantial and Insubstantial' chapter of the *Art of War* it states: 'Appear at points which the enemy must hasten to defend; march swiftly to places where you are not expected.'

具足着様之事
Gusoku kiyō no koto
HOW TO DON ARMOUR
The first stage:

1　*hadagi* 膚着 – under-kimono
2　*momohiki* 股引 – light trousers
3　*habaki* 脛巾 – gaiters
4　*waranjigake* 草鞋懸 – foot coverings

The second stage:
1　*suneate* 臑當 – greaves
2　*haidate* 佩楯 – thigh protectors
3　*gusoku* 具足 – full cuirass
4　*kurijime* 繰締 – armour-securing cords
5　*uwaobi* 上帯 – outer *obi*
6　*hachimaki* 鉢巻 – headband
7　*hōate* 頬當 – faceguard
8　*kabuto* 兜 – helmet
9　*koshiate* 腰當 – sword clasp
10 *ōgi* 扇 – fan
11 *sashimono* 指物 – banner
12 *sai* 采 – war baton

The above are called *jūni-yoroi* – the twelve stages of armour. Items should be donned in this order. There are various other ways, such as *haya-gusoku no kiyō*, 'fast and simplified donning', and *tsuri-gusoku no shiyō*, 'suspended armour'.

Commentator one

Concerning *tsuri-gusoku no shiyō*, armour should be suspended so that it reaches the breast.

Old customs on how a lord should wear armour are found in the ancient document *Azuma Kagami*. When Minamoto no Yoritomo held a memorial service at Shōchōjuin temple, all the warriors of Kamakura attired themselves in fine garments and gathered together. The accompanying brave warriors including Chiba and Koyama joined the procession and the ceremony was conducted with a solemn air. Koyama Gorō Munemasa held the lord's sword, Sasaki Shirō Takatsuna the lord's armour and Aikō Saburō had an arrow nocked to Yoshitsune's bow. While the lord and the procession were inside the temple, Wada Yoshimori and Kajiwara Kagetoki waited outside the gate. When the lord went into the temple hall, Chiba Taneyori advanced and held the footwear the lord took off. Takatsuna waited in the front area with the lord's armour. Some people complained that he had the lord's thigh protectors positioned incorrectly. Takatsuna's pageboy informed him of this, at which he became furious and said: 'If an emergency arises and I need to help the lord don his armour, I can hand the thigh pieces to the lord immediately. Anyone who criticizes me for this is unaware of the old ways.'

[Further information about the above account:]
Wada Yoshimori was the chief administrator of the Kamakura shōgunate.
Kajiwara Kagetoki was the deputy chief administrator of the Kamakura shōgunate.
The event described took place on the twenty-fourth day of the tenth month of Bunji 1 (1185).

膚着
Hadagi
UNDER-KIMONO
This should be secured with strings.

Commentator one
The strings go from the back and tie at the front.

股引
Momohiki
LIGHT TROUSERS
These should preferably overlap the under-kimono.

Commentator one

There are two kinds: *kukuri momohiki* – secured leggings; and *saru momohiki* – pant type. Either will suffice.

脛巾
Habaki
GAITERS

These should be placed under the greaves.

Commentator one

Gaiters are fixed with strings or buttons.

草鞋懸
Waranjigake
FOOT COVERINGS

These should be put on under the gaiters.

Commentator one

Use *karamushi-zashi* cloth, details of which can be found in the scroll *Heigu Yōhō*.

臑當
Suneate
GREAVES

The strings should be tied loosely enough to allow flexibility but not too loosely. When you are in a marsh they should be removed.

Commentator one

Jūōgashira, greaves with knee guards, are desirable for mounted warriors, while standard *shino-suneate* greaves are for warriors on foot.

佩楯

Haidate

THIGH PROTECTORS

These should be placed under the *kusazuri* – tassets. The strings should be wrapped around the back of the armour and tied at the front.

Commentator one

Thigh protectors are attached with *kozaruo* strings.

Commentator two

Sometimes *ita-haidate* – single-plated thigh protectors – are used. These offer the benefit of being quick to remove during battle.

繰締

Kurijime

ARMOUR STRINGS

These should be tightened to the appropriate extent and tied off. The body armour should be secured with these cords.

Commentator one

These are cords used to secure the body armour.

上帯

Uwaobi

OUTER SASH

This should be tightened but still allow flexibility. If it is over-tightened it will be unbearable to wear, even for a single moment.

Commentator one

Secure both your long and short swords with this outer sash.

From Yoshitsune's war poems:

上帯をつよくしむれば暫も居られざりける物としるべし

If the uwaobi *is secured too tightly, be aware that you cannot bear it for even a short while.*

鉢巻

Hachimaki

HEADBAND

There are three ways of knotting the headband:

- *benkei-musubi* 辨慶結 – the knot of Benkei
- *eboshi-musubi* 烏帽子結 – as with the *eboshi* hat
- *hana-musubi* 花結 – the flower knot

Oral traditions exist for these.

Commentator one

The method for tying a headband is described in detail in the scroll *Heigu Yōhō*. According to the *Kōyō Gunkan*, at the battle of Kawanakajima, Uesugi Kenshin had his hair in a *katsura-musubi* style, which seems to be the same as the *hana-musubi* mentioned above. The *ena-musubi* and other knots are explained in detail in another writing.

Commentator two

Concerning the headband:

- The *benkei-musubi* style involves tying at the front in a *jika-musubi* knot.
- The *eboshi-musubi* knot is at the rear and has the ends hanging down.
- The *hana-musubi* knot should be on the left side with the ends hanging down.

頰當

Hōate[102]

FACEGUARD

There are no special comments for this item. It should be secured with the *shinobi-no-o* helmet cord. When the helmet is taken off it is attached to the *takahimo* shoulder cords,[103] the faceguard is attached to the waist. The methods are orally transmitted.

冑

Kabuto

HELMET

It is desirable to look upwards while putting your helmet on. There are various ways of knotting the helmet cords.

Commentator one

The helmet should be donned with your face turned upwards.

Commentator two

To face upwards while donning your helmet is considered auspicious as this posture is fitting for a warrior. What's more, facing upwards allows the helmet cord to be tied quickly. There are various ways to tighten the following cords:

---

102 In the Koga transcription this is referred to as 面頰 *menpō*.
103 The *takahimo* is the cord connecting the chest plate to the back plate.

- *shinobi-no-o*
- *kasa-no-otsuke*
- *mio-no-yatsuke*
- *hankai-garami*

These teachings are all transmitted in another scroll.

腰當
Koshiate
SWORD CLASP
There are certain ways to attach the cords of the long and short swords. Also there are ways to attach the cords of the *koshiate*. There is a certain way to wear the swords without this sword belt, but this is orally transmitted.

Commentator one
How to wear the strings of the sword clasp is one of the things that should be taught when helping someone to don armour.

Commentator two
All of the oral traditions about sword clasps should be conveyed when helping someone to put on armour.

There are fifteen ways to secure the swords without a sword clasp.

扇
Ōgi
FOLDING FAN
There are no special comments for this. Some schools prefer the fan to be worn upside down, with the cord end facing upwards.

Commentator one

There is an alternative way of inserting the fan upside down. The 'string' here means the *udenuki-no-o* wrist strap.[104] How to make a fan is described in the *Dansen no Maki* scroll.

指物
Sashimono
BANNER

There are certain ways to secure the cord. Apart from this there are no special comments to be given.

Commentator one

Details are in the *Kōketsu* scroll.

采
Sai
WAR BATON

There are no special comments for this. Details are found in the *Saihai no Maki* scroll.

鞭
Muchi
RODS

There are ways for wearing *muchi* rods. However, it is for the commander to carry a *sai* war baton and for other warriors to carry the rod. This rod should be worn on the left towards the back.

---

104 The Koga transcription states *uchinuki-no-o.*

[Further points on the above items:]

Sometimes the helmet is attached to either the left or the right shoulder cord when it is removed from the head. Either left or right is fine. The ancient method is to put it on the left side. If the helmet is not secured properly, it will not be held tight and will wobble. No further comments for the way of attaching it to the right side are needed. Securing the helmet in this way is difficult if there is no *shōji-no-ita* shoulder brace attached to the shoulder cord. The main thing is to secure your helmet in a way that suits you. It is good to carry on the old ways of dealing with military gear, but if they bring you little benefit then discontinue them.

Commentator one

Tying your helmet on the left is called *yoichi-gake* – the way of Yoichi. This name comes from an incident during the Kenryaku era [1211–1214]. During the battle of Yashima in the Genpei War, Nasu no Yoichi Munetaka shot an arrow at the target of a fan [on a boat] with his helmet slung in this manner.

It is said that Kakumei was the secretary to Kiso Yoshinaka and he slung his helmet over the right shoulder when he wrote a petition to the Hachiman shrine in Shinohara.

Details on rods are in the *Muchi no Maki* scroll.

Remember, a new method that has merit is better than an old custom that does not.

Commentator two

How to construct a war baton and how to tie the cords are transmitted in another writing.

CHAPTER FOURTEEN

馬装束之次第

Umashōzoku no shidai

THE ORDER IN WHICH TO ATTACH HORSE TACKLE

Below are listed the twelve items of horse gear. Their usage and purpose and the order in which to attach them are discussed in the scroll *Heigu Yōhō* and therefore this information has not been included here.

1 *kutsuwa* 轡 – bit
2 *kutsu* 履 – straw horseshoes
3 *maehabaki* 前脛巾 – greaves
4 *kura* 鞍 – saddle
5 *munagai* 胸掛 – chest band
6 *harubi* 腹帯 – saddle girth
7 *aori* 障泥 – saddle skirt
8 *abumi* 鐙 – stirrups
9 *bamen* 馬面 – face mask
10 *maeabumi* 前鐙 – forward stirrup
11 *ushiroabumi* 後鐙 – rear stirrup
12 *tottsuke-no-o* 取付之緒 – attaching cords

Commentator one
Details about the set manners and customs, including *kuragatame* – saddle-securing –are in the scroll *Heigu Yōhō*.

Commentator two
A decapitated head should be attached to the saddle using the *tottsuke-no-o*

cords. A head can be also attached to the saddle skirt. Designed for attaching a decapitated head, the *tottsuke-no-o* cords are about three *shaku* long and can be made of leather.

行列之事

Gyōretsu no koto

THE PROCESSION OF WAR

When marching in two columns, helmet-bearers should be in the centre and spear-bearers on the outside. If marching in a single column, the spear-bearer should be on the right as normal. When a marching army encounters a narrow path or bridge, it should form a single file; the person on the right should go ahead and the one on the left should move into line after them. Alternate like this in turn.

If you have to attend to something on the way, leave a servant in the procession while you, on horseback, take two or three other servants out of the column and attend to the matter as quickly as possible – then return to your original position. The general should give laws and orders concerning marching in columns, and then you should relay them to your servants.

Before marching, brief your servants about the most important aspects of the upcoming battle. Remember that when you approach the point where the enemy can be seen for the first time, a wave of uneasiness will move through your forces. At this time the servants will often disappear into the confusion but no matter how disturbing the situation becomes, do not move about in distress. If you retain a calm mind, then when an emergency arises you will not act in a disturbed manner. Command your servants firmly and order them not to leave your side.

Commentator one

'Procession' here means marching for a battle. Details are in the scroll *Heieki Yōhō*. If marching before a battle is not conducted in a strict manner, you will not gain victory in the battle itself. Therefore, the laws and orders given should be strictly observed. Other details about traditional customs on marching should be taught separately. Only the things each independent warrior should keep in mind are discussed here. Whether something needs to be done or whether nothing needs to be done, always avoid letting the procession break up in disarray. Never break the procession no matter what happens. Thus, the way of leaving a procession is to be laid out in the rules of the army.

The schools of Ōuchi-Ryū and Yamanoi-Ryū instruct that rules must be given regarding the following four points:

- thievery
- lewdness
- heavy drinking
- gambling

In order to prevent your servants from becoming separated, use passwords and identifying marks such as crests on jackets, scabbards and helmets. Make sure to arrange these fully beforehand. Passwords are a precaution against confusion on the battlefield. Similar situations can happen even at normal times.

CHAPTER FIFTEEN

TAKING UP BATTLE POSITIONS

When taking up position in an existing building, be careful about the section in which you stay overnight. When you arrive at such a location make sure to take a note of the four cardinal directions with a compass[105] and move around the area to check:

- steep and difficult places
- mountains
- rivers
- vegetable and paddy fields

If they are at a distance then enquire about this matter from the locals. It is a tradition to make sure that your horse recognizes each of your servants.

Commentator one

As mentioned earlier, a position taken on a mountain is called a *Go-jinjō*, while one on flat land is called a *go-jinba*. If a position is taken for several days, it is called a *jinsho*. Also, a *hatamoto* is where the general stays in position. The entire area is called a *go-jinchū* or *jinsho*. If in a battle[field] position, the place the lord stays is called the *go-honjin*, while if in a townhouse it is called the *go-shukujin*. The points mentioned here about staying in existing constructions have much in common with battle positions [anywhere]. Therefore, do not think they apply only to when the lord is taking up a position in a townhouse.

Understanding the cardinal points with a compass is an art you should gain at normal times. It is also required when you stay in lodgings while travelling. This is something *samurai* should keep in mind.

---

105 This may be read as magnet.

To ask local people for such information is called *kyōdō no hō.*
Lastly, horses are honest and remember things well.

SETTING UP WAR CURTAINS

When taking up position in an urban area, set up war curtains in front of the building in which you are staying. They should be placed one *ken* away from the house – stand spears and banners between the building and the curtains.

In a camp there should be separate ways for those moving up and down the camp while others stay in position.

Commentator one

War curtains should be set up inside of the buildings as well.

Commentator two

Curtains should normally be set about one *ken* in front of the construction but this distance may vary. In some schools, curtains should be set just outside the entrance of the building. In this case, spears, standards or so on should be placed outside of the curtains. In our school, curtains should be placed one *ken* from the building and spears or standards should be on the inside of the curtains. Washing horse's legs should also be done on the inside of the curtains. Curtains are meant to obscure the enemy's view, so it is a set way in our school to raise war curtains outside at a distance from the building.

Concerning separating parts of the army: in order to let the troops at the upper end of the camp move freely, hold the troops at the lower end, and vice versa. This is in accordance with camp principles.

The knot used for the above curtains should be the *hiramusubi* knot. Details are in the scroll *Maku no Maki.*

BUILDING A FIELD SHELTER

When taking up a position in a field, construct a shelter out of three bamboo posts and two sheets of tannin paper – this is an oral tradition. Provide a sitting mat for each person. Also, grappling hooks should be used to hang up equipment inside the hut.

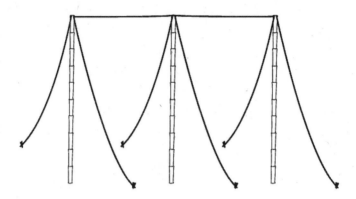

Diagram showing the construction of a field shelter.

Commentator one

Enza – sitting mats – are also called *anshiki*. The number of people occupying a hut can be known by counting these.

Commentator two

The use of sitting mats to check the number of people coming and going is called *anpu no narai* – the teaching of the sitting mat – in Kōshū-Ryū.

The *gaku-no-dō* is a cave-like hut where the bamboo-bundle guards and watch-fire guards are stationed. It is made as in the drawing below.

A *gaku-no-dō*.

This is made of bamboo.

The grappling hook is not a secret tool; it consists of a thin rope with a hook attached.

BUILDING A STABLE INSIDE A SHELTER

A stable should be situated on the left, with curtains called *umaya maku* – stable curtains – stretched out around it. Next a tool called a *dotsunagi*, which is a wood piece about three *shaku* long with an iron ring attached, should be driven into the ground as a point to tether the horses.

Commentator one

The method of constructing this stable is presumably from Kōshū-Ryū. Details are to be found in the scroll *Koyadori no Maki*.

Commentator two

The stable is located on the left side because the left side is more convenient. Stable curtains should be raised so as to prevent horses seeing into the distance ahead of them. The benefits of this are mentioned in detail in the scroll *Heigu Yōhō*.

DRAWING WATER

When you have arrived at the camp quarters draw water as soon as you can and eat some food as soon as possible.

Tradition says that breakfast should be made ready in the evening and the evening meal should be prepared in the morning. In midwinter use hot water to reheat your food.

Commentator one

Rice with hot water is useful not only for heating cold food but also for preventing shortness of breath. To have rice with hot water is always good for *samurai*.

Commentator two

Drawing water is always troublesome. When drawing water from a river, start downstream to avoid muddying the water further down.[106] Order the whole group to take turns drawing water. It is beneficial for meals to be prepared in advance so that you are prepared in case of an emergency. If you think that your turn to draw water will come too late, move to get water before the order is given. Rice with hot water is good for breathing, so always eat this way.

PROTECTING AGAINST THE COLD

Do not take off archers' gloves during the campaign in order to defend yourself against the cold or the heat. When travelling on horseback over a long distance, it is good to dismount and walk from time to time. If you remain in the saddle for extended periods of cold weather, your hands will suffer from chilblains and frostbite and will become swollen and this will impair your control over the reins. There are also medicines you should use to protect you from the cold – these are discussed in detail in another scroll.

---

106 If the drawing of water starts upstream, the churning of the mud will cloud the water and those drawing downstream will draw dirty water.

Commentator one

Archers' gloves should be worn properly at all times. It is detrimental to take them off and put them on again.

In some schools to dismount and walk is known as *sakuragari tazuna* – to view the cherry blossoms with reins in hand.[107]

In battle, Ōta Mochisuke Nyūdō Dōkan noticed that the soldiers under his command had fingers numb with cold, so much so that they could hardly hold on to their reins. He ordered them to tap the saddlebows with their hands. They followed this order and their blood circulation returned and they could again grip the reins. With this in mind, it appears that numbness is caused by a bad circulation of blood. This story has been noted here to illustrate this point.

Commentator two

Medicine for protection from coldness and heat is mentioned in the scroll *Gun'yaku Yōhō*.

MAINTAINING ADEQUATE FOOD SUPPLY

It is said that if you are lacking rations, you should eat leather and items such as saddle skirts, arrow quivers, tree bark, leaves and grasses, or whatever else is available at the time. Alternatively, cattle and horses can be eaten. The above are all used as temporary measures for warding off hunger. To avoid running short of rations in the first place, save food stocks in advance. When defending a castle for a long period, this problem can be hard to avoid. Be aware that you cannot succeed militarily if you have to live in such a manner. There is a recipe used for food, the so-called *hyōrōgan* – hunger pills; details of which can be found in another scroll. I have tried this medicine, but it is not good enough to solve the problem of hunger. Therefore, stock up on food rations beforehand.

---

107 櫻ガリ手綱 – found in Ogasawara-Ryū. To dismount and walk while taking a view of the surroundings.

Chapter Fifteen

Commentator one

A secret recipe for dried rice: carry dried rice with the amount of one third of dried bonito flakes mixed in with it.

Another secret recipe: dry and solidify tofu lees and soak them in water before eating.

Other recipes are found in the scroll *Gun'yaku Yōhō*. Also, use the dried stems of the taro plant as thin ropes, as these can double up as food if necessary.

Commentator two

There is another important point about rations called *tenkōchimei*. However, be aware that these skills are just for one, two or three days at the most. Even if you manage to survive on these recipes know that you will be exhausted and of little use in battle. Since ancient times it has often been the case that due to the shortage of rations, grass, bark, ox or horse meat have been eaten, and various medicines called *hyōrōgan* have been invented. These short-term measures to stave off hunger can be particularly beneficial if your castle is being besieged and reinforcements are expected to arrive within two or three days. There is also a way to make a thin rope of yam stem so you can eat it if necessary.

CHAPTER SIXTEEN

野中ニテ水ヲ尋ル事

Nonaka nite mizu wo tazuneru koto

SEARCHING FOR WATER IN THE FIELD

Use the following methods to find water in a field:

- observing the location of waterweeds
- burying the feather of a crow
- cutting wild grapevines
- squeezing water out of grasses

The above are oral traditions. There are ways to drink water from wells and water found in the wild, but do not drink without care, even if thirst is upon you.

Commentator one

'Waterweeds' means those plants that grow near water, including mallows, arrowheads,[108] Java water dropwort,[109] sweet flags, etc. Search for water by looking for these types of plants.

Dig a hole and insert a crow's feather into the ground and cover over with straw mats or such. Leave it until morning and if dew drops have formed upon it then water is nearby.

Cut grapevines into pieces five or six *sun* in length. Leave a fistful of them in a cup with the cut ends inside the vessel and water will collect within.

Put green grass in a bowl and grind and crumple it so that green water can be collected. Put this green water in a vessel and leave it to stand, then drink the supernatant fluid. It will momentarily relieve thirst yet it will not sustain you.

---

108 *Sagittaria trifolia.*
109 *Oenanthe javanica.*

When you are thirsty after strenuous activity, if you drink truly clear water from a river or any other source, you may die a sudden death. Therefore, place even a small amount of soil or sand in it.

Mix ginger with *shōkisan* medicine,[110] powder it and ingest in order to counteract water poisoning. This method should be used during normal times as well.

Commentator two

Place a crow feather into the ground and cover it with straw mats or so on. Leave it until morning and if dew drops have formed upon it then water is nearby. Then dig a well to find the water vein. Dig about two *shaku* down.

As well as grapevines, loofa[111] vines can also be used.

To counteract poisoned water,[112] roast red adzuki beans and put them in the water.

In the Gushi region of ancient China, Geng Gong positioned his army to defend Shule castle because it had a water source nearby. However, the Huns blocked the stream. Geng Gong had a well dug but even after digging fifteen *jō* water still did not well up. All his men suffered from thirst and drank the juice of horse manure. Geng Gong dressed himself properly and bowed twice to the well and prayed for his men. At that point a great amount of water sprang up and he had men draw water and raise it to show to the enemy that a divine wonder had been achieved.

OBTAINING RICE FROM PILLAGED RICE PLANTS

In order to take rice itself from pillaged rice plants, dig a hole in dry, hard ground and place fresh plants within it, make a fire of this and let it harden. Next, place it all on a saddle skirt, thresh a bundle of it with a wooden club and strip off the ears. In addition to this there are various ways to obtain salt, *miso*

---

110 A common medicine of the time.
111 *Luffa cylindrica.*
112 i.e. naturally bad water, not deliberately poisoned water.

and other foodstuffs. Details are mentioned in the scroll *Gun'yaku Yōhō* and are omitted here.

夜討火事地震可心得事

Youchi kaji jishin kokoroeru beki koto

NIGHT ATTACKS, FIRES AND EARTHQUAKES

Keep in mind that night attacks may be launched when there is a fire – for example, one that results from an earthquake. Also, night attacks often cause fires.

Commentator one

There are appropriate times for night attacks. That is, if you attack at the optimum moment, you can defeat a large-numbered enemy with a smaller number. You can survive and even have a narrow escape when death was thought as inevitable.

Appropriate times for night attacks are:

- when it is windy
- in the middle of an arbitration
- when it is windy and rainy
- when enemy reinforcements arrive
- on the first day of battle
- when a castle is about to fail in defence
- after a large battle
- after a substantial victory

Traditionally these are times when the enemy will not be expecting an attack. However, both sides have now learned to be careful in these situations. Therefore, in the present day, you will need to be creative and flexible to outwit the enemy. It is important to know when you are not expected to attack and to observe when the enemy is negligent. A night attack should be carried out with as much nimbleness as possible. Also, there are set teachings concerning passwords, identifying marks, how to check your men, and so on. In the *Taiheiki* chronicle, it can be seen that the *tachisuguri isuguri* method was used. This involves instructing soldiers to take a certain posture – such as standing or sitting – while giving passwords, in order to identify infiltrators. Teachings on the spaces between camp or fortress gates,[113] passwords and identifying marks are all given to prevent the enemy from following and becoming mixed in with your own men. Choose competent warriors to move out on night attacks or you will not advance and retreat freely. A large attack party should be avoided. Fires especially occur when:

- the enemy is approaching to attack or when retreating
- a castle is falling
- a night attack is taking place

If an army sets fire to its own property it is called *jiyaki* – self-burning; or it may also be called *daimatsu* – the large torch. In the *Heike Monogatari*, the *Jōsuiki* document and other writings it says that Minamoto no Yoshitsune performed this at the battle of Mikusayama. It is a tactic commonly used when attacking an enemy province. However, if done without care, it can be counter-productive; this will depend on the situation.

According to tradition:

A 'scorched-earth policy'[114] should be adopted in a land governed by a strong general, while it should be avoided if your side has driven a weak general into a corner and won a victory.

Thunder and earthquakes are natural phenomena and are difficult to predict. However, you have no need to fear earthquakes if you avoid rocky mountain areas, foothills, the coast, the edges of water bodies or streams or the inside of buildings. Thunder happens often and is frequently used in tactics. For example, if thunder happens to coincide with a brave warrior of your side being killed or the enemy setting fire to a shrine or temple, you can use this to make up a legend with a moral that will influence your people.

---

113 升形ノ習 *masugata no narai*. Castles have an enclosed area between gates – e.g. between the outer gate and the gate beyond. This creates a 'killing zone'.

114 Here, a 'scorched-earth policy' means to destroy everything.

In the *Jōsuiki* record, Minamoto no Yoshihira is said to have transformed into thunder when his enemy Taira no Kiyomori was worshipping at a waterfall. A similar episode concerning Minamoto no Yoshisada is found in the *Taiheiki* chronicle. And there is also the case of Sugawara no Michizane.

Commentator two

The enemy may take advantage of fire to launch a night attack. Fire may occur when an earthquake happens because the shaking of buildings may cause torches and so on to get out of control. Sometimes the night attacks themselves may cause fire because the attackers may set fires. In the latter case, divide your men into two groups: one to fight the enemy, and one to put out the fires, including torches which have been used in the night attack and abandoned by the enemy. Details are found in the scroll *Gunshū Yōhō*.

The three categories of night attack:

- A night attack conducted with ten or twenty people is called a *yogomi* – intruders at night.
- A night attack conducted with one or two hundred people is called a *youchi* – night attack.
- If the attacking force consists of an entire army, the attack is called a *yoikusa* – night war.

夜討城攻之時札ヲ持事

Youchi shirozeme no toki fuda wo motsu koto

CARRYING A NAME TAG DURING A NIGHT ATTACK OR CASTLE ASSAULT

The tag should be small and have your name, including your *nanori* – familiar name. Sometimes it should have where you are from written on the back. Depending on the situation, you may leave the tag in an area you have just attacked.

Commentator one

At the siege of Ōsaka castle, Ban Dan'emon took many name tags with him during night attacks. Likewise, it is a tradition to take a lot of tags for when attacking a castle. The intention is to leave them here and there to show where you have been.

Commentator two

The same thing should be done when attacking a castle. You should leave a name tag as proof that you fought there. Include the place and province you come from and your name. At the siege of Ōsaka castle, Yoneda Kenmotsu and Ban Dan'emon were commanders. Yoneda had many arrows with the name 'Yoneda' written on them before they were shot. Ban had wooden tags that said 'This night raid was led by Ban Dan'emon and scattered them along the way, which made the twenty-one people in his squad famous.

合戦之時矢道事

Kassen no toki yamichi no koto

UNDERSTANDING THE TRAJECTORY OF ARROWS IN BATTLE

Have a good understanding of where arrows are likely to fall. For example, enemy arrows will be directed at the following places:

- where good warriors have taken up position
- where people are gathering in numbers
- where warriors are making a determined advance
- in the case of a castle siege, where people are standing in front of each turret

Remember these positions and try to avoid them.

Commentator one

Those who are experienced are required to know *yamichi* – the path of arrows. However, be aware that your resulting behaviour may be misconstrued as cowardice.

At the siege of Ōsaka castle, Okamoto Hansuke understood the path of arrows.

The concept of the path of arrows can also be used in man-to-man combat. If the opponent is formidable or of colossal strength, do not fight him by grappling but rather observe and make an assessment of him. There is the episode of Manabe Gorōemon Nyūdō Shinnyū of Kishū, who was held in esteem for this concept.

Warriors wearing distinctive armour should be accompanied by a large number of people, not just one or two, when advancing. This is because there will be shooting from every turret tower at the beginning of a battle.

Commentator two

The path of arrows concept is also used in one-to-one combat. A tradition says that if the enemy is strong and powerful, do not grapple straightaway but instead assess them before fighting.

Arrow and musket shots are targeted towards the middle of a formation and the sides may be outside of the range of the path of arrows.

There is a low possibility of being shot if you stick to the corners of castles.[115]

---

115 This could also be read as you and your comrades scattering to every corner of a castle.

CHAPTER SEVENTEEN

出陣合戦場詞之事

Shutsujin kassenba kotoba no koto

CONCERNING THE LANGUAGE FOR DEPARTURE FOR WAR OR FOR ON A BATTLEFIELD

Those at the front may talk to those in the rear, but those in the rear should not answer. Weak words should be avoided in situations of *sukedashi* – fighting to assist someone – and when asking someone to be a witness. For example, *makeru*, meaning 'to lose', can be uttered, but the word *makemajiki*, 'should not lose', must be avoided.

Commentator one

Unacceptable words in a battle camp and on campaign were listed earlier. Here, the following are those words you should keep in mind when departing for war and when fighting on a battlefield.

If someone at the front calls out to someone at the rear, 'Sir [insert name], please move forward', then the person who is being addressed should not answer to confirm that they will advance, they should just move. Also, remember that if you offer to perform *sukedachi* – fight to assist someone – it is most likely that the person will not accept the offer.

Words concerning acting as a witness will vary according to the situation. Generally, many weak words exist, such as:

- *fumu* フム – to tread on
- *nageru* ナゲル – to throw, or give up
- *itameru* イタメル – to hurt
- *komarasete* コマラセテ – to harass
- *makemajiki* マケマジキ – should not lose

These words should be avoided, even at normal times. *Samurai* should simply make a cut or a stab if their patience has been exhausted. Ordering a servant to beat another with a staff is acceptable.

Commentator two

Even at normal times avoid talking in a manner similar to servants or lower people. This is mentioned in the scroll *Heika Jōdan*, therefore no further details are given here.

夜討山林方角之事

Youchi sanrin hōgaku no koto

WHEN CONDUCTING A NIGHT ATTACK CONSIDER THE MOUNTAINS, FORESTS AND DIRECTIONS

You should understand:

- the moon
- the stars
- the mountains
- the forests
- the wind
- fire
- topography

If you move along a dangerous route or in a place you are not familiar with, move in stealth while using *shirushi noroshi* – marker fires.

Commentator one

If the moon is in the east on your way out, it will be in the west on your way back. If you see mountains or fire or feel the wind on the left on your way, then you will see or feel them on the right during your return. Also be aware that if you have ascended, then you will have to descend and so on.

The term *shirushi noroshi* mentioned above is to make and leave fire at several places.

Commentator two

It is often the case that you will lose your sense of direction when infiltrating an enemy province, particularly on a night attack, or in a mountainous or wooded area where you cannot see far ahead. Therefore, keep your eyes and mind attentive. There are teachings on the times of the rising and setting of the moon and its phases, the twenty-eight lunar mansions and the constellation Ursa Major. Take care in the mountains both when ascending and when descending.

Shirushi noroshi is to cut fuses of about four or five *sun* in length, insert them into bamboo sticks, light them and leave them at multiple places along your route.

At the battle of Mikusa, Yoshitsune wondered what to do as the night was so dark. He suggested that his companion Benkei should make a certain type of 'large torch'. By 'large torch', he actually meant setting fire to various buildings.

両陣對シテ合戦初ルト云事
Ryōjin taishite kassen hajimaru to iu koto
RECOGNISING THE START OF BATTLE

As often as a hundred times a day, the two sides may face off and look as if they are about to start fighting. Do not be alarmed at this. Both sides will advance and the *ashigaru* will move into position and shoot their muskets but more often than not close combat will not ensue. However, from the moment you step away from home, you should never drop your guard. Sometimes it will seem as if the battle is never going to begin, but events can turn quickly and combat may break out at any moment. It is also said that within three days after taking up a position, volleys of bullets will be shot. Therefore, do not become flustered at this. An army may fire off a volley of paper bullets to show that it has a large number of muskets. In addition, there will be lots of noise, such as the cries of those on night duty and also goading war cries – this may unsettle the inexperienced.

Commentator one

No one fighting a battle for the first time can show great skill as he will simply be preoccupied with the idea of fighting and have no grasp of the overall situation. In battle, take an overview – observe the *chi* and changes of situation, show good judgement and do not act without thinking. If the enemy is anxious to start battle, have your *ashigaru* go forward while you maintain a solid formation; this is done so that the enemy cannot make a successful attack. Remember that the enemy will most likely adopt the same tactic to counter an attack by your side. Neither army will commence battle until it is confident of victory. In former days, people used to be straightforward and honest and battles would proceed with righteousness. These days, people tend to be better at tactics and so victory does not depend on a single battle. This tendency has developed since the period of Nobunaga, who was from the Taira family. Before a battle actually starts, there may be numerous skirmishes, which will cause you to become tense multiple times each day. Be fully aware of this. Battles may actually start when they seem least likely to, because each side is trying to exploit the other's weak points. There will be no definite signal that a battle has started, even to the rank and file of your own side. Simply remain ready at all times and do not assume that a commotion is another false alarm. Do not allow yourself or any of your people to show negligence at any moment.

Those who are inexperienced are often surprised by the sound of muskets.

Tonoi-doki – night-duty cries – are used to demonstrate to the enemy the level of vigilance that your army maintains.

Sobiki-doki – goading war cries – are used in an attempt to lure the enemy out in order to observe if they are negligent or not.

合戦之次第

Kassen no shidai

THE PHASES OF BATTLE

Both sides will face off in formation, which will be followed by an exchange of musket and arrow fire between the *ashigaru*, after which the *ashigaru* from both sides will peel off to the left and right. At this point the *samurai* will dismount and form a body of men and rush to the advance. Both sides will move forward and *musha*-warriors from both sides will work their way to face each other. This stage is called the *yariba* – the field of spears. This will start when the two sides are approximately thirty *ken* apart, but this is not an absolute rule. When the first pair, one warrior from each side, meets then this is called the *ichiban-yari* – the first spear fight.

Commentator one

These phases of battle are concerned with the commencement of fighting and thereafter. There are important teachings on how your mind should be during these phases. There are also things to keep in mind for both advancing and retreating. Experienced and battle-hardened warriors should be used for the first phase of battle. During this phase, it is sometimes the case that mounted warriors should go on foot or be positioned to the rear of the footed warriors. Such decisions are to be made by the general.

The *hachikō* are the eight forms of achievement that warriors can attain on a field of battle. This subject has been discussed since the period of the warlord Takeda Shingen.

Commentator two

This text is concerned with the early phases of battle. There are very important points to keep in mind, including matters such as advancing and retreating. The first phase of battle is usually reserved for experienced warriors, and mounted warriors may dismount and become footed in some cases, or alternatively, mounted warriors may be placed behind footed warriors. When the two armies advance towards each other, they may sometimes approach with uncontrolled momentum. This results in *yariba* – duels on the field of spears; the distance for this is about thirty *ken*. At this distance the following will happen:

- *ichiban-yari* – first spear fight
- *niban-yari* – second spear fight
- *yarishita no kumiuchi* – grappling by the assistant to the victor of a spear fight

- *tachiuchi* – striking with a great sword

Other types of combat may also happen at this point.
　The three levels of achievement are:
- *jō* 上 – high
- *chū* 中 – medium
- *ge* 下 – low

These should be considered.

CHAPTER EIGHTEEN

According to tradition, the following are the *hachikō* – the eight forms of achievement:

一番鑓

Ichiban-yari

THE FIRST SPEAR FIGHT

When both sides take the formation of *hōshi*, the arrowhead formation, and the two lead men meet, this is *ichiban-yari* – the first spear fight. Whether to enter into a duel or not depends on the situation. It should be determined who achieved *uwa-yari* – upper spear – or *shita-yari* – lower spear – and whether there was an announcement of names or not.

Commentator one

Ichiban-yari may also be referred to as *senpō* – the initiator – although there have been no examples of this terminology since the older days. It is confirmed that it was used in the era of the thirteenth Ashikaga *shōgun* and at the time of Shingen, but it is not known when it was used for the first time.

The bravest warriors will position themselves at the point of the arrowhead formation.

The *yariba* stage normally occurs when the two armies are thirty *ken* apart. If someone passes the halfway point, the battle develops into *yariba wo toru* – fighting the spear duel. If combat does not ensue, this is described as *yariba wo torazu* – not fighting the spear duel. Whoever announces his name first should then say 'ichiban' – 'I am the first!'

Uwa-yari – upper spear – means that your spear is *under* the enemy's spear, while *shita-yari* – lower spear – means that your spear is on *top* of the enemy's.

The reason for this apparent contradiction is that if you attack first your spear will move under the enemy's and that is why it is called upper spear; similarly, if you move second, your spear will move over the top of the enemy's, thus it is called lower spear.[116]

Commentator two

You should never be without armour or spears. You are helpless without them when an emergency arises. If you do not have them in an emergency it will be most disgraceful.

Naga-yari – pikes – are used to make a 'fence' behind which musketeers and archers position themselves. To make a solid formation, lines of pikes should be placed at the front, while *mocha-yari* – spear warriors – are positioned at the sides.

二番鑓

Niban-yari

THE SECOND SPEAR FIGHT

This is the fight following the first spear fight. If warriors declare their names before engaging in the second spear fight, this is considered more prestigious than a first spear fight in which names were not declared. The idea of the upper and lower spear also applies to the second spear fight.

Commentator one

A first spear fight done *without* announcing a name is a lesser achievement than a second spear fight in which a name *has* been announced. The latter should be considered as the first *true* spear fight. First and second spear fights both employ the principles of upper or lower spear and whether to enter into duels or not.

---

116 'Upper' here refers to the person who moves first to get the 'upper hand'.

Commentator two

An example of a duelling situation is when the distance between the two armies is fifteen *ken*, and a warrior goes even one or two *ken* further than the halfway point towards the enemy and has a spear fight.

First and second spear fights do not often happen, as in many cases as soon as the two formations are set up and face off against each other, they begin to break down into *kuzuregiwa-no-yari* – spear-fighting amid confusion.

三番鑓
Sanban-yari

THE THIRD SPEAR FIGHT

[In addition to the above and not counted in the eight achievements is the third spear fight.] This rarely takes place. Sometimes in larger battles, *sanban-yari* – the third spear fight – happens spontaneously. Normally, just as the second spears have joined in combat, the rest of the forces will collide together. If the duelling area is relatively large then a third spear fight may occur, but as an achievement in itself it is not so prestigious.

Commentator one

A third spear fight is not such an impressive achievement and therefore is not included in the eight forms of achievement. However, it is sometimes recognized after a particularly large battle.

鑓下之高名
Yarishita no kōmyō

BEING ASSISTANT TO THE VICTOR OF THE SPEAR

This achievement involves taking a head at speed during the first or second spear fight. There are considerations for this topic. If the feat has been achieved using a great sword or halberd, the term *tsumeru*[117] – to deliver a finishing blow[118] – should be used. However, if a bow has been used, use the term *kotayuru* – to deliver a finishing shot. The soldier who has done this is rated as having attained the status of *yarishita no kōmyō* – assistant to the victor of the spear. This is called *yariwaki sandan* – the three ways to assist the spear.[119]

Commentator one

Yarishita no kōmyō is an achievement where a *samurai* who is not carrying a spear grapples with and decapitates an enemy or kills an enemy with a great sword or halberd while the first and second spear fights are underway.

Commentator two

This is an achievement done by a *samurai* without a spear, where during the first and second spear fights, he holds down and kills an enemy with his great sword or halberd, or any other weapon he might prefer.

The categories for this achievement are:

- great sword
- halberd
- bow
- musket

The greater the distance at which it is carried out, the lower the achievement.

In military language, to assist the spear with a great sword is known as *yariwaki wo tsumetari* – to fill the gap beside the spear; while to assist with the bow is known as *kotayuru* – to respond to the enemy.

---

117 The ideogram 結 used for this term in the Tōkyō transcription is presumably wrong. The one used in the Koga version is 詰, which seems to be correct.

118 In the Koga transcription the ideogram 詰 *tsumeru* is used. However, in the Tōkyō transcription the ideogram 結 *musubaru* is used.

119 The 'three ways' means by sword, by halberd or by bow.

組討

Kumiuchi

GRAPPLING AND STRIKING

There is a difference to be understood between grappling on horseback and fighting on foot. If you venture out on a mission of *ō-monomi* – mounted scouting – combat may erupt between you and the enemy. If you grapple while on horseback and you and your opponent fall to the ground and you succeed in killing the enemy in the end, it is considered a peerless achievement. When fighting on foot, both forces will enter into confusion and enter into sword-fighting, in which both sides will push against each other, to-and-fro, grappling and quickly snatching heads – again, this is considered as a peerless achievement. Grappling on horseback is thought to be less prestigious than combat on foot.

Commentator one

During *kumiuchi* – grappling – a mounted enemy should be pulled down. Sometimes you should wait for the enemy to dismount. There are many other kinds of grappling. Details are given in another scroll.

As well as mounted scouting, there is another kind called *ko-monomi* – scouting in a small group. Details are to be found in the scroll *Heieki Yōhō*. There are many cases where halberds and bows and arrows are used in such actions.

Do not become impatient and discard your spear so as to enter the fight with a great sword. At the battle of Mikatagahara, Arakawa Jin'emon and Daishi Gen'emon were killed because they discarded their spears.

Muskets are beneficial when acting as a *yariwaki* – assistant spear. When you shoot you cannot be sure to hit a specific person – in fact, you can hardly tell which of the enemy you have hit.

Commentator two

Details about large and small scouting groups are provided in the scroll *Heieki Yōhō*.

Achievements secured on horseback are regarded as inferior because they benefit from the strength of the horse itself. There are various points about spontaneous combat. When grappling with an opponent, it is better to force him off his horse.

Sometimes a fight may be started after dismounting; details of this are given in another scroll. Warriors are often injured during grappling on horseback.

一番乗

Ichiban-nori

BEING THE FIRST TO ARRIVE

This means to be the first to advance into a castle when attacking a fortress. Invaders who arrive at the same time as each other are called *ai-nori* – those who arrive together. If you are the second to start climbing the wall but you get your *sashimono* banner over the wall first, you are then classified as the first to advance. This achievement is considered equal to the achievement of *ichiban-yari* – the first spear fight. There is an oral tradition about *metsuke* – mental observation – in connection to this.

Commentator one

On one occasion Gotō Matabei achieved *ichiban-nori* by throwing his banner into the fortress first.

    Metsuke is to observe the layout of the castle in advance and pinpoint the best place to make your climb.

Commentator two

A notable example is that of Gotō Matabei, who once threw his banner into a castle in order to achieve *ichiban-nori*. In Takatō in the province of Shinshū, two men named Yamaguchi Koben and Sasa Seizō achieved *ai-nori* – those who arrive together.

    Concerning *metsuke*, observe the castle beforehand and mark the place where it is best to advance.

Sometimes a banner is thrown in yet not followed by the person who threw it because the situation may be extremely hectic with myriad men clamouring to be the first to enter. Therefore, the banner may be thrown in before the actual person gets in.

A poem states:

城攻ノ一番乗ハ他力ニテ鎗アハスルハジリキナリケリ

To be the first into a castle is not a position gained by strength alone
but by the situation around you, whereas combat with a spear requires strength.

殿リ [120]

Shingari

PROTECTING THE REAR GUARD DURING A RETREAT

If your army is waging a battle in an enemy province and has fallen into confusion, you may have to withdraw. *Samurai* who stay with the lord during the retreat have immense prestige, especially if for some reason the lord's horse cannot retreat. In this situation, give your horse to the lord while you attend on foot. A deed of extreme bravery is to return and retrieve a *sashimono* banner that has been dropped – someone who manages this is considered an *eiyū no bushi* – heroic warrior. Certification should be issued for such a feat and the certificate should say that 'the lord's aim was carried out'.

Commentator one

When a battle is in confusion it is difficult to make a retreat, even when you are alone. It is even more difficult to retreat while helping an injured man. In the *Taiheiki* chronicle and other records there are many accounts of this kind of achievement.

Staying by the lord is also a form of achievement. In the *Taiheiki* there is an account of Oyamada Takaie offering his horse to his lord, Nitta Yoshisada. This kind of behaviour is called *ō no migawari ni tatsu* – sacrificing yourself for the

---

120 The Koga transcription reads 殿之働 – *shingari no hataraki*.

king – and is regarded as similar though not identical to the act of *yaomote*, standing before the lord and taking arrows. Natsume Jirozaemon acted as a substitute for Lord Shinkun[121] and this kind of action is comparable to offering your horse to the lord – both demonstrate a rare loyalty.

The *Taiheiki* describes an episode where someone returns for his banner. Murakami Yoshiteru also performed this feat when Prince Taitō fled to Kumano.

The word *eiyū* from *eiyū no bushi* – heroic warrior – consists of two ideograms:
- *ei* 英 – to have victory over one thousand people
- *yū* 雄 – to have victory over ten thousand people

Commentator two
Generally, know that it is essential to act in this way when your army is in retreat and that you will receive a letter of approval for such actions. The citation 'the lord's aim was carried out' applies specifically to the feat of taking a banner back.

一人之殿

Hitori no shingari

DEFENDING THE RETREAT ALONE

This achievement involves assisting those who are injured and taking heads. When retreating from deep inside enemy territory and many of your allies have been killed or injured, then only great warriors can perform *hitori no shingari* – defending the retreat alone. This is to help an injured person who cannot retreat unaided, travelling back together while fighting an enemy who is in pursuit. It is considered equal to the achievement of the first spear fight, as noble intentions are as good as being first. If you discover that an excellent warrior from your side has been killed then take his head or have a servant decapitate him. *Bushi* who perform the above deeds are called *kaigaishiki mono* – warriors of mental ability and devotion.

---

121 Tokugawa Ieyasu.

Commentator one

Someone who retreats alone is regarded as a *yūshi* – brave warrior; this has been the case since ancient times. Retreating with an injured colleague while driving away an enemy in pursuit and offering your horse to the lord are considered different from retreating alone. To retreat taking an injured ally is even more difficult to achieve than the first spear fight, but should still be regarded as a slightly lower achievement.

When performing *shingari* – defending the retreat – brave warriors also decapitate a dead ally or have their servants do this. Make sure not to decapitate an ally without a witness present. If this is done without care by a young and unachieved man it may cause a problem at a later date, one which may be difficult to explain away. It is desirable to have a retainer of the killed warrior decapitate his master.

Words used to praise brave warriors are:

- *eiyū* – heroic
- *daigō* – immensely brave
- *kaigaishiki* – courageous

Commentator two

When performing *shingari*, sometimes you may be accompanied by a large number in the rear guard, but sometimes there may be only a small number. The type of *shingari* discussed here is when a brave warrior attends the lord deep inside enemy territory, spear-fighting with the pursuing enemy. If a good warrior is injured and has difficulty in retreating, one who is acting in *shingari* helps the injured man to retreat while fighting against the enemy who are in pursuit. Such deeds are truly courageous. *Shingari* is a difficult task to execute even with a large number of allies. He who does it singlehandedly should be regarded as one of the bravest warriors of all time. Helping an ally who is injured and who has difficulty in retreating, fighting with the enemy with spear in hand, being hunted, and having a retainer decapitate an ally who has been killed, these are all things done by an achieved warrior. The level of the intention may be considered even higher than that of a warrior who achieves the first spear fight. Be aware, when taking an ally's head it may provoke an objection at a later point, so it is desirable to have your retainer carry out the decapitation. It is different if a warrior of reputation does this.

The first spear fight is achieved in a state of bursting energy with many allies in support, while acting as rear guard is done in full consciousness. You need to understand the context of an achievement to appreciate its true value.

主君之矢表二立

Shukun no yaomote ni tatsu

STANDING BEFORE THE LORD AND TAKING ARROWS

This achievement is considered to be lesser than the *yari* achievements – careful judgement must be exercised in ranking the different achievements.

Commentator one

An example of this achievement can be found in the *Heike Monogatari*: during the Genryaku period (1184–1185), at the battle of Yashima, Satō Tsugunobu stood before Yoshitsune and took arrows and was killed. Although this sometimes occurred in ancient times, it does not happen today. However, it has been listed as one of the eight forms of achievements here.

Taking arrows is generally regarded as lower than the achievements by spear. Dying in battle can be difficult to achieve, yet it can also be easy. Especially in the Sengoku period, standing before the lord to take arrows and being killed in the process was not as difficult as surviving and going on to attain other achievements. It is also said that if a *samurai* needs to stand before his lord to take arrows to save the lord's life, then this reveals something that the lord has done wrong. A general should be very careful not to advance into arrow range in the first place. To stand before your lord and take arrows intended for him draws attention to the weakness of his tactics. Therefore, such an action may be intended as a means of questioning and correcting the lord's judgement.

Objections to the act of standing before the lord to take arrows:

- It implies that the general is bad at planning
- It implies that the general is trying to save his own life

- It is a method of enhancing your own reputation at the expense of the general's, making him appear to be a coward

For these reasons, Shingen of Kōshū did not value it as an achievement, so think carefully before deciding to take arrows for your lord. Be aware that just to be killed is easy, while to attain achievement is not. The relative merits of different achievements require careful consideration.

Commentator two
In terms of loyalty, *yaomote* – receiving arrows – is the equal of any of the achievements by spear. However, loyalty should be taken as read, while the other achievements set you apart as being particularly honourable. Take note that if receiving arrows for the lord is overvalued, soldiers may deliberately try to be killed in such a manner.

SUMMARY OF THE EIGHT ACHIEVEMENTS
The above are called *bushi no hachikō* – the eight achievements of the warrior. Other achievements are called *shinsō* – achievements through attitude. Within this category there are the *saishinsō* – specific principles of the mind – which include treating dead soldiers with respect and using language to assist an ally in combat.

Commentator one
The eight achievements are:
1 *ichiban-yari* – the first spear fight
2 *niban-yari* – the second spear fight
3 *yarishita* – being assistant to the victor of the spear
4 *kumiuchi* – grappling
5 *ichiban-nori* – being the first to arrive
6 *shingari* – defending the retreat (including collecting heads and helping the injured)

7 *hitori no shingari* – defending the retreat alone (including collecting heads)
8 *yaomote ni tatsu* – standing before the lord and taking arrows

Sukedachi – language to assist in combat – is different from the type of language discussed in the previous chapter. *Sukedachi* involves supporting your allies or friends vocally during a fight, including giving advice on what they should or should not do.

Concerning how to treat the dead with respect: after the battle of Mikatagahara, those *samurai* from Kōshū saw the dead bodies of warriors from the army of Hamamatsu and praised their bravery. This episode is found in the *Kōyō Gunkan*.

Commentator two

Concerning respectful treatment of the dead: Honda Heihachi once saw dead bodies from his own side and had them repositioned appropriately.

Achievements should be judged according to the nature of the situation and the strength of the enemy; also, the general's opinion will be paramount. Be aware that this is not a subject to which set rules can be applied. The above are traditional ideas from older days.

Shinsō – achievements through attitude – include beheading and the third spear fight. *Saishinsō* – specific principles of the mind – include the two points mentioned above.

CHAPTER NINETEEN

場中ノ勝負

Banaka no shōbu

EVENLY MATCHED COMBAT

If two opposing armies position themselves at the boundary between their provinces and engage in daytime battles, withdrawing to their own lands to rest at night and then returning to battle again the next day, then both generals should be considered as excellent. This form of warfare is known as *banaka no shōbu* – evenly matched combat.

In addition, there is something called *banaka no kōmyō* – achievement in full combat. This is also known as *hitori tsuyoshi* – the strength of one man – and involves one soldier taking many heads, an impressive feat even if they are the heads of *aoba-mono*.[122] The feat of capturing many ordinary heads is equal to the taking of one important head. Alternatively, you can take just the nose if you are becoming overburdened with heads. This is called *kezuke* – taking the nose. Even a small-scale battle, if it includes a great feat such as the ones mentioned above, can be considered a *daigassen* – a battle of importance.

Commentator one

Apart from the eight forms of achievement, other ways in which a soldier can draw attention to himself are discussed here and in the following sections:

- *banaka no shōbu* – evenly matched combat
- *hagai no kōmyō* – the achievement of the young hawk
- *hare no kōmyō* – an auspicious achievement
- *hana wo kaku* – cutting off the nose

---

122 青歯者 – literally, 'people of blue teeth', meaning those of the lower class who did not stain their teeth black. Blue was often used to refer to the colour white.

- *shōgeki* – killing the lord-commander
- *kobore musha* – deserting[123]
- *shingari [no ikusa]* – defending a retreat

In most battles, one side will retreat after one or two sessions of combat. Sustained battle with intervals and the continual substitution of troops is only possible if both sides have excellent generals. Such prolonged battles are called *daigassen* – great battles. The number of soldiers involved in the battle is not important.

Hitori tsuyoshi – the strength of one man – is an achievement attained by a single man who fights with and kills many enemies. In such a case, the practice of *kezuke* – taking the nose – may be adopted once you have the general or captain's permission.

Commentator two

Certain battles, such as the ones in Kawanakajima, may not have involved a large number of combatants but are still regarded as great battles.

Nose-taking should be done only after informing your captain or commander. Further details about the practice are given later.

Hitori tsuyoshi is the achievement of one man killing many enemies. As recorded in the *Taiheiki* chronicle, Nitta Yoshisada and Ashikaga Takauji performed in this way at the battle of Minatogawa.

羽下威之高名

Hagai no kōmyō

THE ACHIEVEMENT OF THE YOUNG HAWK

This achievement may be performed in any kind of encounter, from a great battle to a skirmish. It refers to a young warrior following guidance from an older and more experienced *bushi* in order to kill an opponent.

---

123 Unlike the other items in the list, this is a negative action and thus it is prestigious to kill a deserting enemy.

Commentator one

Some of the achievements discussed in this section, including *hagai no kōmyō*, can at times be greater even than the eight forms of achievement themselves.

The *hagai* in the title of this achievement comes from the term *hagai torikai*, which means 'to have a young hawk learn how to hunt from an old hawk'. The convention in this situation is for the experienced *bushi* to seek permission not to carry a *sashimono* banner, thereby giving notice to his superiors that he wishes to let a younger man achieve the feat of *hagai no kōmyō*.

Commentator two

The achievement of the hawk is a way for a father, father-in-law, elder brother, or so on, having already achieved a certain number of deeds, to give up an opportunity for further achievement to a younger family member.

晴之高名

Hare no kōmyō

AN AUSPICIOUS ACHIEVEMENT

This occurs when a member of the *hatamoto* – command group – moves to the vanguard before spear-fighting begins and has a sudden encounter with an enemy. It may be the case that he and the enemy are on scouting missions. He will be recognised for this achievement if he kills or captures the enemy promptly.

Commentator one

Hare no kōmyō takes place in the 'no man's land' between the two armies' positions. Each combatant gives his name to the other and then the fight begins. It is an unusual achievement to attain. Sometimes the lord-commander will order someone to go out to kill an enemy and return with the head, upon which the chosen warrior will venture out on the attack and try to make such a kill.

Commentator two

This achievement occurs when the two armies are confronting each other but the battle has not yet begun. This means an impressive and memorable fight which is achieved in no man's land.

鼻ヲ掻

Hana wo kaku

CUTTING OFF THE NOSE

During a *banaka no shōbu* type battle and after you have informed the rear troops of what you are about to do, put the severed noses of *suhada-mono* – warriors without armour – and *aoba-mono* – people of lower importance – inside the breastplate of your armour. These are people who have no stipend. The reason for doing this is so that you can continue fighting – in other situations this should be avoided.

Commentator one

When cutting off a nose, the eyebrows should also be cut off, so that you can prove that the nose does not belong to a woman. Notify the people to the rear that, as you are engaged in a large battle, you are going to perform *kezuke* – nose-taking. Tell the general, captains or commanders. To perform this without notification is incorrect.

Commentator two

This should *not* be done to the head of an excellent warrior. At the battle of Nagakute, the nose of Mori Musashi [also known as Mori Nagayoshi] was mistakenly cut off by Honda Hachizō, with the result that there were difficulties in determining whose nose it was. It is said Hachizō was killed in the battle of Kanie. If there are not too many heads to deal with, it is questionable whether the noses of even lower soldiers should be cut off.

驗

Shirushi

TAKING EVIDENCE OF WHO HAS BEEN KILLED

This includes taking the head of an enemy soldier after the enemy has been put to rout and chased down. If the enemy is prestigious, take his long sword, short sword or banner as proof and as a way to discover his name.

Commentator one

To take evidence means to bring a helmet, great sword or war baton, together with a head, and bring it back wrapped in a *horo* – arrow cape. For this purpose, there is also a teaching to mark the dead body. Sword cuts should be made on the palms, on the back of the legs or on the feet, or somewhere beneath the armour to serve as evidence.

Commentator two

To mark a dead body, make cuts with a sword on the palms, legs or feet or somewhere under the amour to serve as evidence. This is called *atozuke* – making marks; details of this are explained later in this writing.

In older times, Satsuma-no-kami Tadanori was decapitated by Okabe Rokuyata. When Rokuyata killed Tadanori, Rokuyata realized it was in fact Tadanori by a strip of paper attached to his quiver. Also, on the second day of the seventh month of Kenmu 4 (1337), Nitta Yoshisada was decapitated in Ashiwa district in Echizen province by Ujiie Nakatsukasa-no-jō Shigekuni. Shigekuni presented the head together with Yoshisada's great sword – called Onikiri Onimaru, the 'demon's sword that kills demons' – and thus the head was recognized to be Yoshisada's. To present something from the dead person's gear, as in this example, is called *shirushi*.

将撃

Shōgeki

KILLING THE LORD-COMMANDER

This means to strike a general. Striking down a lord-commander is an achievement worth one thousand achievements, even if it is an *oikubi* – a head taken when the enemy is fleeing. This is such a prestigious honour that he who achieves it will be known as a *myōga no bushi* – a warrior blessed by the gods. If a war baton is brought back with the head then this is again an honour, even if it is an *oikubi* – a head taken when the enemy is fleeing.

People in positions of command are attended by the men of their group and followed by a number of their servants. Those who successfully kill them should be identified as *daigō no rikōmono* – those who are immensely brave and full of wisdom and intelligence. Another act worthy of great admiration is to thrust at a group of twenty or thirty enemy soldiers approaching in a tight formation, thereby causing them to scatter.

Commentator one

It is difficult to kill even a captain or a commander of a small group as they are attended by the men of their units. Therefore, it is even more difficult to kill a lord-commander. Those who can achieve this feat are given the title of *myōga no bushi* – a warrior blessed by the gods. Striking down a lord-commander is usually only possible when the enemy is fleeing. When an army is being defeated, the lord-commander will generally move to protect the rear troops and help defend the retreat – this is the method that an excellent general will use. Because of this, he or his horse may sometimes be hit by an arrow, at which point his luck tends to run out and he will normally end up dead. When the enemy is in retreat, make sure you spot their lord-commander. A soldier with excellent armour, who is carrying a war baton but has no banner on his back and no helmet is probably a lord-commander. If you kill a general you will be rewarded, even if it is the only kill you make during the battle. This kind of military achievement cannot be attained without divine blessing. If you kill a *samurai* who is carrying a war baton, it is a principle to bring the war baton back [together with the head]. Without the war baton, your achievement will not be recognized. This is an ancient way – much like bringing the head back with an arrow cape. Remember – although captains are attended by many men, lord-commanders have even more. Even when facing defeat, they will be accompanied by their servants. Killing a lord-commander is achievable only by those warriors called *daigō no rikōmono* – those who are brave and full of wisdom and intelligence. Therefore, it has been recorded here.

Also, during a battle if there is a group of twenty or thirty people that holds together without scattering, it is most likely that it has the lord-commander or a captain within it.

Only the most courageous warriors serve as defenders of the retreat. Therefore, it is an extremely brave act to chase and fight them with spears or to put them to rout.

Commentator two

If you see an enemy *samurai* who stands out from the rest for the fine quality of his armour or his marvellous war baton or something similar, do not fail to realize he may well be the lord-commander. If you kill the lord-commander, you will be given a vast reward. If you kill someone who has a war baton but present his head without the baton, or if you kill a *horo-musha* – warrior or the cape – and present his head without the cape, this will be called a *kubi-tagae* – ill-presented head – and will not be regarded as honourable.

In a battle, those who advance and are mounted in a group of twenty or thirty are all warriors of prestige. Following them and fighting them is an admirable thing to do.

At the rebellion [of Shimabara] in Amakusa, the head of the lord-commander, Shirō Tokisada, was picked up by a lower soldier. In this case, after inspection of the head it was decided to give a reward to the soldier, though not an official military achievement, as Tokisada's head was of such importance.

コボレ武者

Kobore-musha[124]

DESERTING

Deserters are warriors who avoid intense battles and flee via byroads; in the main they are people of lower standing and are called *kobore-mono* – warriors who detach from the main group. In contrast, true warriors withdraw in formation, which makes them difficult to attack; this is called *shingari* – defending a retreat. Remember, it is admirable to engage in combat with those performing *shingari*, even you do not manage to kill anyone.

Commentator one

According to the *Senkōroku*, *kobore-musha* are those who flee. This type of behaviour often reveals itself when a castle falls. Such people tend to take byways because they expect main roads to be blocked by the enemy. Keep an eye out for deserters, and if you notice one kill him.

Commentator two

Whether to kill a deserter or not depends on the situation. Also, if brave warriors try to defend a retreat at the rear, it should be regarded as an honourable deed to attack them with a spear.

殿ノ軍

Shingari no ikusa

DEFENDING A RETREAT

This is done by warriors who repeatedly return to fight while a retreat is in action. They make statements with dignity and stand against their enemy. Those warriors who support a wounded ally on their shoulders yet are still able to make a kill are called *kusemono* – people of extraordinary ability.

The above are achievements performed by independent soldiers and are exploits that should be carefully studied and kept in mind.

---

124 The Koga transcription has the slightly different title of *kobore-mono* 溢物.

Commentator one

As mentioned earlier, a group of warriors holding together in the rear guard are performing *shingari* – defending a retreat. As these people are brave warriors, to give chase and fight them will be regarded as a feat.

Shingari is also known as *shiriharai* – swiping away those at your rear – and is indeed viewed as the act of a brave warrior. The preceding points related to the enemy retreat, but this point is specifically about a retreat by your own allies. To return and enter into combat while the enemy is giving chase is something that brave warriors do. The principle in such a case is to announce: 'I am [insert name] and I stand and fight in *shingari*.' Then you should fight. Rather than for the benefit of the enemy this announcement is done so that your allies can hear your name.

Sometimes only a single man performs *shingari*. In general, it is more difficult to make a stand against the enemy while your allies are in retreat than it is to move forward while your army is making a forward attack. When defending the retreat it is even more impressive to help injured allies who have difficulty in retreating to withdraw. Since ancient times *bushi* who have achieved this feat have been called *kusemono* – people of extraordinary ability.

Commentator two

According to the *Taiheiki* chronicle, Nonaka Hachirō Sadakuni carried an injured man on his shoulder while he was in retreat.

Commentator one

The eight points above, from *banaka no shōbu* to *shingari [no ikusa]*, are exploits that a soldier should always try to achieve, but are not what captains should seek. Though a brave warrior may try to achieve these things, it is often the case that the enemy will falter and a fight will not take place at all. Therefore, you need some luck to be able to achieve these feats – but you also need ability. One who finds himself in a combat situation but who has the wrong mindset will not be able to fight properly.

The following six points are suspicious 'achievements':

1 *yamai-kubi* 病首 – improper heads
2 *onna-kubi* 女首 – possible female heads
3 *tsukuri-kubi* 作リ首 – falsified heads
4 *hiroi-kubi* 掇首 – discovered heads
5 *ubai-kubi* 奪首 – snatched heads
6 *oitsuke-yari* 追付鎗 – the cornered spear

Keep these in mind and make a proper judgement when fighting.

CHAPTER TWENTY

病首之事

Yamai-kubi no koto

IMPROPER HEADS

These are also called *shirami-kubi* – lice heads. An improper head is one that has been cut without witness and brought after the 'book of heads'[125] has been closed. These may be presented by *samurai* who have failed to make a kill and take a head during actual combat. The truth will be that they have found someone who has had difficulty in escaping and who has been left behind by his allies. They take this person's head and display it so that people will take note. This is the act of a coward.

However, if they have managed to find, capture and behead a good enemy warrior who was hiding with tactics, then this is not a cowardly act but should be regarded as an achievement.

Commentator one

How to make a record in the 'book of heads' is explained in detail in the scroll *Heieki Yōhō*. On a battlefield, heads should be presented before the 'book of heads' has been completed. Bringing heads in later causes great difficulty when assessing the achievement gained, and therefore such heads are called *shōnin naki kubi* – heads without witnesses.

Assessing the capture of enemies who cannot withdraw, such as those who are injured or ill, will depend on who they are. To kill such people is *not* considered a great achievement.

A monk of the temple of Sanjūin of Atsukuma in the district of Ika in the province of Gōshu had maintained a promise with Ishida Jibu Mitsunari since

---

125 首帳 *kubichō* – a record of heads taken in battle.

their childhood. To fulfil the promise, Mitsunari travelled to Ishibashi village after the battle of Sekigahara, but he became seriously ill and was stricken down and lay in his sickbed. Then Tanaka Hyōbu arrived at this place with his army and heard that Mitsunari was going to be transferred from there to hide out with a merchant called Matsumaeya from Tsuruga in Echizen province. To counter this he deployed two of his retainers, Ozawa Seishichi and Tanaka Denzaemon, to lure Mitsunari out at night. They duly captured him and brought him to their lord. This was not the act of a coward but was a grand achievement.[126]

女首之事
Onna-kubi no koto
POSSIBLE FEMALE HEADS
Noses taken from heads in the confusion of a large battle without a witness to verify the act are considered to be *onna-kubi* – possible female heads. Such a head cannot be properly judged: it could be that of an ally, a monk or a woman. Good *bushi* do not engage in such actions.

Commentator one

The term *onna-kubi* is used for noses taken without prior notification to the rear troop and without witnesses. Remember that you should always notify your superiors before taking noses. As a general rule, do not engage in such dubious achievements. If you perform any achievement that may invite suspicion, it is essential for you to describe exactly where it happened and to take evidence from the enemy such as a helmet, piece of armour, great sword or amulet, and then to describe the combat itself. If someone witnesses and reports your deed, your military prowess will reach a deeper level and you will be considered reliable. It has been said from ancient times that with a female head, the iris of the eye is hidden, while on a male head the iris of the eye is visible. When Shinkun[127]

---

126 Ishida Jibu Mitsunari was the commander of the defeated army at the battle of Sekigahara. The point made here is that, even though he was ill, capturing him was still considered an excellent achievement because of his importance.

127 Tokugawa Ieyasu.

attacked a castle which was being defended, there were some heads whose gender could not be identified, even by their hair. Thus the lord decided that the female heads were the ones with the iris of the eye directed downwards, while the male heads were the ones with the iris directed upwards. Those that were determined to be male in this way were discovered to have been correctly identified later on.

Commentator two

Remember that *onna-kubi* are not always female. The point is that it is impossible to determine the gender of a nose – or ear – brought in without notification or proper reason, and so they are classified as possibly coming from female heads.

作り首
Tsukuri-kubi
FALSIFIED HEADS

This involves taking the head of an injured *aoba-mono* – person of lesser importance – and pairing it with a helmet that has been left behind by a [different] fleeing enemy.

Commentator one

Tsukuri-kubi is the act of a skilled but dishonest person, but note that it is not in itself cowardly. Doing this to an enemy head is better than doing it to the head of an ally or a woman. However, it should be avoided since the deliberate misidentification of a head will only cause confusion.

Commentator two

This deed does not accord with the true aim of war. If, upon inspection by the general, a head turns out to have been falsified, this will bring great dishonour to the culprit. Therefore, *samurai* should not undertake such an action.

掇首
Hiroi-kubi
DISCOVERED HEADS

These are also called *shi-kubi* – death heads. If there has been a large battle or even a skirmish, both allies and enemies may be injured and die. Brave warriors tend to leave their kills so that they can move on to kill more enemies. Sometimes other people take these abandoned heads.

Commentator one

There is a common saying:

依品テハ拾首ナリトモセン
Sometimes a hiroi-kubi *may be better than nothing.*

However, it still cannot be deemed to be an achievement. The only exception is the head of a general or captain. In this case, even discovering the head will be an exploit and the finder will be called a *myōga no bushi* – warrior of divine blessing. If a notable enemy warrior is killed in battle but his body is lost in the carnage, the full effect of his death is diminished. Therefore, in order to give encouragement to your army, you should decapitate such a warrior as soon as possible. It is often the case that a heroic warrior who kills enemies with ease, simply leaves them without taking their heads. This is a thing that cannot be achieved by ordinary people and is exactly the point being made here.

Commentator two

At the siege of Ōsaka castle during the Keichō period (1596–1615), a senior councillor of the Satake clan called Shibui Naizen was killed with a musket shot. A man named Hiratsuka Gorobei passed by the dead body while he was chasing down an enemy. Someone saw this and suggested to him that he should take the head of this fallen warrior. However, Hiratsuka turned his face back and asked, 'What worth is there in taking a death head?' He then moved on to fight, to the admiration of people who saw or heard about this.

奪首

Ubai-kubi

SNATCHED HEADS

When you have taken an enemy head in battle, people may approach you as if they are offering to help but instead they snatch the head and run away with it. This can also be called a *musabori-kubi* – coveted head.

Commentator one

It often happens that an enemy or an ally may try to snatch a head from you, so take care. There is a method of carrying a head securely. Insert the *sageo* cord of the sword through the chin and out of the mouth and tie the cord to the top knot of the head. This makes a handle which will not only prevent the head from being stolen but also make it easier to carry such a heavy weight.

Commentator two

During the campaign of Kunohe in Ōshū province, a head was taken by Jinbo Gorozaemon but was stolen by Yuasa Shichiemon. A head should be carried with the *sageo* cord through it so that it cannot be taken. A head is heavy and it may be the case that the head is stolen either by an enemy or by an ally – therefore, be careful. At the battle of Nagashino, Ōkubo Shichirōemon had a head stolen, but he was able to find out who the culprit was: a *rōnin* from Kōshū under the command of Sakakibara Shikibu Daisuke. He reported the theft to Shinkun the Great Lord [Tokugawa Ieyasu], and as a result those *rōnin* who joined from Kōshū were dismissed and Ōkubo Shichirōemon was honoured in the end. Keep this in mind.

追付鎗之事

Oitsuke-yari no koto

THE CORNERED SPEAR

If you corner an enemy group while it is trying to cross a fence, ditch or earth embankment or while it is withdrawing after being routed, the soldiers may reform, set their spears and engage in combat. This should not be classed as *hon-yari* – true spear. In addition to this there is *oikake-yari* – the chased spear. If this takes place on horseback it is not considered as combat with spears, but is instead called *han-yari* – the half-spear.

Commentator one

This is also called *inu-yari* – the dog spear. In Kōshū-Ryū it is known as *mamako-yari* – the adopted spear. Even this can be an honoured exploit, but it will depend on the situation. Spear-fighting across a barrier like a fence does not often lead to an actual confrontation. As an example of spear-fighting across a gate understand that Tsumura Yūkan entered into this in his youth at the siege of Ōsaka castle when he attacked Sanada's outlying earthwork defences. Fighting with spears across a barrier of some description is not difficult to do and therefore it is not considered to be true spear-fighting. There is a difference between chasing and fighting an ordinary withdrawing group, as discussed here, and chasing and fighting those who are defending the enemy retreat.

Commentator two

The cornered spear is different from the chased spear. The chased spear is when the enemy army collapses and you follow in pursuit and enter into combat with a group of retreating soldiers. This is not considered as true spear.

One example of the cornered spear comes from the Odawara campaign, when Gamō Ujisato engaged in spear combat with Hirosawa Owari-no-kami over a ditch.

A spear fight that is had with an enemy in retreat is also not considered true spear.

Half-spear is considered half the achievement of true spear.

敵ノ道具ヲ取ル事

Teki no dōgu wo toru koto

TAKING ENEMY EQUIPMENT

It is regarded as an achievement to take any equipment that belongs to the enemy lord-commander. It can also be an achievement to take the equipment of other *samurai*, but this depends on the situation. Do not discard items without consideration, thinking that there is no use in keeping them.

Commentator one

In many cases taking enemy equipment can be a valuable tactical ploy to bring about a victory. As recorded in the *Taiheiki* chronicle, during the battle of Chihaya castle Kusunoki's troops obtained abandoned flags and curtains from the Nagoya forces, which enabled Kusunoki to deceive the enemy.

Commentator two

To capture any of the following items of enemy gear can be regarded as an achievement:

- upper-level achievement 上 – flags and curtains
- mid-level achievement 中 – *horo*-capes and war batons
- lower-level achievement 下 – swords and armour, etc.

Up until this point there has been a general discussion of the kinds and levels of achievement that a soldier can obtain. Specific achievements that have not been mentioned should be judged according to the principles discussed here. Things that should be kept in mind about military achievements are covered at a later point in this scroll. From here on is written a discussion on the things a soldier should keep in mind.

CHAPTER TWENTY-ONE

一兵陣中心掛之事

Ippei jinchū kokorogake no koto

THINGS THAT INDEPENDENT SOLDIERS SHOULD KEEP IN MIND WHILE ON CAMPAIGN

According to tradition, independent soldiers should understand the importance of the following three things while on campaign:

- eating quickly
- removing armour as late as possible
- unsaddling a horse as late as possible

Commentator one

There are many things that an independent soldier needs to keep in mind. However, many of these will depend on the situation. Consider and use the above as basic principles.

Those who eat slowly will be unable to deal with emergencies.

Those who remove amour or saddles too early will not have enough time to prepare in an emergency.

These are the most important things to keep in mind during a campaign.

Commentator two

The basic principle is always to be prepared for emergencies even during times of peace.

It is said that if you take off your armour you will become tired.

The lord-commander should lay down the three points above as orders. These come before the rest of the points – of which there are approximately fifty to follow – because they are essential things you should never forget throughout a campaign, even for a moment.

将ヨリ給ル采拝頂戴之事

Shō yori tamawaru saihai chōdai no koto

HOW TO RECEIVE A WAR BATON WHICH HAS BEEN GIVEN BY A GENERAL

There is a method of courtesy and respect to this and is an oral tradition.

Commentator one

When you are given a war baton from a general, you should bow to the other *samurai* present and say something like: 'I wonder why I should deserve to receive such an honour.' The way of speaking in this situation follows the principles found in the traditions of *kurai no kotoba* – the language of class.

Commentator two

When a *samurai* is promoted to the rank of captain he is presented with a war baton. During this ceremony, you should bow to the other *samurai* three times and say something like: 'I was told to take over the group from [insert name] and was given this war baton. I am not sure if I am the right person to give orders to these great people, but it is the lord's will and therefore I will try my best to be worthy of his expectations.'

If the people reply that they will follow your orders, you should talk with *kurai no kotoba no narai* – the tradition of the language of class – which is found within our school. When everyone comes together, you should have a *shōgi* stool prepared and give orders with the war baton in your hand. Then you should say that if anyone acts against your orders, they will be punished without exception. At the same time you should earnestly describe the rewards to be had. This is what oral tradition says on the matter. If you do not observe tradition and proper courtesy, your orders will sometimes not be accepted.

太刀之事

Tachi no koto

CONCERNING THE GREAT SWORD

If the lord offers a *tachi* great sword to someone who is in a position of command, he should decline it – this is an oral tradition.

Commentator one

If you receive a great sword from the lord, you are obliged to bathe it in blood by killing an enemy. However, if you are in a position of authority over a number of people, you cannot fight for yourself, which means that you cannot bathe the sword in blood. Therefore, you should decline the sword by saying: 'If I am to take this I shall have to be excused the burden of command.' Alternatively, you can request that the sword be entrusted to the lord's squire.

Commentator two

You should also say: 'Until a victory has been won in this battle, I would like to entrust this sword to the lord's squire'. The lord will then normally give one of the following orders:

'You should entrust your group to someone else and concentrate on your own fighting.'

'The sword does not have to be baptized with blood.'

'Entrust the sword to my squire.'

This is called *tachi no kokoroe* – points to keep in mind about the great sword.

馬乗様之事

Uma noriyō no koto

RIDING A HORSE

Details of horse-riding are given in the 'Lord's Messengers' chapter of the scroll *Heieki Yōhō*. Principles for an independent soldier are the same as for any other person riding a horse.

Commentator one

Details of this are written in the scroll *Heieki Yōhō*. Riding a horse is the same for both normal *samurai* and the lord's messengers. After dismounting, warriors should band together.

Commentator two

Generally, you should ride a horse slowly to begin with and then increase speed. Know that in a steep place you should dismount and walk.

戦初ヲ知ル事

Tatakai hajime wo shiru koto

KNOWING WHEN BATTLE HAS BEGUN

The following are indications that a battle has started:

- when a *tsukai-musha* – warrior messenger – does not return to his position
- when two or three flag-bearers advance and retreat
- when flag-bearers stop and move into position
- when the spacing between the vanguard and the second troop opens up

Commentator one

When serving as a messenger to convey an order to start the battle, it is a principle not to return to the lord.

When flags divide and separate from their normal set position toward the rear, know that the battle is commencing.

When the above said flag-bearers for each troop stop to take up position, the battle will commence at any moment.

When battle begins, a space opens up between the first and second troop to avoid the second troop collapsing in a 'landslide' if the vanguard has fallen.

Commentator two

In addition to the four points mentioned above, another sign that battle is about to begin is when warriors dismount from horses and get together, forming in line with spears.

Concerning the four points:

- It is a rule that a messenger who is sent from the lord to the vanguard to inform them to start the battle does not return but instead remains with the vanguard. However, there may be exceptions to this rule.
- Know the battle has commenced when flags that are located towards the rear and in formation are divided.
- If the above mentioned flags move out to the sides, then fighting is imminent – the flags are sent to the sides when a battle is about to begin.
- The second formation will be set back from the vanguard by a distance of three *ken*. This is in case the vanguard collapses towards the second troop.

It is important to be able to recognize when a battle has begun, as notification of the start of battle will not be given to each soldier. Understanding the four signs described here will prevent you from thinking that a battle is about to begin whenever you advance on the battlefield, which is mentally fatiguing. Concerning leaving room between the vanguard and the second troop, details are provided in the scroll *Heieki Yōhō*.

鎗前之事

Yari-mae no koto

PREPARING FOR SPEAR COMBAT

Remove your *hōate* face guard and your *haidate* thigh protectors.

Commentator one

Your should remove your face guard because it muffles your breathing when fighting. If it is a *gyakuzura* – open face mask – then you do not have to remove it. In other schools when thigh protectors are taken off they are folded up and put over the shoulders, but this can inhibit your fighting. Instead you should have a servant carry them, or otherwise throw them to one side.

Commentator two

The phase of *yari-mae* – preparation for spear combat – is a critical phase of battle, like being 'in the mouth of a tiger',[128] and is where an independent soldier can attain great achievements. Information about the face guard and thigh protectors from our school is given here. Face guards are detrimental as they impede your view, and also inhibit breathing. *Ecchū hōate* chin guards are acceptable and should not be removed. This is such an important subject that more has been written on it than even on the first spear fight – further details are given in another scroll.

---

128 虎口場 *koguchiba* – literally, 'the mouth of a tiger', meaning a very dangerous situation. This is also the name given to the space outside the entrance to a castle.

CHAPTER TWENTY-TWO

戦之時敵ニ目ト心ヲ不放ト云事

Ikusa no toki teki ni me to kokoro wo hanasazu to iu koto

NEVER TAKE YOUR EYES OR MIND OFF THE ENEMY DURING A BATTLE[129]

Things that can be observed with your eyes in the day:

- sun
- mountains
- forests
- grassland
- trees

Things that can be observed with your eyes at night:

- stars
- moon
- distant or close features
- wind and rain
- fire
- the form and colour of clouds
- snow

Commentator one

Sun: in the daytime, the time of the day can be observed.

Mountains: observe the steepness.

Forests: check for ambush.

Grassland: observe whether the grass is deep or shallow.

---

129 Not the enemy itself but enemy territory.

Trees: observe whether they are short or tall, in a wood or in a forest.

Stars: there are important points concerning *hagun*, the seventh star of Ursa Major, and also about *ōboshi*, the star Sirius.

Moon: observe for the time, distances, wind and rain, cloud and snow. Some add thunder to this list.

By paying attention to these points with your eyes and mind, you can attain your own achievements and win battles. Remember 'observing with perception'[130] is different from 'seeing'.[131]

Commentator two

Most people attempt to fight to the death upon a battlefield and therefore there is a tendency for some to become mentally disconnected. Just pull yourself together and fight. Check things at each of the four cardinal points and embed them in your mind and eyes. Gauge the time, the steepness of mountains and the depth of forests; at night observe the stars – including *hagun* – and also moonrise and moonset, head winds and tail winds and cloud formations, etc. If it is snowy, be careful and take note of the depth of the snow.

武者色之事

Musha iro no koto

OBSERVING WARRIORS

This includes observing the following aspects:

- the appearance of the soldiers themselves
- the appearance of the flags
- the direction and timing of arrow and musket shots

Commentator one

There are various points about the appearance of warriors. To judge which

---

130 察 *satsu* – to perceive beyond observation.
131 観心 *kanshin* – originally a Buddhist word meaning 'to penetrate the true nature of your mind'.

are strong and which are weak, know that those who move into a formation with speed so that the captain can observe them are to be considered strong soldiers. These soldiers form a tight and close connection, they look 'blackish' and appear calm. Weak soldiers are restless and appear 'whitish', they look upwards and have a loose formation. In summary, the strong are substantial and 'blackish', while the weak are insubstantial and 'whitish'.

Concerning the above three points:

- The term *gusoku no aiiro* refers to the helmets of the troops and the gaps that appear between them.
- It is desirable that the flags themselves flutter, whereas the bottoms of the poles are held steady. This applies to both the enemy and the allies; anything that goes against this should be avoided.
- Arrow and musket shots are not always fired in the same direction but instead may criss-cross in confusion. This is the way a weak enemy will show signs of possibly moving to retreat. When you see this, it may be appropriate to attack suddenly with horses, as a disorganized and confused enemy will find it difficult to work in unison to repel such an attack.

Commentator two

The techniques of *musha-iro* are used to judge whether someone is strong or weak, substantial or insubstantial. The following are the traditions for the three points in the main text:

- Substantial soldiers look 'blackish', their 'six tools' are clustered tightly like ripe fruit on a branch,[132] and they also have a look of composure. Insubstantial soldiers have many gaps between their 'six tools' and appear restless. *Gusoku no aiiro* means 'gaps within the armour'.
- It is desirable to have flags held tight and stable at the lower part and for them to move at the upper part; methods are to be transmitted in the *Kōketsu* scroll.
- Shots from insubstantial soldiers are scattered and without aim, while those from substantial soldiers are well directed. However, the tips of the spears

---

132 This is a play on the similarity between the ideograms for 'substantial' and 'ripe'. The 'six tools' are listed in chapter two.

of insubstantial soldiers look unified. Be aware that those soldiers who shoot arrows or muskets in an organized way but do *not* hold their spears in unison with each other are substantial. This is a point you should keep in mind when sending mounted warriors to break through an enemy or when deciding which formation to use against the enemy.

両人争テ首ヲ取タル時之事
Ryōnin arasoite kubi wo toritaru toki no koto
TWO PEOPLE COMPETING TO TAKE A HEAD
If someone is competing with you for a head, make a mark with your sword on the foot of the victim or inside his armour – do this before you return and without being noticed by your rival. This is a slightly different situation from *aiuchi* – combined killing of an opponent. However, even if it is a case of *aiuchi* the above cutting should still be done. These are called *shinobi shirushi* – hidden marks.

Commentator one
When two people combine to kill an opponent, the first person to strike should be the one to be recognized for the achievement. To avoid any future argument, you should make marks or take evidence. How to do this will depend on the situation.

Commentator two
In the combined killing of an enemy, the first person to strike should be regarded as the one who made the achievement. There is often an argument about this, so make sure to make your mark first. One way is to mark with a sword or the like on the back of the armour. An example of this type of thing is when Kani Saizō put bamboo grass in the mouth of a dead body. The following is an example of two people competing to take a head: at the battle of Nagakute, when Ikeda Shōnyū was facing defeat, he moved to a small hill and called for a new horse. At this point Uemura Den'emon, Andō Hikobei, Nagai Denpachi,

Hachiya Shichibei and possibly one other rushed him. Andō stabbed with his spear and both he and Nagai tried to decapitate Ikeda Shōnyū, both falling over each other, but in the end it was Nagai who took the head. He then also cut the fingers off. This type of thing should be kept in mind in combat.

疵見様之事

Kizu miyō no koto

IDENTIFYING INJURIES

When examining dead or injured allies or enemies, you should understand the following points about different types of injuries:

- A spear wound will be triangular[133]
- A musket wound is circular and deep
- A halberd wound is wide
- A great-sword wound is long
- An arrow wound is fairly deep

Commentator one

Identifying the nature of an injury is useful not only for treating an injured ally but also as evidence for when an argument arises about an enemy head. If someone says that he killed the enemy with a certain weapon in a certain way, then an examination of the wound may prove or disprove his claim. Therefore, *samurai* should have this kind of knowledge in advance.

A halberd wound can easily be mistaken for a sword wound, but as a halberd is used for stabbing as well as cutting, the wound it makes has small differences and is of a different depth. Swords are also sometimes used for stabbing, but such wounds are thinner.

The entrance wound from a musket bullet is round and small, while the exit wound is large and ragged.

As it is not unknown for a warrior to attack one of his allies, do not believe everything that you hear – even those words spoken by your allies.

---

133 Spear wounds may also be diamond-shaped.

餌二餉ト云事

Eba ni kurau to iu koto

USING SOMEONE AS BAIT

In a difficult situation some people may ask a warrior-comrade to shoot his bow or musket, knowing that this action will get the comrade killed. They leave the body on the earthen embankment as cover. This is considered a distasteful move that only a devious person would make. Do not fall for this stratagem.

Commentator two

A *samurai* should never play this trick, but you must guard against it at all times. This is just one example of the ways that deviously skilled people cause difficulties to young colleagues or fool them into advancing to difficult places. Some people may act this way out of jealousy at the achievements of a fellow *samurai*. If you do not respond to their provocation, you may be called a coward; but if you do respond you may find yourself stuck in a dangerous situation. Be aware that such things may happen. Make sure not to be provoked when this type of situation arises. This is a situation that requires proper judgement, the judgement of an experienced person.

CHAPTER TWENTY-THREE

沼渡リ之事

Numa-watari no koto

CROSSING A MARSH

Take off your face guard and greaves and secure your feet with rope. There is a set of tools called *numa-gutsu* – marsh platforms; these are made of wood.

Commentator one

If you try to cross a marsh in heavy armour, you will sink into the mud deeper than you expected. Your face guard will limit your view, so you should take it off.

To bind your legs, tie thin rope below the knees and also around the middle of the instep.

Marsh platforms are wooden plates that you lie your chest and head on to cross a marsh. They are not designed for comfort nor are they particularly ingenious; they are recorded here for situations when you do not know what to do on a night attack or when you come to a place you cannot cross easily.

Commentator two

This technique should be used during night attacks on castles and so on. Sometimes the enemy will grow complacent if it knows its castle is protected by a marsh. In such a situation you should use the tactic of *numa-watari* – marsh-crossing. Make two lattices of woven bamboo measuring one *ken* square. When crossing a marsh on horseback, a warrior in armour will sink into the marsh deeper than he expects. Remove your face guard so that it does not block your view, and take off your greaves so that you can move your feet freely. Bind cord around your feet and sandals so that the sandals will not come off. Crossing with two boards by putting one board forward after the other will work.

川越之事

Kawagoe no koto

CROSSING A RIVER

Methods of crossing a river include:

- *sanjaku-watari* 三尺渡リ – three-feet crossing
- *uki-watari* 桴渡リ – crossing by floating
- *uki-gutsu* 浮沓 – floating platforms

Details are found in a different writing.

Commentator one

Concerning *sanjaku-watari*: tie your sword cord to your sash and tie the other end to the man behind you. Something else in substitute of the sword cord may be used. Cross over together.

Uki-watari is a spear 'raft'. People hold spears horizontally and cross side by side. Details are in another writing.

Commentator two

If you fall over while trying to cross a river in armour, you can end up drowning unexpectedly. Therefore, use the technique of *sanjaku-watari* – three-feet crossing. This involves a group of soldiers binding each other with rope at roughly three-*shaku* intervals. This technique is also useful when travelling at night. To do this tie the sash and sword cord together and to each other when crossing a river. Raft-crossing and spear-crossing are explained in detail in the scroll *Heieki Yōhō*. *Uki-gutsu* – floating platforms – are discussed in the *Kōketsu* scroll.

人ヲ改ル詞之事

Hito wo aratamuru kotoba no koto

WORDS TO TEST PEOPLE

Call people by using your own name.

Commentator one

Be it at a time of war or peace, when you give your name you should say it loudly and repeat it until the opponent responds. Also, if you call to someone with your own name and they reply with an affirmative, simply capture them.

Commentator two

To question a suspicious person, call out with your own name. *Shinobi no mono* or other secret agents may respond to your name. If this is the case capture them and thoroughly question them.

道ニ迷ヒタル時之事

Michi ni mayoitaru toki no koto

FOR TIMES WHEN YOU ARE LOST

When you are lost:

- use a horse to find your way again
- make enquiries of local people
- follow the flow of water
- observe the appearance of grass and trees

Commentator one

Let an old horse go ahead of you and follow the horse as the horse will know the path. Use a horse of seven or eight years old or even older.

Asking local people is the technique of *kyōdō no kan* – spying by using local people as guides.

You will always get to a village if you follow a river, whether upstream or downstream.

'Appearance of grass and trees' here means the length they have been cut to.

Commentator two

Concerning the use of a horse: let an old horse lead you.

Concerning the use of local people: this is *kyōdō no kan* – spying through locals.

Concerning the point of following the flow of water: you will surely find a village if you follow the flow of water.

Concerning the point of observing the appearance of grass and trees: there are teachings on this in our *shinobi* scroll. If the grass is mowed evenly, that means it is far from a village; while if the cut of grass does not look even, then it is close to a village. Therefore, make a comprehensive judgement from your environment.

A poem says:

行違ふ野原を雪ハ埋まるとも老いたる馬は道を知るなり

If you get lost when travelling in a field covered heavily with snow, an old horse will know the path ahead.

雪道之事

Yuki michi no koto

FINDING THE WAY IN SNOW

Use the following methods:

- follow people's tracks
- probe to discover the road
- use a horse

Commentator one

When snow is covering the path, probe the ground with the butt of your spear. Tracks used by people feel hard.

To find the path when it is covered in snow, let an old horse go ahead of you.

Commentator two

Even if only a short time has passed since any earlier allied troops have moved through an area, know that snow may cover and hide their tracks. If you do not know which way they have taken at a fork in the road, find it by probing the road in this manner. Specifically, probe the snowy ground with a spear or cane, and if the troops have passed there, the top layer of snow is shallow while the layer below will be hard. However, if the troops have not passed that way, the top layer of snow will be deep. If snow is falling only lightly in the evening, and you identify horse hoof prints that have not yet been covered by a full layer of snow, probe the snow of the hoof prints themselves. If the tracks are recent, the snow beneath will not crack; while if they are old hoof prints, the snow beneath *will* crack.

覆兵伏隠之事
Fukuhei fuse kamari no koto
TYPES OF AMBUSHES
There are three types of ambush:

- *fuku* 覆 – ambush with a [large] group
- *fuse* 伏 – ambush with *samurai*
- *kamari* 隠リ – ambush with *dōshin*[134] and *ashigaru* foot soldiers

Details on locations are recorded in a different writing.

Commentator one

Concerning *fuku*: this consists of two to three hundred warriors who lie in wait with a leading captain. This can also be called *fukuhei* – soldiers who crouch.

Concerning *fuse*: this consists of twenty to thirty good warriors or even fifty to sixty. They ambush and attack where the enemy is not well defended or attack the command group.

---

134 A lower rank of *samurai*.

Concerning *kamari*: this is to attack with *ashigaru* foot soldiers. When an army withdraws, sometimes it will leave people at places as ambushes. These are called *sutekamari* – ambushes deposited to the rear.

Generally, the terms *fusekamari* or *fukuhei* are used.

Commentator two

Fuku is to have one hundred to two hundred people in hiding.

At the battle of Sekigahara, Shima Sakon, a senior counsellor to Ishida Mitsunari, had about a hundred *ashigaru* hide in a forest on the riverbank at Kasanui-zutsumi, in order to attack and hold Yabu Takumi's troops at bay. This is an example of *fuku*.

組討之事
Kumiuchi no koto
GRAPPLING AND STRIKING

Do not roll the opponent over, and make sure to decapitate him *after* he has been killed – there are oral traditions.

Commentator one

'Not rolling the opponent over' means you should avoid rolling around yourself.

To decapitate the enemy you need to kill him first because if you do not wait until he is dead before taking his head, he may stab you or throw you off while he is under you. Also you can smash him in the eye with your pommel. There are secret methods in our school about grappling and sword-striking with military tools.

塀乗亦塀ヲリノ事

Heinori mata heiori no koto

CLIMBING UP AND DOWN WALLS

There is an oral tradition in which a spear is used.

Commentator one

To climb up a wall, secure cord around the spear handle so that you can use the wrapped rope as a foothold when climbing.

To climb down a wall, hold the spear handle lightly. Place the spear butt on the ground and lean the spear against the wall, then slide down the spear handle.

A long sword can be tied to a grappling hook.

Details on this kind of thing are written in the *Shōninki* scroll.

Commentator two

Traditions for this are in our *shinobi* scroll.

CHAPTER TWENTY-FOUR

川ノ淺深ヲ知ル事

Kawa no senshin wo shiru koto

DISCOVERING WHERE A RIVER IS SHALLOW OR DEEP

Methods include:

- using a rope with markings
- using the technique of *hyōri*
- understanding the flow of water

Details are written in the scroll *Suisen Yōhō*.

The enemy may have hidden *rangui* – spikes – or *sakamogi* – thorny branches – in the water. Their presence may be indicated by swirls or ripples on the surface of the water above them and the water may sometimes have colour.

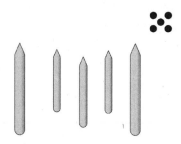

Sakamogi – thorny branches.

Commentator one

Use thorny bushes or Japanese honey locust[135] boughs under the surface of the water.

---

135 *Gleditsia japonica.*

'Water that has colour' means water that has deliberately been made muddy in order to hide spikes and thorny branches. Leave a rod or something else like it and return. This is done so that when other people are sent there they will find it with ease.

Also, observe and remember the location of mountains, forests and topological features. Do this so that if you make an achievement but have not been able to bring any evidence back with you, you can instead describe the surroundings to support your account.

Commentator two

Concerning the three points within the main text:

Attach a weight to a string just like a fishing line and as the riverbed slopes towards the centre measure the depth at set intervals, so that you can discover the formation of the ground below the water. This can be done even if the river looks irregular. For example, if the river becomes five *sun* deeper over a distance of one *ken*, the estimate for the distance of ten *ken* will be an increased depth of five *shaku*.[136]

Hyōri here means to look up and down the river and also to observe the source and stream. If the river flows east to west, the *hyō* [being the main] is the *east*, while the *ri* [the lesser] is the *west*. If the river runs south to north, south is *hyō* [the main], while north is *ri* [the lesser]. The shallow is *hyō* while the deep is *ri*. Details are in the scroll *Suisen Yōhō*. There are large and small shallows. Downstream of a large shallow area the stream is slow, while it is rapid upstream of this large shallow area. This upstream area is called the *semakura* – pillow of the shallows.

'Water with colour' means muddy water. Water is made muddy so that hidden traps cannot be seen.

Spikes should be put in arrangements of five, as shown below.

●   ●
  ●
●   ●

---

136 The original measurement multiplied by ten.

Thorny branches appear as a tangle.[137] Place the *mokkoku*[138] bush within the spikes.

合戦能キ場所ニ験可残事

Kassen yoki basho ni shirushi nokosu beki koto

LEAVING MARKS OF EVIDENCE AT APPROPRIATE POSITIONS DURING A CAMPAIGN

Five features which can help you to remember people are:

- the appearance of their horse's hair
- their armour
- the mark on their spear
- their banner
- the crest on the front of their helmet

[To help you mark a route,] you can tie grass.

Commentator one

To remember people, observe them and concentrate on memorizing them very carefully with the above five points in mind.

Tying grass is similar to the way that pilgrims leave pieces of paper at places where they have travelled.

Commentator two

You need to observe these things carefully. As mentioned before, when travelling in an enemy province, you should make a note of dangerous or useful locations such as mountains or places where horses can gather, because such information can be of great use later on. Once you have taken up position in a large army on the actual field of battle, it will be difficult to find such positive and negative

---

137 The original manual simply states 'appear as' and then a small drawing of a tangle is given.

138 *Ternstroemia gymnanthera.*

places. Therefore, you should observe and remember the advantages and disadvantages of any given place beforehand. Remember such things as rises of a certain gradient in a certain direction from a specific tree, or notable features a certain distance from a specific point.

Also, leave *kōgai* spikes or something similar as evidence that you have attained an achievement in that location.

Carefully observe the mountains, forests and topography and remember such points as markers. This is called *ba ni shirushi wo nokosu* – leaving a mark at a place.

You should remember a warrior by the five points in the main text. If you do not pay attention to the appearance of people, you will not be able to identify them later on.

If you keep these points in mind and try to use them, then even if someone is just passing by on another route you will remember them easily.

Tying grass is a method for marking a *direction* or a *way*. This is done in order to inform any troops who are following your troop of the direction you have taken. This is similar to the way pilgrims leave pieces of paper as markers.

無證據所高名之事
Shōko naki tokoro nite kōmyō no koto
FOR ACHIEVEMENTS WITHOUT WITNESSES
If you attain an achievement without someone to witness it, do the following:
- leave marks
- take a mental note of the area

Commentator one
Observe and remember the site of your achievement and leave marks behind, such as *kōgai* spikes or a *sansho*[139] charm or a *kozuka* knife.

Make mental notes of the:
- mountains

---

139 三所 – literally, 'three places'. Presumably an abbreviation of *Kumano Sansho Gongen*, the three major worship sites of the deity Gongen, which are all situated in the Kumano area of Kishū province. Therefore, a *sansho* is a charm received from one of these three shrines.

- forests
- rivers
- valleys
- grasses
- trees

Use the above, among other things, as evidence.

Commentator two

To make a mental note of the area, you should observe and remember what a certain place is like, including such details as the locations of mountains, forests and recesses of mountains, etc. Also, leave marks, such as charms, spikes or fans. This is all intended to serve as evidence when you report later on.

首ヲ取様之事

Kubi wo toriyō no koto

HINTS FOR CUTTING OFF A FACE

When cutting off from the upper lip, make sure to take the skin from the lower jaw as well. If you are to take the nose then make sure to take the skin up to the eyebrows. Also take a single *shikoro* – helmet neck plate.

At the battle of Nagakute, Honda Hachizō cut the nose from the head of Mori Musashi. This was because the lord had given an order for that day to cut off noses instead of heads. However, Honda was not able to prove that it was Mori Musashi's nose and when it was later put back on Mori Musashi's head it did not fit correctly. As a result, Honda was in disgrace. He was later killed in another battle in Kanie.

Commentator one

If a head is cut poorly the chin will be left behind, still attached to the neck and the body. In such a case, to avoid arousing suspicion, the chin should be cut off separately and brought along with the head.

Commentator two

A dead enemy's helmet may be brought back to serve as evidence that he was armoured. However, as discussed previously, helmets are heavy and therefore sometimes just the bottom bands of the helmet are brought back instead of the full helmet itself.

Concerning cutting off the nose, details are mentioned earlier. One of the helmet neck plates should be presented together with the head as evidence of *kabuto-kubi* – the captured head of a warrior. If you bring back the whole helmet, it will be too heavy.

首奪ハレザル事
Kubi ubawarezaru koto
PREVENTING YOUR PRIZE HEAD FROM BEING STOLEN
Thread your sword cord through the mouth and out of the throat.

Commentator one

There is a way to thread a head using your sword cord. Details were mentioned earlier. The sword cord is also used to bind prisoners by their legs ready to be presented to the lord-commander.

高名ノ品々之事
Kōmyō no shinajina no koto
VARIOUS POINTS ON ACHIEVEMENTS
Do not worry about trying to take a prestigious head right from the start of battle; you can take a more prestigious head later on. Remember, if you take a better head at a later point you can always discard an earlier head. If you are only willing to aim for a prestigious head, you may end up taking no heads at all.

Chapter Twenty-four

Commentator one

This point on gaining achievements holds true even during times of peace. In short, you should take anything within your grasp that is positive and do so without hesitation, because if you hesitate you may never achieve anything at all.

CHAPTER TWENTY-FIVE

死出立可嫌事

Shiniidetachi wo kirau beki koto

AVOIDING THE 'COSTUME OF DEATH'

The 'costume of death' involves cutting the helmet cord and saddle girth shorter than normal and tying the cords of the arrow cape to your stirrups.

Commentator one

There have been examples of the 'costume of death' since ancient times. For the 'costume of death' all the cords of the *rikugu* – six tools – should be cut to a fist's length. One theory states that the arrow cape cords should also be cut. In Kōshū-Ryū there is a manner called *horo wo dai ni aguru* – placing the arrow cape on a pedestal.[140] This is found in the *Kōyō Gunkan*. In all cases, the cutting of cords conveys the message that you do not intend to tie them again. Also, banners with reference to arrow capes are shunned in battle as they are regarded as 'banners of death'.

Commentator two

The cords of an arrow cape are tied to the stirrups; therefore, stirrups have holes for these cords. In Kōshū-Ryū, there is a taboo against cutting the cords of an arrow cape, a practice that is known as *dabi-aguru* – cremation. Banners that refer to arrow capes are shunned because they carry the connotation of being 'only for a single day'.

The 'costume of death' is also considered as an outfit worn by someone who has a grudge against his lord and is determined to die. If you find a soldier in this outfit, discretely notify the general.

---

140 ・ 二上ル i.e. 'out of reach', meaning that it cannot be adjusted.

味方相色ノ事

Mikata aiiro no koto

THE APPEARANCE OF ALLIES

Note that there will be a change in the movement of flags and banners. The gaps between troops will also change.

Commentator one

If flags are moved to different positions or gaps between the troops are widened, be aware that the battle is about to commence. This is the same as the point on spacing between the vanguard and the second troop included in the previous chapter.

Commentator two

Ai 相 from *aiiro* in the title means 'appearance', and means to observe what a formation is like, such as the movement of flags and the spacing between the vanguard and the second troop, as explained earlier.

敗軍ノ心得之事

Haigun no kokoroe no koto

POINTS TO KEEP IN MIND CONCERNING DEFEAT

When your army has been defeated, do the following:

- ride in a circle
- if the enemy are spread out, hold your position
- there is a point here to understand on the announcements to be made
- stay with the general and those who are experienced

Commentator one

When your army has been defeated and is in retreat but you wish to return towards the enemy, you will find it difficult to ride against the tide of your fleeing allies. Therefore, there is a way called *wanori no narai* – the teaching of riding in a circle –which involves moving out to the side of the crowd and then doubling back towards the enemy.

You should not go back towards the enemy when the enemy is in full force. Instead, wait until you see gaps between the enemy troops.

Concerning how to make an announcement: let your allies know you are doing this by saying: 'I [your name] will stay to defend the retreat.' You should stay with the general and the senior warriors because they are experienced and will come up with excellent ideas. Also, when undertaking the achievement of defending the retreat and other kinds of accomplishments at the time of a defeat, it is a principle to stay with senior people as well as the general.

Commentator two

It would be better to stay close to the general or older people because you can benefit from their advice and also they have a proper judgement about the levels of achievement. 'Older people' means senior counsellors.

若武者へ指南之事
Waka-musha e shinan no koto
INSTRUCTING YOUNG WARRIORS
When instructing young warriors, remove your own banner.

Commentator one

This is the same as the achievement discussed earlier called *hagai no kōmyō*. To remove your own banner is customary in such situations.

殿ノ事

Shingari no koto

DEFENDING A RETREAT

To defend a retreat:

- stay by the generals or the captains
- consider the language to be used when speaking to your allies

Commentator one

When defending a retreat, stay close to a general or captain so that you can be sure your achievements will be noted.

If you speak to your allies, you should say something like: 'Sir [insert name], you are normally a brave man, but you look nervous. Stand firm.'

To stay and defend a retreat is something an individual achieves of his own will and it is difficult to make such deeds known. This is the reason for the point about staying close to the general or captain.

城責之事

Shirozeme no koto

ATTACKING A CASTLE

There are three points to tell your servants. They are to do with climbing a wall when a castle is about to fall, being aware of the danger of gunpowder when fire breaks out, and how to counter the last pitched attack of a defeated enemy, which will put your allies on 'their back foot'.

Commentator one

Three points when attacking a castle.

- Tell your servants to help you climb up a wall. Also, you should tell them to throw your banner or something like this into the castle compound. If you drop any weapons or gear, instruct them to retrieve them and bring them to you.

- If a fire breaks out when a castle falls, the gunpowder store will explode. Tell your servants not to be surprised by this.
- The enemy will fight back if their end is in sight. In such a battle, they will be in mortal desperation and the attacking side will always be affected by this. In this situation instruct your servants to stay close to their master instead of attempting to attain achievements or exploits.

Commentator two

Be aware that being killed at this final stage of a battle when it is possible for you to fulfil achievements is inappropriate and of no value.

CHAPTER TWENTY-SIX

吾備前之事

Waga sonai mai no koto

CONCERNING THE FRONT OF THE ALLIED FORMATION

Do not have anyone stationed to the front of your position and do not allow anyone other than *tsukaiban* – messengers – to cross in front of you.

Commentator one

If someone is passing across the front of your position and within the army formation, make sure to question him at once and kill him if the situation demands it. Messengers who have been given an order from the lord are exempt.

Commentator two

This does *not* only apply to the period just before a combat or during a procession; it is always rude to the general to pass across the front of a troop in formation. Sometimes, however, it will turn out that these people who have crossed to the front are *samurai* who have been given an order to scout ahead for the lord.

The standard carried by the lord's messengers is a golden *kamuro*.

As soldiers may argue among themselves, maintaining discipline is paramount.

陣替ヱノ事

Jingae no koto

MOVING TO A DIFFERENT MILITARY POSITION

Take care, as people may drop equipment during the move. Even if you travel for less than a day's march, carry rations and have porridge or soya beans for horses.

Commentator one

People drop equipment not only when moving to a different military position, but also when travelling to a different lodging during times of peace. Therefore, make an item checklist and use it. Prepare rations and include extra amounts, so that you are prepared for unexpected situations.

Commentator two

Concerning rations, dried rice or *dōjōji*[141] is desirable.

小屋出陣之事

Koya shutsujin no koto

DEPARTING FROM CAMP QUARTERS

Although it is considered proper to leave before others, do not rush to achieve this. If you are too far in advance and have to wait for others to arrive this can be undignified. It is best to depart at a *relatively* later time and travel quickly. Lastly, do not take too long getting prepared inside the camp quarters themselves.

Commentator one

Leaving a camp shelter too early and waiting for others to arrive is not considered good because it looks like you are waiting around for others to arrive to aid you in facing the enemy. Being late is also inappropriate as it appears to display unpreparedness. Generally, apart from *ichiban-yari*, first spear, or *ichiban-nori*, the first to advance, being too eager to be first and to be in advance is not considered proper if it does not comply with your allies' actions. This is why this discussion has been written here.

---

141 Possibly similar to *dōmyōji-ko* – small pellets made of steamed, dried and ground rice.

Commentator two

Apart from in *ichiban-yari* and *ichiban-nori*, if you advance and no one follows, you will be killed.

乱取之事
Randori no koto
PILLAGING

When the general gives an order to pillage, the first things you should take are military gear and then rations. Do not become obsessed about gold and silver.

Commentator one

After the instruction to pillage has been given from the general and the order in which people will take turns has been set, pillaging should be done with full respect for the order in which it is to be done. Pillaging without authorization is prohibited.

Commentator two

There should be rules set for the first group and second group, and signals should be given with bells and drums – do not pillage according to your own wishes. Pillaging should be conducted according to the orders of the general and should be done in turns, with proper courtesy shown between the different groups. Pillaging without authorization is prohibited.

Equipment to be pillaged:

- military gear
- rations
- gold, silver and treasures

A brave warrior should show proper judgement in dealing with gold, silver and treasures. In older times, there was a retainer of Uesugi Kenshin whose name was Oka Sanai. He liked gold and silver so much that he collected it avidly. Everyone chastised him about this but he did not pay attention, which led to many arguments with his colleagues. In the end, it turned out that he donated all of the money to benefit the path of the *samurai*, which showed that he did not actually care about the money itself. It became apparent that he had a solid determination, one that was akin to a slate of stone. Everyone was impressed with how devoted he was to *budō* – the path of the *samurai*.

When Mōri Motonari defeated Sue Yoshinori in Itsukushima of Aki province, military gear was pillaged.

It is said that gold and silver should not be taken, but this depends on the situation. If you see some, it is acceptable to take it.

表裏之事
Hyōri no koto
DECEPTION
It is not only the enemy who tries to deceive you, but also sometimes your allies – there are oral traditions on this.

Commentator one
Be aware of deception from the enemy. They may prepare their own men with incorrect information, such as the direction of south instead of north, right instead of left. There are various forms of deception, never be inattentive concerning this matter.

Commentator two
Deceptions may be attempted not only by the enemy but also by your allies. Remember the episode of Sasaki and Kajiwara at the Ujigawa river.[142] Do not let your guard down. Some people use old or young men as bait and achieve a victory of the spear for themselves.

---

142 Sasaki and Kajiwara were both trying to get to the other side of the river. Kajiwara lied to Sasaki that his horse girth was loose and then moved on to be the first into battle through this deception.

Chapter Twenty-six

虚実之事

Kyojitsu no koto

INSUBSTANTIAL AND SUBSTANTIAL

In a one-to-one combat between warriors, take the enemy's substantial mind and make it insubstantial. In this way, you can defeat them. There are insubstantial soldiers and substantial soldiers. To overthrow others, consider this in depth.

Commentator one

Concerning the discussion on insubstantial or substantial, those who show slovenliness in their equipment and who are restless should be considered as insubstantial soldiers, while those who look 'blackish' and are calm are substantial soldiers. Do not try to defeat substantial soldiers with a substantial force, instead attack them when they become insubstantial. The extreme secrets of *kyojitsu* are found in the *Kōketsu* scroll.

CHAPTER TWENTY-SEVEN

戦中ニテ首ヲ見スル事

Senchū nite kubi wo misuru koto

DISPLAYING DECAPITATED HEADS IN BATTLE

Display decapitated heads during battle by lifting them high with the left hand. If someone else displays a head in this manner, treat this as a signal to lift up the head you are holding.

Commentator one

When you are in a large number of people during a battle, if someone lifts a head up high, you also should lift the head that you have taken before they lower theirs. This should be done to serve as evidence at a later point, and also so that people will say that they observed many decapitated heads.

Commentator two

You should hold the head in the left hand as you will have an unsheathed blade in the right. Do not drop your weapon while holding the head aloft. If you kill an enemy with a spear or an arrow, then when you show the head you may have your servant hold the spear or the bow so that you can lift up the head with your sword in hand.

The presentation of a head [other than being lifted up during battle] is called *taimen-kubi* – the presented head. *Taimen* refers to the heads of the noble or high ranking, while the terms *jikken* or *mishiru* are used for the heads of lower-ranking people.

首ヲ馬ニ付ル事

Kubi wo uma ni tsukeru koto

ATTACHING A DECAPITATED HEAD TO A HORSE

One way to carry a head while on horseback is to put it in a *kubi bukuro* – head sack. Another way is to bind it to the horse. A general's head should be placed on the left side and an ordinary soldier's head should be placed on the right side. Both should be attached to the *shizuwa* – back support of the saddle.

Commentator one

Head sacks can be made of rope and formed like a net or they can be made of cloth, like a feed bag. They are one *shaku* two *sun* in length and nine *sun* in width. There are differences according to the school.

Alternatively, thread a thin cord through the mouth and attach the cord to the *shiode* – saddle horn. Using the strap of the saddle flap is also permissible.

Commentator two

Heads can be attached to the *mottsuke* or *tottsuke* rings, which are attached to the saddle horn. If there are two heads to carry, one should be attached to the *tottsuke*, and the other to the *mottsuke*. If both are attached to one side, it can create an imbalance. Attach the head of an important *samurai* to the rear, because if it is attached to the front it may be damaged by the stirrups.

勢気可見知事

Seiki mishiru beki koto

OBSERVING THE ENERGY AND *CHI* OF AN ARMY

Identify the state of an army's *chi* by observing whether it is strong or weak at the front, the rear, the left and the right.

Commentator one

Energy and *chi* rise like clouds of dust and stream out of an army in the direction opposite to the one in which it is heading, whether east or west, left or right.

Whether the energy is strong or weak can be assessed by observing flags. If the energy is strong the flags will be streaming, while if it is weak they will be drooping.

Commentator two

Assess the enemy's energy to help you decide whether to advance or retreat.

While the vanguard is attacking the enemy, the flags should remain in place and continue to be 'tight' in their formation so that there will be no weak sections for the enemy to observe. Those who move around extensively are weak soldiers.

騎馬ト歩武者トノ事

Kiba to kachimusha tono koto

MOUNTED *SAMURAI* AND *SAMURAI* ON FOOT

During a battle *samurai* on foot should take the higher ground, even if it is only slightly higher. Be aware that mounted *samurai* are at an advantage on a plain. It is taught that mounted *samurai* will ride in a circle with the intent of killing footed *samurai*. There are oral traditions for both sides of this.

Commentator one

Concerning a battle between a mounted warrior and a footed warrior: there are ways to ride in a circle, to stab a horse and not to have your horse stabbed. These should be passed on by demonstrating the actual movements.

If a footed warrior takes a higher position, he will cancel out a mounted warrior's height advantage.

Commentator two

The ways for both mounted and footed *samurai* are given in another scroll.

舩軍之事

Funa-ikusa no koto

NAVAL WARFARE

During naval warfare, take off your *kote* gauntlets and use *yugote* – archer's sleeves. Carry a *kaginawa* grappling hook; this is also called the *shinobi nawa* – *shinobi* rope. Carry it in a hidden bag below the shoulder guard.

Although there is no definitive place to stay on a ship there are some areas that are considered to be advantageous.

Use the centre line. This concerns the distance to the enemy.

There are ways and places to use the grappling hook.

Medicines for seasickness are described in detail in the scroll *Gun'yaku Yōhō*.

Use the concept of *hachibun* – eight-tenths – when you board or alight from a ship.

Apart from the above, remember that when the captain of the ship gives instructions, it is as if you were taking orders from a captain on land – details of this are in the scroll *Suisen Yōhō*.

Commentator one

Details about naval warfare are found in the scroll *Suisen Yōhō*. The points here are just basic information.

The order to take off your gauntlets will be given by the general. The purpose of this is to make sure everyone is ready to man the rudder or the oars when the time comes. Gauntlets restrict your freedom of movement.

To aid embarkation and disembarkation, carry grappling hooks on your waist. They can also be used in an emergency if the *hayao* – quick cord – breaks.

Concerning *hachibun*: disembark the ship when about three out of ten people have disembarked, and embark when seven or eight people out of ten have embarked. The reasoning behind this principle is that if you disembark too early, your allies will not be there in time to support you and you may be killed; whereas if you disembark too late, it will appear like you are using the ship for shelter, which will appear inappropriate.

One ship is equal to one troop in a land battle and each ship has one leader, just as each troop has a captain.

Chapter Twenty-seven

Commentator two

Archer's sleeves should be adjustable to fit each person's hands and fastened with cord on the inside. They should be made of satin or unbleached cotton or linen. This has a frill at the end.

Both thick and thin grappling hooks are useful and you should carry them on your waist as spare ropes for an emergency. They can also be used for embarkation and disembarkation. Further details are given in the scroll *Heika Jōdan*.

The uses of the grappling hook:
- securing saddles
- as quick rope
- climbing a wall
- cooking in a battle camp
- boarding or alighting from a ship
- securing luggage
- locking doors or *shoji* sliding screens
- carrying a decapitated head

There are various kinds of medicine for seasickness.

Gauntlets should be removed and stowed in the prow of the ship. Thigh protectors are useless when sitting for a prolonged time.

There is a teaching called *jūmonji no narai* – the teaching of the cross – which is for a combat between an allied and an enemy ship.

CHAPTER TWENTY-EIGHT

首實撿之事

Kubi jikken no koto

HEAD INSPECTIONS

When presenting a head, hold it with your right hand while putting your left hand on the cut of the neck. Allow the lord-commander to glimpse the right cheek of the head and then withdraw to the left. Do not kneel down. The person presenting the head should not look at the face of the lord-commander but instead focus on the head itself.

Commentator one

Detailed principles concerning head inspections are written in the scroll *Gunbai Yōhō*, therefore only an outline is given here. Those who are young and inexperienced should seek guidance from older, more knowledgeable colleagues. There may be small differences in protocol between different schools, clans or even individual generals.

Sitting without kneeling means to squat on the haunches. This way the person presenting the head can withdraw quickly.

It is a principle not to look at a general's face when presenting a head.

Note that the three main reasons for head inspections are:

1 to gather allies who may have become scattered after their return
2 to notify the people of achievements made, in order to boost their courage
3 to secure the enemy area and demonstrate the *chi* of your victory to the enemy

Head inspections have been conducted since ancient times for the above purposes.

Commentator two

Those who have brought back heads should remain in their armour and put the head on a *kugyō*, *ashiuchi* or *kannagake* tray. These trays are often edgeless on one side, so turn that side towards the lord. Place a sheet made of [unintelligible text] or paper under the cut of the head.

The right[143] side of the head should be shown [to the lord]. The presenter should kneel on the left knee and have the right knee drawn up [in a crouched position]. Stand up with the right foot. A cup of *sake* should be served after the presentation. Show the head quickly and leave without delay. If the head has a malignant look or has something that might arouse pity in the lord-commander's mind, or reduce his courage and thus it is to be avoided. It is a principle not to show faces of this nature.

There are a few different kinds of head inspection: if it features the head of a lord-commander it is called a *taimen*; whereas the inspection of soldiers' heads is called a *jikken* and an inspection of lower people's heads is called a *mishiru*. However, the general term is *jikken*.

Only the right cheek, and not the front of the face, should be shown to the lord. The distance between the general and the head should be two or three *ken*.

The presenter of the head should be armoured to show courtesy to the general, but this depends on the situation. You should ask for instructions from a senior counsellor or an official. Not too many heads should be submitted for inspection at once. After a while the lord-commander may start to feel compassion for the victims, which will be detrimental to the war effort.

When a head inspection is conducted in a field, cut pieces of pear wood to the length of three *shaku* and six *sun* and sharpen the ends. Stand them in the direction of the ram and the monkey[144] and put the heads on the stakes and display them in a non-linear fashion. The same thing should be done after capturing a castle with haste.

When heads are inspected from a *zashiki* room, the head of a lord-commander may be brought through the gate, while ordinary people's heads

---

143 The original text states 'left', but this is considered to be a transcription error as the main text states 'right'. However, commentator two does state 'left' twice.

144 Southwest.

should be kept outside the gate. This is the same in a battle camp.

The person presenting the head should remember to chant the mantras called *honkaku no bun*:

南無本覺法身　南無本有如来
Namu honkaku hōshin, namu honyū nyorai.

These should be chanted in your mind.

Commentator one

The *honkaku no bun* are sentences of enlightenment and words of thoughtfulness. If you forget them while chanting then we have an oral tradition for this.

If a head is simply placed on a tray, it will easily fall over. Therefore, it is a set custom to flatten the cut section of the neck and put a spike through from the bottom of the tray to secure the head.

Commentator two

The twelve reasons for a head inspection:

- to celebrate a victory in battle
- to collect scattered soldiers together
- not to become lost in triumph and to promote care
- to bring people back together so as to settle them down to follow the prescribed laws
- to praise achievements, as there is no other way to approve them
- for the lord-commander to show and acknowledge his soldiers
- to enhance the dignity of the lord-commander in the eyes of the soldiers
- to reinforce the discipline of the soldiers by displaying fresh blood
- to investigate and gain details of military achievements
- to listen to the talk of the soldiers
- to encourage those soldiers who are idle
- to be in position to attack the enemy if it returns[145]

---

145 This section is a reconstruction. The original text is damaged by worm bites.

Something to keep in mind when bringing in heads: as your mind will be in a state of *kyo* – insubstantiality – and hard to settle, chant the *honkaku no bun* mantra three times. This is a chant of enlightenment. For the meaning of the words, ask a monk. If you do not remember the words we have an oral tradition to help with this.

In ancient times, there were ghost stories and legends telling of when Mikenjaku hid a sword inside a head to kill the enemy, and when Geifu inserted poison in a head in order to kill Gao-zu of the Han Dynasty. Also in Japan there are episodes recorded, such as people becoming paralyzed through contact with a young general's head or the effects of a malignant head. All these superstitions derive from an insubstantial state of mind. Therefore, you need to keep yourself solid and brave and the above mantra will help you to do so. It is said that Ishida Jibu Mitsunari held a head inspection before the battle of Sekigahara, at which point all the presented heads appeared to change through five colours. People at the time took this to be an ill-fated sign.[146]

After chanting the above mantra three times, open your eyes and observe.

After the inspection, the heads are taken away promptly; at that point other warriors should step forward from both sides and give three war cries.

For a head inspection, 'to make up the head' means to flatten out and even up the cut section – this is done so that the heads of lord-commanders or other high-ranking people do not fall over when they are placed on platters.

Commentator one

To show the heads of warriors of the cape, wrap them in an arrow cape and have only a part of the cheek and the forehead on show in the direction of the lord-commander. After this, leave. There is a specific way to wrap them with a *fūtei* cloth. Details of this are written in the scroll *Gunbai Yōhō*. In other respects the method of displaying the head from a warrior of the cape is the same as for any other head.

---

146 These scenarios are based on earlier Chinese legends in which a weapon or poison is inserted into a decapitated head, which comes back to life when it is being presented and kills its enemies.

Keshō no kubi are heads where the blood has been washed off and the hair correctly prepared. The way of setting the hair is to soak a comb in water and then smooth back the hair with the back side of the comb. This is the reason why smoothing the hair with the back of a comb that has been soaked in water is shunned these days.

The platter for the head should be made of chinaberry wood.[147] This is why all tools made of chinaberry wood are shunned in *samurai* families of today.

Generally, if the manners for a head inspection are not correctly observed, this may cause ill luck for the lord-commander. Therefore, these customs should be followed with much care.

Commentator two

Concerning the heads of warriors with an arrow cape: these should be styled in accordance with *keshō no kubi*. Details of this are found in the scroll *Gunbai Yōhō*. During a head inspection, heads should not be presented without care, since this can cause bad luck to befall the lord-commander. Therefore, those in charge of head inspections should be present to teach those who are unfamiliar with the ritual of head examinations before the heads are actually presented. No further comments are given here.

As well as the above points in the main text, the principles for a head inspection should be carefully observed. In older times, when Yukiwaka-maru, the seven-year-old heir of Amako Yoshihisa, held a head inspection, there was a malignant head, which suddenly opened its eyes and stared at the young boy. As a result Yukiwaka-maru died soon afterwards. Also, when Fuchibe Iga-no-kami saw the head of Prince Daitō he said that it would be against the ancient customs to bring such a head to the lord-commander, so he threw it into a grove.

Wrapping a head with an arrow cape is not always the convention.

One theory states that only three colours of arrow cape are acceptable:

- red
- pink
- white

147 *Melia azedarach.*

Colours other than the above three should not be used. Additionally, the compatibility of the colour with the Five Elements in association with the warrior should be considered.

When you have killed a warrior of the cape, cut a section from the cape, fold it over to form four layers, cut one layer from this and cover the face with it. Then wrap the head with the remaining three layers. At a head inspection, open the three-layer section to show the head and lift the single layer above the left eye. This is also called *keshō suru* – styling the head.

The term *mishiru* refers to the inspection of lower-ranking heads. For these ceremonies the lord-commander need not be in armour, but the heads should still be presented on a tray.

In an inspection of one hundred heads, pick out three of the higher-ranking heads to be presented to the lord on a tray. The other heads should be placed together in line so that they can be inspected at the same time. If there are more than one hundred heads, choose seven for the standardized procedures of the head inspection. If there are too many heads, line them up so that the lord-commander can inspect the heads from horseback with an unsheathed sword in the hand. He should start at one end and inspect them on the left.

Whether to attend to the hair of a head depends on whose head it is. Usually, brave warriors and lord-commander's heads should have their hair prepared. Whether to groom unseemly hair or not depends on the situation.

Kubi-taimen is the inspection of the head of an enemy general, which is to be done by an allied commander. *Jikken* is an inspection of soldiers' heads. These ceremonies should be conducted by a *gunbaisha*, therefore details are in the scroll *Gunbai Yōhō*.

首實撿ニ不入首
Kubijikken ni irezaru kubi
HEADS THAT ARE NOT TO BE INSPECTED
The following types of heads should not be offered for inspection:
• heads with their eyes and mouth open

- malignant heads with flesh, blood or such oozing from the cut
- heads with their tongues protruding

These are called *yashin no kubi* – malignant heads – and are not the preferred type. For those with their eyes open, pull out the eye lashes and tap the eyes with the handle of your great sword – at this they will close. For those with protruding tongues, force the tongue back in with a *wari-kōgai* – split hair pin.

Commentator one
Apart from the above three categories there are also:
- *tengan* 天眼 – upward-eyed
- *chigan* 地眼 – downward-eyed
- *sagan* 左眼 – left-eyed
- *ugan* 右眼 – right-eyed
- *butsugan* 佛眼 – Buddha-eyed

Malignant heads differ from other heads taken in battle in that they sparkle with moisture and have an intense look in their eyes as if they were still alive.

A *hodare-kubi* is a head that keeps oozing blood or other matter from the cut and does not stop. Heads with protruding tongues often stay the same colour as they were before death and the teeth may clench.

For those heads with their eyes open, pull out the eyelashes and strike the eyes with a sword handle. For those with protruding tongues, put the tongue back in with a *wari-kōgai* – split hair pin.

Fix problems like this before head inspections. Heads that cannot be adjusted in the above ways should not come anywhere near the lord-commander.

The customs to be used are given by *gunbaisha* and are set out as rules. Being unaware of the details is no excuse for breaking the rules.

Commentator two
There is a poem about how heads can predict fortunes in battle:

右ハカチ左ハ負ル佛和談地マクル故ニ天ハ永引

Right-eyed predicts victory, left-eyed brings defeat, Buddha-eyed means reconciliation, downward-eyed is downfall, and the upward-eyed is a sign of a prolonged battle.

Another theory associates different types of head with the Five Elements:

- right-eyed is of Wood
- left-eyed is of Metal
- upward-eyed is of Fire
- downward-eyed is of Water
- Buddha-eyed is of Earth

CHAPTER TWENTY-NINE

敵ノ首捨ルニ友引之方ノ事

Teki no kubi suteruni tomobiki no hō no koto

THE DISPOSAL OF DECAPITATED HEADS IN THE DIRECTION
OF *TOMOBIKI*

By hours[148]

In the hours of:

- rat
- horse
- hare
- cockerel

Use the *ninth* direction [from that animal].

In the hours of:

- ox
- ram
- dragon
- dog

Use the *fifth* direction [from that animal].

In the hours of:

- tiger
- monkey
- snake
- boar

Use the *third* direction [from that animal].

---

148 The Koga transcription states that these are all days and not hours.

Commentator one
Enemy heads should be discarded in the direction of *tomobiki*; allies' heads should not.

Commentator two
Further details, such as *shibiki* – drawing in death – and *henpōbi* – the day of revenge – are in the scroll *Gunbai Yōhō*.

During a head inspection, present the heads from the direction of *tomobiki* and discard them in the direction of *shibiki*.

The directions allied heads should be discarded:

- on the day of *tsuchinoe* and the boar, discard in the direction of the rat
- on the day of *tsuchinoe* and the ram, discard in the direction of the dragon
- on the day of *tsuchinoe* and the cockerel, discard in the direction of the dragon
- on the day of *tsuchinoto* and the ox, discard in the direction of the ram

Those who were killed in a battle, including horses and hawks, should all be left in the above directions.

If it is the day of the rat, the ninth sign from and including the rat is the direction of the monkey, so the direction of the monkey is *tomobiki* in that case.

If it is a day of the horse, the ninth sign including the horse is the direction of the tiger, so the direction of the tiger is *tomobiki* in that case.

If it is a day of the ox, the fifth sign including the ox is the direction of the snake, so the direction of the snake is *tomobiki* in that case.

If it is the day of the tiger, the third sign including the tiger is the direction of the dragon, so the direction of the dragon is *tomobiki* in that case.

手負不臥方

Teoi fusezaru hō

THE DIRECTION IN WHICH INJURED PEOPLE SHOULD NOT BE LAID DOWN

During the three months of spring, injured soldiers should not be laid with their head towards the east.

During summer, autumn and winter, continue to avoid the direction of *ōbun*, just as in spring.

The direction of *ōbun* is as follows:

- in spring it is in the east
- in summer it is in the south
- in autumn it is in the west
- in winter it is in the north

Commentator one

The directions of *ōbun* in the *doyō* seasons are the inter-cardinal points; remember that each of the cardinal points is associated with one of the four seasons.

Commentator two

The direction of *ōbun* is as follows:

- in spring it is east and of the Blue Emperor[149]
- in summer it is south and of the Red Emperor
- in autumn it is west and of the White Emperor
- in winter it is north and of the Black Emperor

The *doyō* seasons are of the Yellow Emperor.

Each direction has an element associated with it and that element matches the element of the direction of *ōbun* [as described above]. This doubles the power of that element and is thus found to be propitious in most cases.[150] However, these combinations of directions and times of synergetic *chi* should be avoided when treating injured people. Because the *chi* of the injured has been defeated, powerful *chi* affects them adversely.

In spring, the element of Wood is doubly powerful in the east; therefore,

---

149 The directions and seasons are associated with the Five Chinese Heavenly Emperors 天帝.

150 Spring is of the element of Wood; east is also of the element of Wood. This means that the direction of *ōbun* has two associations with the element of Wood, doubling its power.

placing the injured in that direction at that time of year should be avoided, as the energy is too great. A period of *doyō* will follow the example of the season to which it is attached; so, for example, the eighteen days of *doyō* leading up to spring belong to the element of Wood, as the element of Wood is attached to spring.

感状之事

Kanjō no koto

LETTERS OF APPRECIATION

These are written by the general after returning from a campaign. Sometimes, and according to the circumstances, they may be awarded on the battlefield. There is an oral tradition of things you should keep in mind about this custom.

Commentator one

The details concerning different levels of appreciation letter are found in the scroll *Heieki Yōhō*. Matters like this are called *budō ginmi* – examinations on *budō*.

A letter of appreciation given to Miyabe Zenshōbō for his actions at the battle of Shinozu stated that he was unequalled in the world. Katō Samanosuke was given a similar accolade when he captured an enemy ship in Busan Bay. However, he pointed out that there cannot be two unequalled people in the world and Taikō[151] agreed. As a result Taikō ordered that the letter be rewritten to state that Katō had attained a countless number of similarly great achievements. These letters of appreciation were drafted by Yamanaka Yamashiro-no-kami, who was Taikō's secretary.

Commentator two

If a letter of appreciation does not do justice to your achievements, do not accept it. If, on the other hand, it is too complimentary, you should also decline the honour.

---

151 Toyotomi Hideyoshi.

On the twenty-sixth day of the eleventh month of Keichō 19 (1614), a retainer serving the Uesugi clan whose name was Sugihara Hitachi was given a letter of appreciation from the Great Lord [Tokugawa Ieyasu] in Ōsaka. Hitachi received it from the Great Lord in person, opened it and briefly looked at it. He declared that the letter was absolutely perfect, that nothing had been left unsaid. He then left. This episode shows how knowledgeable Hitachi was and how he knew that the letter was written with excellence at only a mere glance upon receipt of it. However, you should generally accept such a letter only after examining the words within it.

There are various ways to write a letter of appreciation, but in the main they should follow the general's preference.

Words to be used in letters of appreciation, organized by level of excellence:

上

Jō

Upper level

- *murui no kōmyō* 無類高名 – unparalleled achievement
- *batsugun no hataraki* 抜群働 – fighting above and beyond the level of the masses
- *eiyū no bushi* 英雄武士 – heroic warrior
- *wasuregataki hataraki* 難忘働 – unforgettable achievement

中

Chū

Middle level

- *ikki tōsen no hataraki* 一騎當千働 – one warrior in a thousand
- *hirui no hataraki* 非類働 – achievement without bounds
- *me wo odorokasu hataraki* 驚目働 – a glorious achievement to behold
- *hitori no hataraki wo motte* 以一人働 – you single-handedly achieved [insert accomplishment]

下

Ge

Lower level

- *shinmyō no hataraki* 神妙働 – a blessed achievement
- *kaigaishiki hataraki* 戒々敷働 – an achievement of competence
- *kitoku no hataraki* 奇特働 – an achievement beyond the norm
- *kidai no hataraki* 希代働 – a rare achievement for our age

CELEBRATING A SUCCESSFUL CAMPAIGN

Upon returning from a successful campaign with your reputation enhanced, you should hold a celebration just as you did at the departure for war. In such a celebration, all family members – including wives and children – should be gathered together to engage in a drinking party. Achievements that servants have attained should be examined and rewarded accordingly. Any promises you made before departing for war should now be honoured and you should give out rewards. If any of your servants were killed during the war, track down their offspring and compensate them. It is a principle to mourn the dead.

Commentator one

It is a custom to gather all – including wives and children – and to have the same kind of celebration as was given before departing for war.

Servants that have been killed should be mourned with the same respect that is given to your ancestors. The intention behind this is to bind their surviving relatives to you.

Commentator two

Warfare is of critical importance to a nation. The commander-in-chief will reveal his wisdom or ignorance through his actions during war, and this is even more true for an independent soldier.

Chapter Twenty-nine

In warfare you should:
- value your name
- think little of your life
- not hesitate to expose your flesh and skin to the destruction of a blade
- advance to attain achievement with haste
- display colossal bravery

Warfare is more dangerous than treading on thin ice in order to see into a deep pool. Therefore, if you return with success and have gained achievement know that you have unified with heaven's principle and truly been blessed by the gods. Just as you did before departing for war, you should have a celebration by bringing together your wife, children and relatives to partake in a feast. To those servants whom you have pledged to reward, give out rewards as promised. This is one way to make them have faith in your reward system. For those servants who were killed in action, as a leader you should show benevolence by performing a memorial service and expressing condolence.

Ishikawa Heisuke was killed at the battle of Shizugatake during the Tenshō period (1573–1591), but the lord was so impressed by his achievement he gave rewards to his brother, Ishikawa Nagamatsu, although he was still only young. This was done to transfer reward to his family for an outstanding achievement.

Concerning having a memorial service for your servants: at the battle of Yashima, Satō Tsugunobu Noto-no-kami was hit and mortally wounded by an arrow. Minamoto no Yoshitsune was taken by a deep grief and held Tsugunobu's hand in his last moments, stroking the injury and crying at his passing. Afterwards, Yoshitsune held a memorial service to commemorate Tsugunobu's death and donated a horse called Tayūguro to the monks in memory of the deceased Tsugunobu. Many soldiers who saw this were deeply touched and felt inspired to sacrifice themselves for this lord because it showed that, even if they were killed, their lord Yoshitsune would give out and display great benevolence. Consider this episode and know that the lord's benevolence is most essential. It is this mindset that causes servants to become attached to their masters. Therefore, it is a principle to hold a memorial service for *samurai* and other soldiers who have been killed.

SELECTED GLOSSARY

aigyō 愛敬– friendly, approachable attitude

bu 分 (i) – unit of length equivalent to approximately three millimetres

bu 武 (ii) – from *bushidō, bushi, budō*; pertaining to the military

budō 武道– from its context and positioning within the original scrolls, this term is generally translated as 'way of the *samurai*' in this book and not as 'martial arts'

bugei 武芸 – military arts

bugyō 奉行 – commander or magistrate

buke 武家 – warrior families

bushi 武士 – alternative name for *samurai*

chi 気 – the well-known Chinese concept of an energy that flows through the body and the universe can be expressed in many ways, but it is most commonly understood as 'life-force'; although often considered a mystical, metaphysical, atmospheric energy, *chi* can also refer to practical, physical energy

chōtō 長刀 – can mean either halberd or long sword; however, from analysis of context, the Natori texts appear to use *chōtō* to mean halberd or pole-arm rather than spear or long sword

chūgen 中間 – servants

chūgi 忠義 – the concept of loyalty and justice

Five Elements (*Gōgyō*) 五行 – the foundation of all creation, namely: 木 Wood, 火 Fire, 土 Earth, 金 Metal and 水 Water

gandō chōchin カントウ挑灯 – light housed in a tapered and flat-ended tube and kept upright by means of a gimbal system; it was used much like a modern handheld torch to illuminate specific directions

genkan 玄関 – entrance of a house

gunbai 軍配 – esoteric side of warfare; see also *gunbaisha*

gunbaisha 軍配者 – person who understands the 'esoteric and magical military ways' of gunbai, such as divination and warfare rituals

gundō 軍道 – the military way or path

gunjutsu 軍術 – military skills, practical warfare methods

gunpō 軍法 – 'military ways', the tactics of war

gunpōsha 軍法者 – person who understands the 'military ways' of *gunpō*

gunsha 軍者 – *samurai* of normal level who understands military ways and is considered core military personnel

hakama 袴 – wide, flowing trousers worn by the *samurai* class

hara-kiri 腹切 – to commit suicide through the ritual of *seppuku*; see *seppuku*

hei 兵 – soldier or weapon, or a military mindset

inshi 隠士 – literally, 'hidden warrior'; in this manual the term refers to a master-less *samurai*

ippei 一兵 – independent soldier, i.e. a retained soldier of warrior status and trained in the arts of warfare, who is in the service of a specific lord

jō 丈 – unit of length equivalent to approximately three metres (or exactly ten *shaku* in the Japanese system)

kan 貫 – unit of currency and weight; one *kan* is equivalent to 3.75 kilograms

kashira 頭 – captain of men

katakiuchi 讐討 – act of revenge

katana 刀 – long sword

kenka 喧嘩 – spontaneous combat

ki 気 – Japanese spelling of *chi*

kishōmon 起請文 – written oath to the gods

ko-kyo 孤虚 – method of establishing lucky and unlucky directions

komono 小者 – servants, literally 'small people'

Kōshū-Ryū 甲州流 – military school comprising teachings from retainers of the Takeda clan

kumade 熊手 – rake-like hook

kyojitsu 虚実 – concept of substantial and insubstantial

mononofu 武 – alternative reading for *samurai*; see also *bu*

ōsō 王相 – concept in which the energy of each season is associated with a particular direction

rōnin 牢人 – *samurai* without a master, one who is not employed or retained (the ideogram used here differs from the normal version)

sanjaku tenugui 三尺手拭 – section of cloth normally measuring approximately one metre by thirty centimetres *sasumata* サスマタ – U-shaped pole-arm used to capture people

seii-taishōgun 征夷大将軍 – formal name of the *shōgun*

seppuku 切腹 – ritual disembowelment with a knife, normally assisted by a *kaishaku* – second – who completes the ritual by decapitating the *samurai* who is performing *seppuku*

shaku 尺 – unit of length equivalent to approximately thirty centimetres

shinobi 忍 – secret agent, spy and commando-infiltrator; also known as a *shinobi no mono* and commonly known today as a ninja

shinobi-gaeshi 忍返 – spiked defences to prevent *shinobi* infiltrators from entering a position

shinobi-guchi 忍口 – secret or hidden entrance

shōbu 勝負 – combat or confrontation

sukedachi 助太刀 – person who assists another during combat

sun 寸 – unit of length equivalent to approximately three centimetres

tachi 太刀 – great sword; longer than a *katana*, a *tachi* is generally worn blade-edge down when in armour

taishō 大将 – the main leader or lord, translated in the text as lord-commander

Ten Celestial Stems (*Jikkan*) 十干 – a set of ten concepts born of Chinese thought, consisting of five pairs which directly relate to the Five Elements, e.g. Fire-larger, Fire-lesser, Water-larger, Water-lesser, etc.; the Ten Celestial Stems also form the basis of a ten-day cycle and are often used in conjunction with the Twelve Earthly Branches

tenugui 手拭 – broad cloth normally around sixty to seventy centimetres long; see also *sanjaku tenugui*

tōzoku 盗賊 – thieves and gangs of robbers

tsukubo 突棒 – T-shaped pole-arm used for capturing

Twelve Earthly Branches (*Jūnishi*) 十二支 – understood as equivalent to the signs of the zodiac; the hours, days, months, years and directions are all divided into twelve and allocated one branch, each of which is represented by an animal; starting in the north and moving in order they are: rat, ox, tiger, hare, dragon, snake, horse, ram, monkey, cockerel, dog and boar; often used in conjunction with the Ten Celestial Stems

uchihatashi 打果 – feud-fighting, normally where both parties understand that conflict will arise in the future; sometimes written declarations are made
wakatō 若党 – assistants; literally 'youthful aid', although the term can be applied to assistants of all ages – 'old' and 'young' are sometimes used to refer to 'important' and 'unimportant' retainers
wakizashi 脇差 – short sword
Way/way (*dō*) 道 – a path of life or a subject deeply studied; in the text we have capitalized the term when it refers to a spiritual or moral path and used lower case for a more practical set of techniques, e.g. 'the way of tea', 'the way of the sword', etc.
zakō 座功 – master who passes on traditional wisdom through oral teachings, including poetry
zashiki 座敷 – formal reception room in a Japanese house

A NOTE ON THE COMMENTATORS

Natori Masazumi's main text remains the same across multiple versions. However, various different commentators have added oral traditions, notes and explanations in the margins of each respective transcription and are numbered accordingly. The main text should be considered the words of Natori himself and the commentaries should be understood to be adding to Natori's original writings in an effort to record the school's oral traditions.

The commentary labelled 'commentator one' contains oral traditions from the Tōkyō transcripts. The 'commentator two' material consists of oral traditions from the Koga transcripts, probably dating from around 1700.

It is apparent that commentator one predates commentator two: the syntax of the two commentaries shows that commentator two had access to, or was taught by, commentator one, or at the very least there appears to be a connection between the two. As a result, some of commentator two's commentaries exactly replicate those of commentator one. These have been omitted from the text.

INDEX

Terms are mainly given in English, except where Japanese terms do not bear translation.

'n' refers to footnotes.